NRTS-20/UNUP-422

Natural Resources Development in the Sahel: The Role of the United Nations System

Lee H. MacDonald

THE UNITED NATIONS UNIVERSITY

FROM THE CHARTER OF THE UNITED NATIONS UNIVERSITY

ARTICLE I

Purposes and structure

1. The United Nations University shall be an international community of scholars, engaged in research, post-graduate training and dissemination of knowledge in furtherance of the purposes and principles of the Charter of the United Nations. In achieving its stated objectives, it shall function under the joint sponsorship of the United Nations and the United Nations Educational, Scientific and Cultural Organization (hereinafter referred to as UNESCO), through a central pro-gramming and co-ordinating body and a network of research and post-graduate training centres and programmes located in the developed and developing countries.

2. The University shall devote its work to research into the pressing global problems of human survival, development and welfare that are the concern of the United Nations and its agencies, with due attention to the social sciences and the humanities as well as natural sciences, pure and applied.

3. The research programmes of the institutions of the University shall include, among other subjects, coexistence between peoples having different cultures, languages and social systems; peaceful relations between States and the main-tenance of peace and security; human rights; economic and social change and development; the environment and the proper use of resources; basic scientific research and the application of the results of science and technology in the interests of development; and universal human values related to the improvement of the quality of life.

4. The University shall disseminate the knowledge gained in its activities to the United Nations and its agencies, to scholars and to the public, in order to increase dynamic interaction in the world-wide community of learning and research.

5. The University and all those who work in it shall act in accordance with the spirit of the provisions of the Charter of the United Nations and the Constitution of UNESCO and with the fundamental principles of contemporary international law.

6. The University shall have as a central objective of its research and training centres and programmes the continuing growth of vigorous academic and scientific communities everywhere and particularly in the developing countries, devoted to their vital needs in the fields of learning and research within the framework of the aims assigned to those centres and programmes in the present Charter. It shall endeavour to alleviate the intellectual isolation of persons in such communities in the developing countries which might otherwise become a reason for their moving to developed countries.

7. In its post-graduate training the University shall assist scholars, especially young scholars, to participate in research in order to increase their capability to contribute to the extension, application and diffusion of knowledge. The University may also undertake the training of persons who will serve in international or national technical assistance programmes, particularly in regard to an interdisciplinary approach to the problems with which they will be called upon to deal.

ARTICLE II

Academic freedom and autonomy

1. The University shall enjoy autonomy within the framework of the United Nations. It shall also enjoy the academic freedom required for the achievement of its ob-jectives, with particular reference to the choice of subjects and methods of research and training, the selection of persons and institutions to share in its tasks, and freedom of expression. The University shall decide freely on the use of the financial resources allocated for the execution of its functions. . . .

NATURAL RESOURCES DEVELOPMENT IN THE SAHEL: THE ROLE OF THE UNITED NATIONS SYSTEM

Lee H. MacDonald

THE UNITED NATIONS UNIVERSITY

Lee H. MacDonald is in the Department of Forestry and Resource Management at the University of California, Berkeley, California, USA.

The arid and semi-arid lands together constitute about one-third of the earth's land surface but support only about one-eighth of its population. These dry lands contain a significant proportion of the poorest countries of the world.

The United Nations University Arid Lands Sub-programme chose the theme "Assessment of the Application of Existing Knowledge to Arid Lands Problems". A number of research studies were commissioned under this theme, examining the various interfaces that exist between scientific investigation and the application of its findings, often within a regional context.

The study *Natural Resources Development in the Sahel: The Role of the United Nations System* also focuses on the problems of socio-economic development, environmental conservation, and the application of scientific knowledge and technological resources in the Sahel. In this it follows the views expressed by the UN Conference on Desertification (UNCOD, Nairobi, 1977), which provides a good example of the difficulties of follow-up co-ordination on the international level.

The author's conclusion is that development aid must be provided in a spirit of co-operation and without any preconceived ideas. Although the UNU's special Sub-programme on Arid Lands has now been concluded, the new programme on Resource Policy and Management has undertaken to maintain this international dimension in research, training, and dissemination, stressing the interaction of resource management, conservation, and development.

© The United Nations University, 1986

The views expressed in this publication are those of the author and do not necessarily reflect the views of the United Nations University.

The United Nations University
Toho Seimei Building, 15-1 Shibuya 2-chome, Shibuya-ku, Tokyo 150, Japan
Tel.: (03) 499-2811   Telex J25442   Cable: UNATUNIV TOKYO

Printed in Japan

NRTS-20/UNUP-422
ISBN 92-808-0422-7
United Nations Sales No. E.86.III.A.3
01000 P

CONTENTS

PREFACE

In 1983-1985, drought in sub-Saharan Africa was a topic of world-wide concern as it had been in 1968-1973. In both cases, it was only after several years of deficient rainfall and poor harvests that the resilience of the people was sapped and the human suffering became dramatic enough to capture widespread attention. In 1983-1985, however, many of the public and private aid organizations had sufficient presence in the field to fully recognize the extent of the problem as it developed. Memories of the 1968-1973 drought in the Sahel helped give credibility to field reports, and past experience facilitated communication and co-operation among relief agencies. While the severity of the situation and the difficulties of responding effectively cannot be overestimated, it is clear that the response of the international community was a considerable improvement over the relief efforts of 1973-1974.

These periodic severe imbalances between food production and human requirements are usually termed "natural disasters", and it is generally assumed that the problem will disappear once nature returns to "normal". Those who have worked in the sub-Saharan zone known as the Sahel realize that the problem will not disappear with the first growing season with adequate rains. Even a cursory review of basic facts will quickly indicate that millions of people are caught in a spiral of poverty and malnutrition.

Since 1975 more than US$1,000 million in development assistance has been provided annually to the eight member countries of CILSS (the Permanent Interstate Committee for Drought Control in the Sahel). This unique political group, formed after the 1968-1973 drought to rationalize development efforts, includes — from east to west — the countries of Chad, Niger, Burkina Faso (formerly Upper Volta), Mali, Mauritania, Senegal, the Gambia, and Cape Verde. While the first priority of CILSS is to attain self-sufficiency in food production, after ten years there is little to suggest that this objective is being achieved.

Improvements in health care, education, nutrition, the standard of living, and life expectancy have also been sporadic at best. Given the relatively large influx of development assistance and the fact that 80 per cent of the population is directly dependent on agriculture, one must wonder whether the natural resource base is suf-ficient to even begin to meet human needs for food, clothing, and shelter during any but the best years.

These were the general concerns that led me to undertake the present study. I have focused on the efforts of the United Nations system partly because of the need to make the vast subject more manageable and partly because of my familiarity with the UN system. In many ways the UN efforts are a microcosm of all aid flowing to the Sahel, for the diversity and interactions of UN organizations and their funding sources reflect virtually all possible development topics and methodologies. Hence much of the present monograph is devoted to documenting the diverse UN activities and their respective modes of operation.

Similarly, the thematic focus of the report is on natural resources development because the vast majority of the population are, and will continue to be, directly dependent on the existing soil, water, and vegetation resources for their livelihood. There seemed to be a need to question whether aid programmes have been able to develop stronger, sustainable production systems, or whether they have contributed to the region's instability by permitting much higher human and animal populations which are then destined to decline precipitously during periods of unfavourable climatic conditions.

As the study progressed, two serious limitations became apparent. The first was a lack of scientific data to evaluate either the trends in resource quality or the effects of different development activities on the resource base. This difficulty can be ascribed partly to the limited research capability in the Sahelian countries, partly to a justifiable emphasis on development rather than scientific studies, and partly to the problem of gaining access to scattered research that does not find its way into the mainstream of science. The problem of access was also the basis of the second major limitation, namely that each of the parties involved in development assistance has reasons to restrict access to its detailed project reports. Thus it has proved nearly impossible to evaluate the impact of development projects on the natural resource base in the way originally envisaged, and consequently more attention has been paid to political and administrative questions. I have provided some discussion of assistance to the Sahel from sources outside the UN system and of sectors not related to natural resources, but this is primarily to provide context and contrast.

The completion of a manuscript, particularly one with a relatively long gestation period, leaves one with innumerable debts of gratitude but limited space for acknowledgement. Dr. Walther Manshard stands out as pillar of support and inspiration; and his secretary for several years, Mrs. Phyllis Talley, helped type an earlier version of the manuscript. Dr. Stephen Preston, Dr. Kenton Miller, and Dr. Asit Biswas provided much of the initial feedback which eventually led to this publication. Among others, Dr. Jack Mabbutt, Dr. Brian Spooner, and Dr. Douglas Johnson provided guidance and insights gained from their extensive work in arid lands. A number of libraries and documentation centres have humoured me in my quest for non-existent or simply obscure references; these have included the OECD Development Centre in Paris, the Sahel Documentation Center at Michigan State University, the Office of Arid Lands Studies at the University of Arizona, and most recently the Documents Library at the University of California at Berkeley. The staff at the United Nations' Dag Hammarskjöld Library in New York were extremely helpful in guiding me through the UN documentation system and providing me with a pleasant nook in which to work; Mr. Nick Christonikos deserves special mention in this regard. Similarly, the staff of the United Nations University liaison office twice helped with extended stays in New York, and M. E. Leung provided assistance and support that has not been and cannot be fully acknowledged. The UNU staff in Tokyo have also been most supportive, despite my difficulty in meeting self-imposed deadlines. Sumiko Yokoyama and Motoko Kuroda still hold warm spots in my heart for typing and retyping the first version of this report. Kathleen Landauer has kept the administrative problems at bay and provided some early and crucial enthusiasm. At Berkeley, Dr. Louise Fortman graciously read through the manuscript, while Rosemary Warden deserves credit for cleverly converting my hard-copy writings and revisions into an organized, electronic form. Finally, thanks must be given to my wife and friends who have been given additional burdens or been forced to adapt to my schedule so that I could work on this project.

This preface would hardly be self-respecting or complete without the acknowledgement that, in the final analysis, what I have written is solely my responsibility. Inevitably, dealing with such a complex topic will result in some omissions or errors in interpretation, but these should not obstruct the broader picture. I only hope that this work will help lead to a more open and realistic debate on UN development assistance, and to clearer links between development assistance and an improvement in the lives of the people of the Sahel.

1. THE SAHEL: HUMAN AND ENVIRONMENTAL OVERVIEW

Introduction

In the oral tradition of Niger, drought and hunger are familiar topics. Before foreign conquest there were the periods known as Ize Mere, "the sale of children"; Goosi Borgo, "grinding up the water gourd"; and Yollo Moron, "sit and stroke your plaits" — for there was nothing more that could be done. Colonization did not change the pattern, for there was famine first in 1913-1914 and then in 1931-1932, when the locusts came in hordes, leaving the people with hunger. In 1942 west of Niger there was Wande-Maasu, "leave the wife, push her aside"; and in 1951-1952 there was Gaari-Jire, "cassava meal", when the only way to survive was to eat high-starch cassava meal brought in from Dahomey (now Benin) and Nigeria (Salifour 1975). The drought that lasted from 1968 to 1973 might have been unusual in its length (UNCOD 1977a) but cannot be considered unique (Nicholson 1983).

It was the 1968-1973 drought that focused the world's attention on the region immediately south of the Sahara. An unusually poor series of wet seasons led to the failure of crops and the death of livestock on a massive scale, and the pictures and stories of malnourished children and dead cattle stimulated a tremendous outpouring of emergency relief. This short-term reaction has been followed by an unparalleled international effort to aid the long-term development of the countries that are now commonly called the Sahel.

Originally the term Sahel — an Arabic word literally meaning "shore" or "bank" — had a specific geographic reference: the southern boundary, or "shore", of the Sahara, the variable zone between the extremely arid desert and the more humid savannahs to the south. As a somewhat arbitrary zone within the continuum between desert and rain forest, it has been variously defined by different authors (Grove 1978; Bernus 1971). No matter what rainfall or phyto-geographical limits are used, it should always be kept in mind that rainfall is extremely variable from year to year, and this has a direct effect on the vegetation and the types of human activities that can take place.

For the moment we shall define the Sahel as that area immediately south of the Sahara which has an average annual precipitation of more than 100 mm and less than 600 mm. The northern half of this area can be considered useful primarily for nomadic grazing, with a gradation from camels to goats, cattle, and sheep as one moves from north to south. Rain-fed agriculture is possible only on the wetter sites, and then only in the wetter years. In the southern portion of the Sahel rain-fed agriculture is possible in most years, but yields will vary considerably.

On average this zone is some 450 km wide, and, by the definition above, it should extend — at least in a physiographic sense — in an east-west band for roughly 5,500 km between the Atlantic Ocean and the Red Sea, including significant parts of Senegal, Mauritania, Mali, Niger, Chad, and the Sudan as well as the northernmost parts of Burkina Faso,* Nigeria, Cameroon, and Ethiopia. Bernus (undated, citing Monod 1975), suggests that this transitional zone could even be considered to extend around the Ethiopian plateau to north-east Kenya. While it can be argued that the 1968-1973 drought had at least as severe an effect on certain provinces within Ethiopia, semi-arid Ethiopia is generally considered separately from the Sahel; and even the Sudan is separated on political grounds from the West African Sahel, despite the obvious geographical similarities. Figure 1 is a map of West Africa south of the Sahara showing estimated isohyets of mean annual precipitation.

South of the Sahel zone we can define a more wooded Sudanian zone, where the average annual precipitation of about 600-950 mm permits a more varied and less risky rain-fed agriculture, often integrated with the raising of livestock. Still further south is the rather heavily wooded Guinea zone, with its much higher productivity but also a much greater incidence of debilitating human and livestock diseases. The Guina zone could be considered the beginning of the rain forest, perhaps patchy at first because of natural and anthropogenic fires, but rapidly becoming an unbroken canopy in the natural state.

It should be emphasized that this definition of the Sahelian, Sudanian, and Guinea zones is arbitrary.

---

* Burkina Faso was known as Upper Volta until 1984. The older name will be used where appropriate throughout this book for references relating to the time before the change.

1

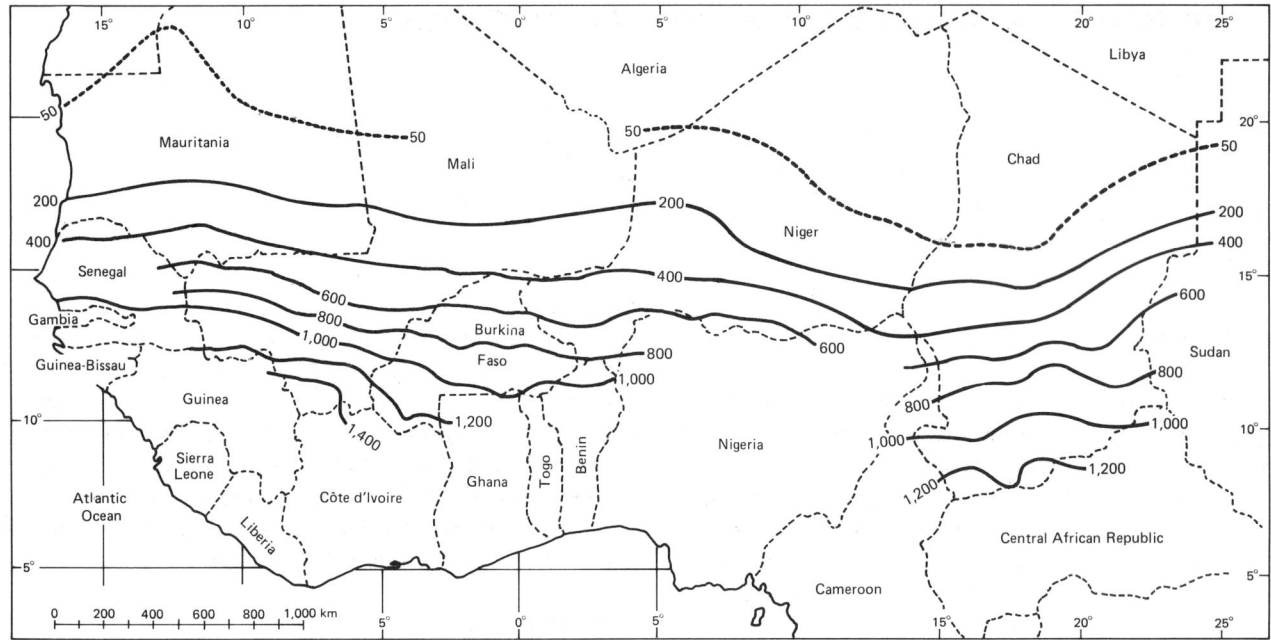

FIG. 1.　Map of West Africa, showing isohyets of mean annual precipitation in millimetres
(Adapted from Boeckm et al. 1974)

Boundaries in the natural state are indistinct, and they are further blurred both by annual variation in precipitation and by human activities. The general pattern of east/west-trending geographic zones is also disrupted by the major river systems such as the Niger, the Senegal, the Gambia, the Volta, the Chari, and the Logane, as well as well as Lake Chad. Nevertheless, the concept of the zones is useful to indicate generalized landscape types which can then be associated with human activities.

In recent years, the term Sahel has come to refer also to the group of countries which encompass this "shore" of the Sahara. While technically this should include the Sudan, in practice the countries primarily referred to are Senegal, Mauritania, Mali, Niger, and Chad. Nigeria and Cameroon are excluded, because only a small percentage of their total area and population falls into the Sahel zone. On the other hand, Burkina Faso is relatively arid and is linked to the other Sahelian countries by both its colonial legacy and its basic socio-economic conditions. Similarly, the Gambia, although slightly more humid and with a British rather than a French colonial heritage, is included because its future is inevitably linked with that of Senegal and it faces very similar problems of development. Cape Verde, an island country more than 600 km west of Senegal, has also been politically linked to the Sahelian countries and shares similar environmental conditions, but because of its geographical isolation and the author's lack of direct experience with it, it will not be considered in any detail in this report.

Thus, these seven countries — Burkina Faso, Chad, Gambia,

Mali, Mauritania, Niger, and Senegal — form a relatively cohesive geographical and political grouping. All of them underwent severe dislocations as a result of the 1968–1973 drought and have now banded together in an effort to more effectively improve existing socio-economic conditions and minimize the adverse effects of future droughts. As a group, they are beyond doubt among the "poorest of the poor".

In 1981 life expectancy in these seven countries averaged 44 years, and per capita gross national product ranged from $110* in Chad to $460 in Mauritania. In all seven countries adult literacy rates were below 20 per cent in 1980, and daily caloric intake in 1977 ranged from 5 to 26 per cent below FAO standards. Population per physician was 13,000 or more, and safe drinking water was available to no more than 37 per cent of the population (World Bank 1981, 1983a). Even more unsettling is the fact that per capita food production was lower in all countries in 1979–1981 than in 1969–1971 by between 4 and 24 per cent. From 1960 to 1981 gross national product did not keep up with population growth in Chad, Niger, and Senegal (table 1).

Even without taking the 1968–1972 drought into consideration, this is clearly one of the poorest areas in the world and one that has made little progress in the effort to improve the standard of living. Continued economic growth

---

* References to dollars are to US dollars throughout this book.

TABLE 1.   A statistical overview of the Sahelian countries

	Chad	Gambia	Mali	Mauritania	Niger	Senegal	Upper Volta[a]
Population (thousands)	4,500	600	6,900	1,600	5,700	5,900	6,300
Area (thousand km^2)	1,284	11	1,240	1,031	1,267	196	274
Average annual population growth rate, 1970–1981 (%)	2.0	2.5[b]	2.6	2.3	3.3	2.7	2.0
GNP per capita (US$)	110	370	190	460	330	430	240
Average annual GNP growth rate per capita, 1960–1981 (%)	−2.2	2.5	1.3	1.5	−1.6	−0.3	1.1
Life expectancy at birth (years)	43	42	45	43	45	44	44
Adult literacy rate (%)[c]	15	15	10	17	10	10	5
Food production index per capita, 1979–1981 (1969–1971 = 100)	96	77	88	77	93	76	94
Percentage of labour force in agriculture, 1980	85	—	73	69	91	77	82

Sources: Manshard 1979; World Bank 1983a

All figures from 1981 unless otherwise indicated.
[a] Now Burkina Faso
[b] 1970–1975
[c] Dates of estimates range from 1978 to 1982.

in the industrialized world leaves these countries further and further behind in relative and real terms. Some form of external assistance is therefore necessary if they are to meet the basic needs of the existing population, to say nothing of improving the prospects of the next, much larger, generation.

Climate

In physical terms the Sahel is a mixture of elements from the Saharan and Sudanian zones, with seasonal changes determining which of these is uppermost. Life in the region is essentially dependent on the annual movements of the Intertropical Convergence Zone. In April moisture-bearing winds come in from the south-west, pushing against the hot, dry air mass that covers most of North Africa. The convergence of these air masses causes thunderstorms, and in fits and starts, the Intertropical Discontinuity moves north. In the southern part of the Sahel the first rains usually fall in late May or early June, while in the north the rain may begin only in July. Peak rainfall is almost invariably in August, and the retreating intertropical front means a cessation of rain in early September in the north and early October in the south.

Following the rainy season there is a brief transitional period of warm temperatures that is often accompanied by dry winds from the north-east. The cold season lasts approximately from late October to early March, and during this time surface water disappears and the vegetation dries up. Another transitional period is between March and the onset of the rainy season. The lack of cloud cover causes this transitional period to be the hottest time of

the year, and it is usually also the time of greatest stress. Both water and forage are scarce, which means that milk production is at its lowest ebb and the animals are at their weakest. Depending on the previous year's harvest, the granaries may also be nearly empty, although the grain must hold out through the rainy season until the new harvest is ready.

One of the primary characteristics of arid and semi-arid zones is extreme variability in rainfall, and the Sahel is no exception. Generally variability increases as one goes from south to north, at least until the hyper-arid (less than 100 mm) zone is reached. It is still a matter of controversy whether the low rainfall years are due to stronger highs over the Indian Ocean (Schove 1977) or lower surface temperatures in the Atlantic (WMO 1975), but neither of these are likely to have much value in terms of forecasting drought. Different authors have also analysed the available climatic data in an effort to find cyclical patterns (Faure and Gac 1981; Schove 1977) and these studies have helped us to understand the extent and frequency of variability. However, the cyclical patterns that have emerged are weak and based on a relatively short record; so again the predictive value is severely limited. Figure 2 shows the variation in annual rainfall for the different zones from 1901 to 1980.

Climatic predictions are further hampered by the fact that changes in the movement of the Intertropical Convergence Zone are not well understood (Rasool 1982). Some authors have postulated a positive feedback loop, whereby drought causes a decrease in the vegetative cover, which then may increase the albedo, increase the dust content, or decrease the amount of freezing nuclei. These in turn would cause

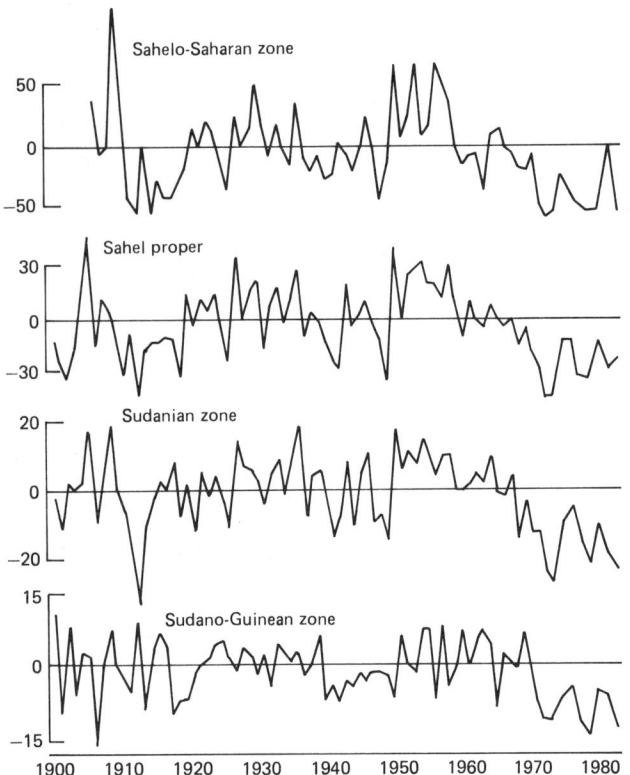

FIG. 2.   Variation in annual precipitation (percentage above or below normal) in four different zones of West Africa, 1901–1980. Note the decreasing scale of variation from the Sahelo-Saharan zone to the moister Sudano-Guinean zone. (From Nicholson 1982)

a further decline in precipitation (Nicholson 1983). While current models indicate that such processes could have an effect, there is no real evidence that this is the case. The fact that droughts don't persist indefinitely suggest that there are other, more powerful processes at work.

Climatic change is another popular incantation that is brought forward to "explain" the recent droughts in the Sahel, but this carries little validity except over the very long term. From 20,000 to 12,500 years ago, for example, the climate of the Sahel was probably very much drier, with active dunes 500 km south of where they are now (Grove 1978). These fossil dunes, now stable and covered with vegetation, are an important feature in today's land-scape. From approximately 12,500 to 9,500 years ago, the climate fluctuated, but gradually became wetter than at present, and this relatively humid period contined until some 4,000-5,000 years ago. Since then the climate in the Sahel has been roughly similar to today's climate. Wetter periods do exist, but these do not exceed the historical variation nor provide any indication of a long-term trend. Figure 3 shows the annual and long-term variation in the level of Lake Chad, and this does not show any major drying trend prior to 1970.

While annual precipitation means, such as those indicated in figure 1, can provide a valuable first approximation to the climate in the Sahel, they can also be very misleading. First, the amount of precipitation must be considered in the context of the extremely high annual evaporation figures (3,000-4,000 mm). Second, one must take into account the extreme variability of precipitation in arid

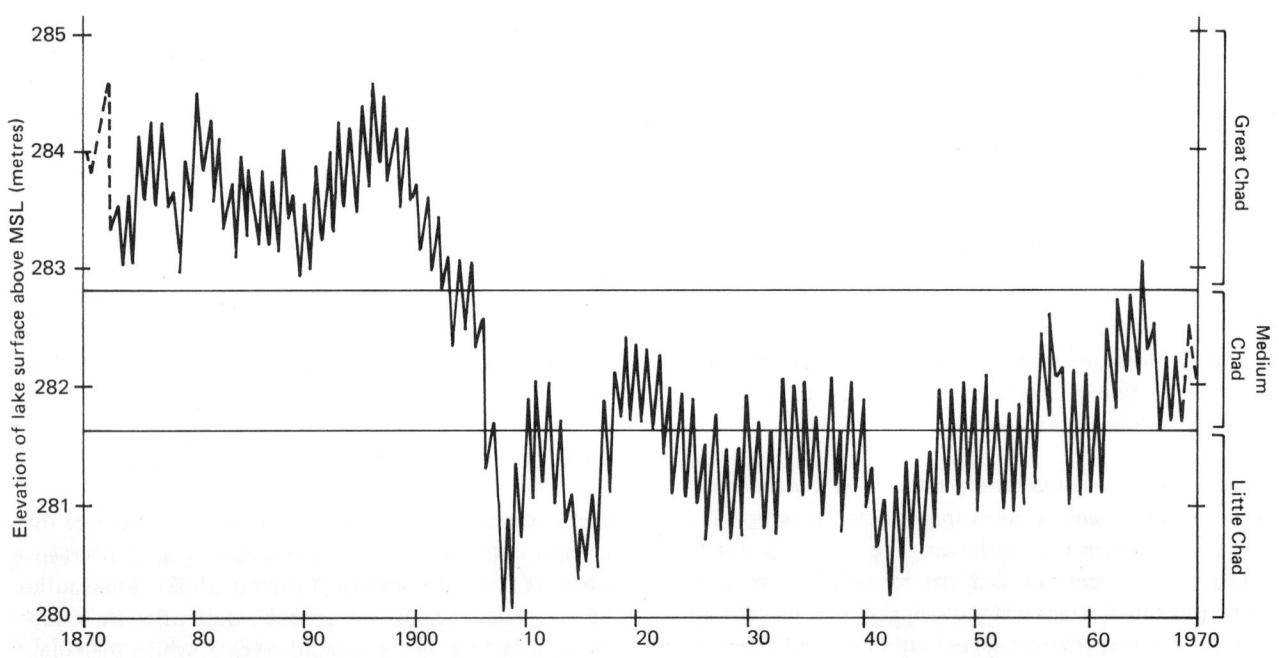

FIG. 3   Surface levels of Lake Chad (annual maxima and minima), 1870–1970 (From Sikes 1972)

TABLE 2. Climatic data for Agadez, Niger

	Mean temperature (°C)[a]	Evaporation rate (mm)[b]	Rainfall[c] Days[d]	Rainfall[c] mm
January	20.0	284	0.1	0.1
February	22.8	304	—	—
March	27.4	370	0.1	—
April	31.1	413	0.1	1.2
May	33.9	415	1.5	6.1
June	33.5	346	2.3	7.3
July	32.2	247	6.2	43.1
August	30.7	170	9.7	90.3
September	31.3	267	2.5	15.7
October	29.7	342	0.1	0.3
November	25.0	315	—	—
December	21.3	289	—	—
Annual	28.2	3,762	22.6	164.1

Source: UNCOD 1977a

[a] 1926–1954
[b] 1963–1964
[c] Mean 1921–1954
[d] Number of days with rainfall over 1 mm

TABLE 3. Rainfall (mm) over ten-day periods in Tudu, Niger, 1969–1974

Month and day	1969	1970	1971	1972	1973	1974
April						
1–10	0	0	0	42.6	0	0
11–20	0	0	0	0	0	0
21–30	0	0	0	0	0	1.0
May						
1–10	0	0	0	3.2	0	5.0
11–20	0	0	0	2.0	1.8	0
21–31	0	37.9	0	20.5	0	0
June						
1–10	13.0	0	0	8.2	0	2.0
11–20	0.3	6.5	0	52.6	0.8	3.5
21–30	17.0	0	0	51.6	0	0
July						
1–10	63.0	51.5	29.6	12.6	3.6	27.0
11–20	24.5	39.7	0.4	0	9.4	11.1
21–31	82.1	169.0	29.0	29.7	23.0	52.1
August						
1–10	29.4	52.0	47.7	104.9	25.6	159.7
11–20	77.6	52.3	74.4	21.8	32.5	79.3
21–31	43.3	27.9	37.5	47.8	4.5	15.0
September						
1–10	35.9	9.5	26.4	0	27.6	26.8
11–20	20.3	46.8	21.4	2.3	27.6	33.5
21–30	25.0	0	1.5	0	0	0
October						
1–10	10.5	0	0.5	0	0	6.5
11–20	0	0	0	0	0	0
21–30	6.0	0	0	0	0	0
Total	447.9	493.1	268.4	399.8	156.4	422.5

Source: Faulkingham 1977

lands, both spatial and temporal. As an example, it is worthwhile to look at two stations in depth, Agadez and Madona in Niger. At Agadez, in the western part of Niger (17°N, 8°E), annual precipitation has a 53-year mean of 158 mm, with a maximum of 288 mm in 1958 (182 per cent of the mean) and a minimum of 40 mm in 1970 (25 per cent of the mean). Table 2 presents monthly average temperatures and precipitation and evaporation-rate figures for Agadez.

With a standard deviation of 57.2 mm, in any given year the chances are one out of three that rainfall will exceed 215 mm or fall below 101 mm (UNCOD 1977a). At Madona, in south-central Niger, records from 1944 to 1974 indicate a mean of about 450 mm per year but with a maximum of 825 mm in 1950 (183 per cent of the mean) and a minimum of 156 mm in 1973 (35 per cent of the mean) (Faulkingham 1977).

From a plant's point of view (or, for that matter, a dry-land farmer's) the timing of the precipitation is at least as important as the total amount. A dry spell of ten days or more can seriously retard the development of a crop, and, if prolonged, will kill it. Such dry spells after the onset of the rains were documented in 1970, 1972, and 1973 in a village near Madona (table 3), and each time the dry spell necessitated a second or even a third sowing, further depleting whatever stored grain was available until the next harvest.

Pasture species are usually much more resistant to drought,

but a dry spell after the onset of spring growth will reduce the number of annuals and lower the reserves of perennials (UNCOD 1977a). Undoubtedly annual seeds have a large degree of variability with regard to time and moisture requirements for germination, but a series of such breaks in the rainy season can lead to a relative increase in perennials. The timing and intensity of rainfall interacts with other factors such as slope and soil type to indirectly affect not only germination and primary productivity but also soil erosion, species composition, patterns of grazing, etc.

Spatial variation in precipitation is also very important, as indicated in table 4. P1, P2, and P3 were stations located less than 10 km apart in a small drainage basin 30 km from Agadez. The data for August again suggest that variability tends to be inversely proportional to rainfall, as one storm on 14 August 1973 dropped 50 mm on P1 and P3 but only 24 mm on P2. In areas with a higher average annual rainfall, these variations would tend to even out.

TABLE 4.   Rainfall (mm) at stations near Agadez, Niger, 1973

Station	April	May	June	July	August	September	Total
P1	—	—	0.5	32.5	80.4	0.0	113.4
P2	—	—	4.2	31.2	45.8	0.2	81.4
P3	—	—	2.3	25.0	91.5	0.0	118.8
Agadez	8.1	—	10.8	39.4	17.9	0.1	76.1

Source: UNCOD 1977a

In summary, rainfall in the Sahel is highly variable with regard to its timing, amount, and spatial distribution. In general, as the annual average precipitation decreases, the variability increases. In turn, this amount of variability suggests that one or more dry years will occur with a certain statistical frequency. This does not, however, imply any sort of periodicity or regularity of drought, nor any predictive capability other than an estimation of probabilities based on the past record.

This variability also makes it mathematically impossible to make any claims of short-term climatic change. In all likelihood any past climatic change took place over hundreds of years, so the change over a period as short as 50 years would be at most a few millimetres of rainfall. Our understanding of the global weather system is such that this also doesn't allow any predictive capability. It may be that dry years tend to come in series rather than randomly (Nicholson 1983), but the cause of this is uncertain. Finally, this variability in climate, combined with the lack of predictability, has critical implications for resource use and development planning.

Vegetation, Land Use, and Resource Development

A brief outline of the vegetation in the Sahel is important for two main reasons. First, since vegetation is a function of soils, climate, and previous land use, it serves as an important indication of productivity and potential land use. Second, some 85 per cent of the people live in the rural areas and are therefore dependent on the natural vegetation for virtually all their energy, most of the feed for livestock, and a variety of medicinal and nutritional purposes.

Consistent with the Sahel's position between the desert and the tropical forest, the vegetation is a mixture of Sudanian and Saharan elements, together with a very small number of endemic species. Nevertheless, Monod (1975) concludes that a distinctive Sahel zone can be floristically identified. Within this zone three main vegetation zones are typically distinguished. From north to south these are the Sahelo-Saharan zone, the Sahelian zone, and the Sahelo-Sudanian zone (Bernus undated; Bradley 1977). To a large degree these ecological zones are consonant with land-use zones, briefly described below.

The Sahelo-Saharan zone has a mean annual rainfall of approximately 100-200 mm. It is an area of widely scattered shrubs and sparse perennial tussock grasses. Vegetation cover is usually less than 30 per cent, with shrubs and trees found mostly along the wadis (seasonal watercourses) or other edaphically favourable sites. The herbaceous biomass is no more than 400–500 kg per hectare (Adefolalu 1983). Soils are largely undifferentiated, low in organic matter, and generally poorly developed. The dominant woody species are low trees or shrubs of Acacia tortilis, A. ehrenbergiana, and Maerua crassifolia, while the key grass species are Aristida pungens and Panicum turgidum.

As in the Sahara itself, nomadic grazing is the dominant form of land use. In a good year, large herds of cattle, sheep, and goats will range northwards throughout this zone, making use of the diffuse and ephemeral vegetation. Once the seasonal water starts to dry up, the herds will slowly shift back to the south.

The Sahelian zone can be roughly defined as that area with an average annual rainfall of 200-400 mm. It has a basically prairie vegetation of annual grasses but with larger and more numerous trees and shrubs than the areas further to the north. In addition to the three woody species already mentioned, one commonly finds Acacia raddiana, A. senegal, A. seyal, Balanites aegyptiaca, Zizyphus mauritiana, and Boscia senegalensis. Dominant grasses include several species of Aristida, Cenchrus bifloris, and Schoenefeldia gracilis. Soils are often gravelly, low in organic matter, and deficient in nitrogen and phosphorous. Most soils have a high sand content and are classified as aridisols. As in the Sahelo-Saharan zone, the poor chemical and physical properties result in a high susceptibility to wind and water erosion (Stoop 1981). In small depressions or low-lying areas the finer sediments tend to accumulate and form vertisols, clay loams, or alluvium (Berry 1975). This increases the water-holding capacity and allows better plant establishment and growth. Other reports note that all soils are more or less eroded (SSO 1973).

Dryland agriculture has often been attempted in this zone, but crop yields are highly variable and fail altogether in dry years. Once the land has been cleared, aeolian erosion can become a serious problem. Except for a few localities with better soil and water reserves, this zone should be devoted to animal husbandry.

In the Sahelo-Sudanian zone, annual rainfall averages 400–600 mm. The vegetation can be classified as an open savannah. Soils in the sandy areas are generally ferruginous, and these are interspersed with vertisol clays, clay loams, or alluvium (Berry 1975). The natural tree cover is perhaps 10–12 per cent on sandy soils, and as much as 60 per cent on the clay or silt soils. Less xerophytic species are found, such as *Combretum glutinosum*, *Guiera senegalensis*, *Grewia* spp., *Adansonia digitata*, *Anogeissus leiocarpa*, *Pterocarpus* spp., and *Terminalia* spp. There is a dense cover of perennial grasses, including *Andropogon*, *Eragrostis*, *Pennisetum*, and *Zornia glochidiata*. In this zone rain-fed agriculture is possible, but in the drier years yields will be considerably reduced.

Figure 4 is a generalized schematic drawing of the major tree and grass species in the three zones defined above. This pattern is of course modified by topography, geology, and micro-climate, as well as annual variation in precipitation. If there is a series of more humid years, such as the period 1960-1967, these zones will shift northwards and the less xerophytic vegetation will colonize drier sites. When conditions then return to "normal" or there is a drought, there will be some mortality, and care must be taken to ascertain whether this is in fact a normal process or a sign of increasing desertification.

Unfortunately, there have been very few long-term research projects that have been able to distinguish between climatic and anthropogenic factors. One such study was carried out in an area of northern Senegal that receives an average annual rainfall of 400 mm. Fortuitously, detailed work began in 1969, just before the dry years of 1970, 1971, and 1972, when total annual rainfall was 209, 202, and 33 mm respectively. Between 1969 and 1970, rainfall was effectively reduced by 45 per cent, but herbaceous production dropped only 20 per cent. In 1972 above-ground production was practically nil, yet the major proportion of grass seed remained on the ground and viable. For the woody species, mortality was highly variable according to the species and the site (dune summits, slopes, or depressions). Maximum mortality was sustained by *Guiera senegalensis* on dune summits — 63 per cent — but more than sufficient numbers of this species survived to ensure continued seed production and dominance. The adaptability of the woody overstorey is indicated by the reduced time actually in leaf (40–45 per cent reduction in 1972-1973), reduced leaf biomass production (35–76 per cent reduction in dry-weight production in 1972-1973, depending on the

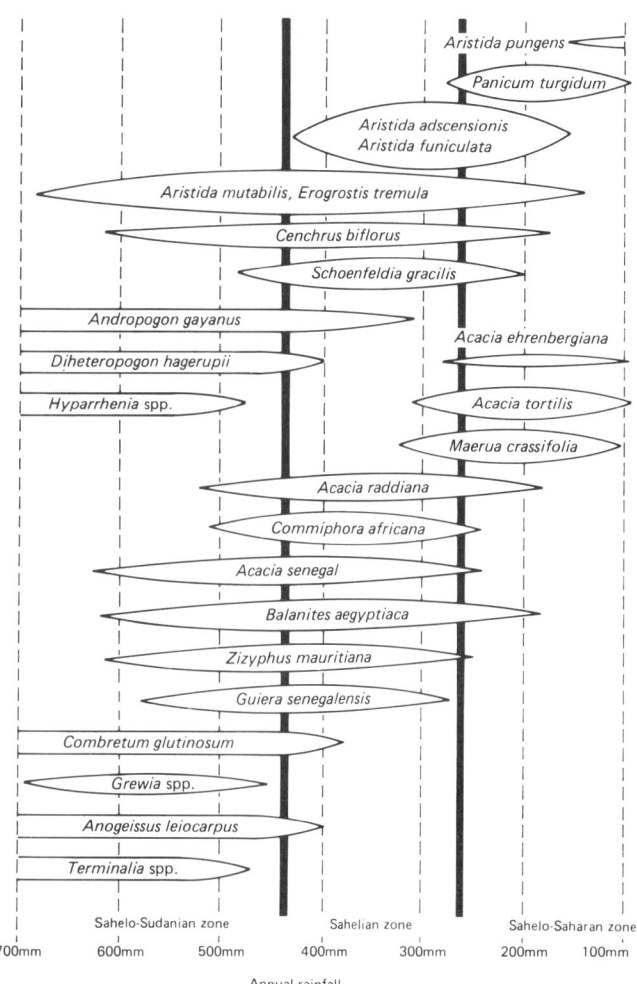

FIG. 4.   Ranges of some principal plant species in the Sahel in relation to average annual precipitation (From Bradley 1977)

species), and greatly reduced flowering and fruiting. In summary, the response of both the herbaceous and the woody layers suggest that the initial effects of any drought are dampened, and in cases of continued drought the growth and reproductive processes simply slow until more water becomes available. Mortality does occur and can be significant, but the potential for rapid regeneration remains. To retain this resilience and integrity of the natural vegetation, the harvest of products must be reduced during successive dry years.

As implied above, most of the woody species in these zones are dry-season deciduous, with the timing of leaf flush and leaf drop dependent on precipitation. In the drier areas only *Balanites aegyptiaca* and *Maerua crassifolia* are evergreen. The growing season may be reduced to as little as one month in the northern Sahel and roughly three months in the Sahelo-Sudanian zone.

TABLE 5.   Variations in plant biomass (kilograms per hectare) in the northern
Sahel by time of year and topographic location

	August	September	October	November	December	February
Dunes	150	400	600	650	550	380
Depressions	300	3,000	3,400	2,800	2,400	2,200
Shaded surfaces	400	1,600	1,800	1,600	1,000	800

Source: Boudet 1975b

In addition to these three zones, there are other types of vegetation, which are found only in very specific conditions. One of the most important of these is the flood-plain vegetation along the Senegal, Niger, Chari, and other main rivers. The abundant water supply makes these areas highly productive, but they are also easily exploited. The riverine forests of *Acacia nilotica* have been heavily cut, and this has significantly increased erosion and sedimentation rates (NAS 1983). The flood plains are also the source of valuable pastures. Dominated by *Echinochlua* spp., these areas are important in providing high-quality grazing and thereby shortening the time that animals are dependent on browse and low-quality dry fodder (Office of International Studies 1978).

South of the Sahelo-Sudanian zone is the Sudanian zone. Here rainfall ranges from about 600 to 950 mm, and this supports a much denser woody vegetation. For the most part the trees are still dry-season deciduous. The herbaceous cover is generally taller, and *Andropogon* spp. could be considered the characteristic grass (Ruthenberg 1974). The denser vegetation combined with the long dry season means that fire is relatively common and may burn much of the area (Cockrum 1976).

Still further south is the Guinea zone, and this may be subdivided into the Doka woodland zone (950–1,400 mm average annual rainfall) and the Guinea woodland zone (1,400–1,800 mm average annual rainfall). The former can be considered a mixture of savannah and forest, with fire a key element in maintaining the grassy open areas (Cockrum 1976). The Guinea woodland zone tends to be mostly forested. Only Senegal, the Gambia, and Burkina Faso have more than 10 per cent of their land area in the Doka woodland zone, and for obvious reasons these areas are relatively densely populated. These wooded zones are the source of much of the charcoal for the urban centres, and they are also much less subject to drought. Hence these areas, as well as the countries further to the south, historically have absorbed much of the influx of people and animals when there is drought further north.

As noted above, land use is closely correlated with vegetation. In the northernmost parts — with less than 300 mm annual rainfall — grazing is virtually the only practical form of land use. Only on flood plains or in exceptionally favoured locations can crops be grown without some form of irrigation. Further south rain-fed agriculture is the dominant occupation of the rural population, with livestock often an important component. Only when one gets into the Guinea zone do the problems of animal diseases force a more complete reliance on crops. Following is a brief description of grazing and agriculture, and then a discussion of the other major components of the Sahelian economies.

Grazing

In the absence of wells, pumps, and other technological inputs, grazing is the only effective way to utilize the very dispersed, ephemeral resources north of the 300-mm isohyet. Different ethnic groups have developed a variety of strategies to cope with this harsh, high-risk environment. On one extreme there are the true nomads, who usually do not follow any set routes in exploiting the vegetation; their numbers are estimated at 2.5 million in the seven countries considered here (Caldwell 1975). At the other extreme are the farmers who raise crops on the flood plains and wetter areas and maintain only a few animals as a supplement to their diet and insurance in case the crops fail. In between is transhumance, involving regular seasonal migrations. In this system it is common for part of the tribe, clan, or family to tend the animals while the remainder stay in one place to grow crops during the rainy season.

Given the short-term availability of high-quality pastures, such systems of movement are eminently reasonable and ecologically sound. Dry-weight primary production in the northern Sahel can reach as much as 2,000 kg per hectare, enough to support one to two tropical livestock units* per hectare (UNCOD 1977a). However, after the rainy season the quantity of forage declines rapidly, as shown in table 5, and the lack of woody vegetation means that little

---

* A tropical livestock unit (TLU) is defined as 250 kg live weight of livestock, so that 1 TLU is approximately 1 camel or horse, or 1.33 cattle, or 8.5 sheep or goats (cf. Boudet 1975a).

forage is available in the dry season, especially in the Sahelo-Saharan zone.

There is also a marked seasonal change in the quality of forage. For example, the crude nitrogen content of *Cenchrus biflorus*, a characteristic Sahelian grass, drops from 16 per cent in growing plants in the rainy season to 4 per cent in straw in November and only 2.6 per cent in straw in April (Boudet 1975b). For cattle, a nitrogen content of at least 5 per cent is required to prevent weight loss. Without supplemental feed, cattle under these conditions will clearly tend to lose weight and may not survive if they must be driven long distances to market. In Senegal the weight changes of two-year-old Zebu cattle were recorded during rotational grazing on a pasture that had a peak above-ground herbaceous biomass of 1,300 kg per hectare in an area with an average annual rainfall of 430 mm. The seasonal summary was as follows:

— August and September: daily gain in weight of 900 g/day with a stocking rate of 50 kg/ha.
— October to December: daily gain in weight of 400 g/day with ingestion of 60% of herbaceous production (straw) at a stocking rate of 300 kg/ha.
— January to June inclusive: daily loss in weight of 170 g/day with ingestion reduced to 30% of the forage stocks, at a stocking rate of 90 kg/ha.
— January to late April (before the very hot period): maintenance of weight with consumption of 35% of the forage stocks, at a stocking rate of 80 kg/ha. [Boudet 1975b, p. 33]

Of the four animals commonly grazed — camels, goats, sheep, and cattle — camels are the most hardy, able to survive 10 days without water even in the dry season, and able to eat almost anything. On the other hand, cattle usually stay below the 200-mm isohyet and, as indicated by animal deaths in the last drought (see chap. 3), they are the most susceptible. Sheep and goats range everywhere, with the latter being noted for their ability to reach and consume all types of vegetation. Gillet (1975) blames the goat's preferences for buds as a major factor in the degradation of the vegetation cover. Sheep, on the other hand, are castigated more for their gregariousness than their feeding habits.

The traditional grazing pattern is that at the end of the dry season the animals are either near the permanent villages feeding on dry matter and browse or far enough south to find range and water but not so far as to encounter the tsetse fly. The migration north begins and continues as long as the grass ahead is as green as the pastures at hand. When the northernmost grass and water are consumed (usually in November or December), there is a slow movement southwards to the home range, where there should be crop stubble and a full growth of grass to carry the animals through the dry season (Clyburn 1974). Traditionally, the different clans or ethnic groups usually have their respective grazing areas, and, depending on their environment, they also tend to specialize in certain animals. For example, the Fulani in northern Nigeria and southern Niger are known for their cattle, while the Tuareg, who live north of the Fulani, rely more on camels. In times of drought all the herders tend to shift further south than usual. In 1971–1973, for example, Mauritanian herdsmen were reported in Liberia and Nigerians in Zaire (Clyburn 1974).

Cattle productivity is notoriously low, with a calving rate of 0.5, a kilograms-feed-per-kilogram-weight-gain ratio of 20 to 1, and four to five years needed for the animals to reach sexual maturity. Often the Sahelian herders have been castigated for being backwards, for over-grazing, and for a general lack of efficiency; but it is now recognized that they are acting rationally, given their environmental milieu and social paradigm. Swift (1976) explains:

The fact that pastoralists are more concerned with protecting themselves from these risks than with making an immediate profit determines a number of salient features of nomad economic strategies. Three are relevant here: (a) flexibility in managing animals so as best to exploit a varied vegetation; this is accomplished by herding several species of domestic animals, each with its own economic and ecological characteristics. Pastoralists commonly spread risk by herding sheep and cattle, which sell well but need lots of grass, water and labour, and camels and goats, which sell less well but which can survive very bad conditions. Goats in particular are hardy, able to survive a drought and can breed again rapidly, thus producing milk five months after the first good rain. Various combinations of these species give Sahelian pastoralists a flexible range of economic strategies to follow according to the needs and conditions of the moment. (b) A second important feature of traditional herd management strategies was the accumulation of large herds above those needed for immediate subsistence in good years. This habit has given rise to misunderstanding and talk of cattle worship. It is nothing of the sort. As several researchers have pointed out, large herds are the adaptive response of a subsistence economy to the demands of a difficult and variable environment; among other virtues, large herds enable food to be stored "on the hoof" and make it possible for a network of reciprocal gifts and loans of animals to be set up between families, which serves as insurance against individual disaster. Pastoralists use animals [that are] surplus to immediate subsistence needs to build social relationships which can be turned back into food in time of need. (c) A third characteristic of Sahelian pastoral economies is their relative lack of success in regulating grazing pressure. The variability of rain and pasture, and the need for flexibility in management, make any precise attribution of land to a particular group of pastoralists difficult. . . .

Grazing land is generally considered the property of the clan, other clans not being permitted to graze without permission. . . . In fact, even if a clan has complete jurisdiction over the pasture of one particular area, members of that clan may still overgraze. The problem of limiting use of common property resources to an ecologically correct rate of exploitation is at variance with group interest and a solution can be found within the framework of a strong political power . . . able to impose limitations on the individual in the interest of the collectivity.

Cattle can be considered the dominant livestock species, and an analysis of the problems and trends in cattle production can serve as a useful indicator of animal husbandry in general. The basic paradox of livestock in arid lands is that pastures vary considerably on an annual basis but it takes several years for a given herd to respond. In theory it should be possible to reduce the animal population quickly in dry years, but this is generally unacceptable to the herder for both social and economic reasons. In the past, they would respond to changed conditions by shifting their animals to the north or the south depending on whether it was a good or a bad year. For a variety of social and political reasons this is ceasing to be an option.

Estimates place the current cattle population of the Sahel at approximately 23 million animals (USAID 1980a). This is slightly less than the peak of 24 million in 1968 but significantly more than the estimated 20 million at the end of the 1968-1973 drought. It has been suggested that stocking rates should be kept at 80 per cent of the average carrying capacity in order to protect the land in times of drought, but even in 1973, when the cattle population was at its nadir, the animal population was estimated to be within 10 per cent of the range capacity (USAID 1980a).

An increase in productivity has been attempted as a means of improving the standard of living of the herders without increasing the cattle population. So far the results have not been sufficient to compensate for population growth, and per capita meat and milk production have each declined 26 per cent over the last 15 years (USAID 1980a). Increased domestic consumption — primarily in urban areas — has significantly reduced export earnings. Milk imports have rapidly increased, and, if present trends continue, the Sahel will become a net meat importer by 1990.

In 1977 the livestock industry accounted for 16 per cent of the GNP of the Sahel countries. An estimated 21 per cent of the population are dependent on livestock production as their major means of support. Nearly half of these are sedentary, leaving about 3 million people engaged in nomadism or transhumance (USAID 1980a). These latter groups are the most difficult to reach with services and progressive change, and, for a variety of reasons, governments are encouraging them to adopt a more settled life-style.

Agriculture

While grazing is the dominant land use in most of the Sahelian countries, rain-fed agriculture is the dominant means of livelihood in all the Sahelian countries except Mauritania. In the seven countries discussed in this report, it is estimated that 80 per cent of the population were engaged in sedentary agriculture in 1975, farming 13 million hectares (Club du Sahel 1980). Sorghum and millet are the main food crops, and yields of the latter are 78 per cent of the average yield in Africa and only 44 per cent of the average yield in the developed countries (Lateef 1980). Legumes are often grown in combination with other grains and are important more for their nutritional value than for their absolute production.

Inputs are generally very low, with animal traction used rarely, pesticides and herbicides virtually unknown, and fertilizers used only in very limited quantities. FAO (1977) estimated that fertilizer use averaged 1 kg or less per hectare of cropland in Chad, Mali, Mauritania, Niger, and Upper Volta (Burkina Faso), 10 kg per hectare in the Gambia, and 16 kg per hectare in Senegal. Fertility has traditionally been maintained by the use of fallow periods, supplemented by kitchen residue in the near fields and manure from animals grazing on crop stubble or fallowed fields. Population growth and the increased area under cash crops have greatly reduced the use of fallowing, and this has had a number of negative environmental effects (see chap. 5).

The modernization of agriculture is also hampered by the spatial pattern of cultivation. Farmers, in order to reduce risk, often plant a number of different plots in a variety of soil and topographic conditions, thereby ensuring some yield in all years (Faulkingham 1977). In a study in south-eastern Upper Volta, Delgado (1978) found that the average farm had 17 different fields, averaging less than 0.25 hectares each, although not all of these would necessarily be in production in any given year.

In addition to sorghum, millet, and the other subsistence crops, cash crops — primarily groundnuts and cotton — are widely grown. While they contribute only 10-15 per cent of the gross value added in agriculture, they are very important in terms of exports and hence earnings of foreign exchange. In the case of Chad, cotton provides 85 per cent of export earnings. Groundnuts and cotton — together with cowpeas in Niger — account for 50 per cent of the export earnings of Senegal, Mali, Niger, and Burkina Faso. This reliance for export earnings on cash crops has meant that the vast majority of research and development efforts, as well as economic incentives, have been directed towards cotton and groundnuts rather than millet and sorghum.

Rice, sugar, and wheat are also generally grown as cash crops, but these are rarely exported. Population growth, urbanization, and changing food habits have caused rice consumption to increase at an average rate of 8 per cent per year. The bulk of the rice is grown domestically, but imports are increasing. Wheat consumption has risen a phenomenal 11 per cent per year, with virtually all of this imported. In contrast, sugar production has nearly doubled in the last decade and now meets approximately one-third of the domestic demand (Club du Sahel 1980).

Irrigated agriculture offers the twin benefits of higher production and relative independence from the uncertainties of climate, but at present less than 2 per cent of the farmland in the Sahel is under some form of irrigation. According to recent estimates, 71,200 hectares can be considered to have complete water control, while another 154,000 hectares have partial water control (Club du Sahel 1980). Nearly 90 per cent of the irrigated farmland is found in Mali or Senegal. The area under irrigation has nearly doubled since 1960, but during the past few years the development of new areas has barely surpassed the rate at which older areas are being abandoned. Rice is the main crop in irrigated areas (Club du Sahel 1980).

Another 200,000 hectares are under traditional forms of irrigation, including flood-recession farming (Club du Sahel 1980), and these are generally the areas targeted for the development of irrigated agriculture in the next few years. The importance of an adequate water supply is illustrated by the fact that 10 per cent of the population lives on the 3 per cent of the land with relatively abundant water resources.

Fishing

Despite the popular conception of the arid Sahel, the major river systems, Lake Chad, and the rich coastal waters all combine to make fishing an important industry. Fish is a major source of protein for much of the population, with an annual per capita consumption of 15 kg of fish versus 17 kg of meat. The fishing industry also contributes just 4 per cent of the regional gross product but generates 16 per cent of the region's exports. The resource is distributed unevenly, with Mali and Chad having 90 per cent of the inland waters between them, and Senegal and Mauritania having almost all the coastal waters. The inland catch is 220,000 tons (the estimated potential is 390,000 tons), and the catch in coastal waters is 1.7 million tons (with an estimated potential of 2.1 million tons) (Lateef 1980). The coastal fishing industry is still dominated by foreign vessels, but efforts are being made to build up the fishing industry in Senegal and especially in Mauritania (see chap. 3). This concentration on Mauritania is due to the fact that the fishery resources off the north-western corner of Africa are one of the world's last major under-exploited stocks, and, under the Law of the Sea accord, much of this stock is under Mauritania's control. Mauritania is actually one of the very few developing countries which has significantly benefited from the recent Law of the Sea accords.

Industry

Overall industry is still at an early stage of development in the Sahel. While real growth has been taking place and the industrial sector now accounts for 23 per cent of the total gross domestic product for the seven countries, most of the industrial activity is related to either the exploitation of minerals or the processing of various agricultural products. In countries that have no mining, such as Chad and Mali, the contribution of the industrial sector to

TABLE 6.   Distribution of labour force (1980) and gross domestic product (1981) by sector (%)

	Agriculture		Industry		Services	
	Labour force	GDP	Labour force	GDP	Labour force	GDP
Chad	85	70[a]	7	11[a]	8	19[a]
Mali	73	42	12	11	16	47
Mauritania	69	28	8	24	23	48
Niger	91	30	3	32	6	38
Senegal	77	22	10	26	13	52
Upper Volta	82	41	13	16	5	43

Source: World Bank 1983a

[a] 1979 data

the gross domestic product drops to 11 per cent (table 6).

There is some production of goods to sell locally and thereby save foreign exchange, but even in Senegal the industrial sector contributes only one-quarter of the GDP, and the processing of agricultural goods is nearly half of this (Lateef 1980).

One of the major problems in industrial development is the relative isolation of many of the Sahelian countries. Chad is some 1,500 km from the nearest seaport and lacks any railroad. Goods generally come by railroad and then are transferred to lorries, but this is a time-consuming and expensive process. Burkina Faso is also land-locked, although it does have a rail link to Abidjan in Côte d'Ivoire and the internal road system is relatively good. Similarly, Mali is connected by a railway through Senegal to the port of Dakar, and the Senegal River can be used for transportation during the flood season of July to October. Within Mali there is also 1,600 km of the Niger River, and much of this is navigable from July to January. The Gambia, Senegal, and Mauritania all have deep-water ports, but the transportation system to the interior is much less developed in Mauritania (with the exception of the links between the mines and the coast). In summary, transport to countries such as Niger and Chad is difficult and may double the cost of imported goods. During the rainy season internal transport within all the countries tends to get bogged down except along the main arteries. Tens of millions of dollars have been contributed from outside to improve this situation (chap. 3), but the extent to which this will lead to improved incomes and standards of living remains to be seen.

Tourism is another component of the industrial sector. In all likelihood this will remain insignificant except for Senegal, which can offer beautiful beaches and the pleasant climate of Dakar, and the Gambia, which attracts a limited number of English-speaking tourists. The problem with tourism is that it is extremely sensitive to fluctuations in the world economy and hence unreliable in terms of employment and foreign-exchange earnings.

In recent years mining has become increasingly important as a source of export earnings and hence funds for development. As with the fishing industry, there is considerable variation between the seven countries covered in this study. Mauritania has developed its iron and copper deposits, and mining now accounts for 27 per cent of its gross domestic product and 70 per cent of its export earnings. Niger has been supplying some 20 per cent of France's uranium requirements, and Senegal's phosphate exports are becoming increasingly important. Burkina Faso was expected to begin exploiting manganese and minor gold deposits, but recent unfavourable prices may delay these plans. Other phosphate deposits have been found in Mali and Niger, and while they may not be rich enough to justify export, they could be exploited locally for use as fertilizer.

National Economies

As indicated in the introduction to this chapter, the total gross national product declined between 1970 and 1981 in Chad, and the per capita GNP declined over the same period in Niger and Senegal. In large part this decline can be traced to the agricultural sector, as growth in the service and industrial sectors generally exceeded the population growth rate. The development of uranium deposits in Niger has spurred rapid industrial growth, while Mauritania has suffered a significant decline in industry from 1970 to 1981. On the other hand, Mali has averaged 4.6 per cent growth in the GDP per year since 1970, with strong growth

TABLE 7.   Selected economic indicators and trends in the Sahelian countries, 1970–1981

	Balance of payments (million $)		Imports, 1981 (million $)	Debt service		Average annual GDP growth rate (1970–1981)
	1970	1981		% of GNP[a]	% of exports	
Chad	2	4	137	2.9	14.4[b]	−0.2[b]
Mali	−2	−216	370	0.8	3.8[a]	4.6
Mauritania	−5	−6	265	8.0	15.8[a]	1.7
Niger	1	−152	449	3.8	3.6[b]	3.1
Senegal	−14	−619	1,035	4.2	13.7[b]	2.0
Upper Volta	9	−263	338	1.1	3.8[c]	3.6

Sources: World Bank 1981, 1983a

[a] Data from 1981
[b] Data from 1978
[c] Data from 1979

in both agriculture — especially cash crops — and services. Burkina Faso has also made significant progress in the last decade, with agriculture and services again leading the way (World Bank 1983a).

With the exception of Chad and Mauritania, all the Sahelian countries have experienced a significant decline in the balance of trade between 1970 and 1981 (table 7). Oil imports have been a major factor in this decline, accounting for 20-25 per cent of all imports. Machinery and manufactured goods are the most important imports in financial terms.

Both growth rate and per capita income seem to be related to indebtedness. Mali and Burkina Faso, the two countries that have experienced the highest growth rates, are the least indebted. On the other hand, Mauritania and Senegal, the two richest countries in terms of per capita gross domestic product, have the highest indebtedness. For the most part the high debt-service ratios — which are higher than those of Brazil, Mexico, or Argentina — have not caused concern because the absolute amounts are relatively small compared to those of Latin America. The Sahelian countries have also benefited from the tendency of the industrialized countires to simply cancel or refinance their debts. Inflation has not run rampant as in so many other countries, largely because of the economic links between most of the Sahelian currencies and the French franc. These links are largely due to the history of the region, the topic of the next chapter.

2. A HISTORY OF AID

Pre-independence

In looking at the current situation in the Sahelian countries it is important to realize that the present systems of organization and administration, while essentially based on a European model, have not been imposed on an unstructured amalgam of nomads and agriculturalists. Rather, current boundaries and political structures are the uppermost layer of history in a region that has already experienced at least a thousand years of kingdoms and empires. These large, relatively sophisticated political entities were established not just to resist outside influence and provide protection but also to regulate trade and commerce. For example, the kingdoms of Kanem, north of Lake Chad, and Ghana, on the upper reaches of the Senegal River, were already well established by the tenth century, and they served as the initial focus for trans-Saharan trade once North Africa was organized into Muslim dynasties. Here the exchange of gold from the south for salt from the north was carried out, and the profits from this and other types of commerce supported the development of towns, palaces, and a productive agriculture. Even through the early period of European settlement and trade, the succession of empires and ethnic groups controlling this commerce remained relatively undisturbed. There was, however, a continuing displacement of people to the south, where they pushed against the mostly forested coastal states (Davidson 1974). European presence was established by the Portuguese as far north as the Gambia River by 1500, but this was limited to small-scale trading and had virtually no effect on the interior. The Portuguese were then pushed out of the West African trade by the Dutch, and the large profits available through the growing slave trade subsequently attracted English and French traders, who were in turn supported by their respective royal navies.

From 1677 the French dominated trade north of the Gambia, in the area of the Senegal River, with the primary exports being hides and gum arabic. More established settlement was hindered by occasional British occupation of the French forts, but the relatively limited commercial possibilities (i.e., comparatively poor supplies of slaves and gold) led to a failure of the British colony of Senegambia and continued dominance by French traders (Davidson 1974).

In the hinterland these coastal struggles had little effect. More important was the occupation of the Niger bend by Moroccan tribes and the overall shift in the balance of power from the southern, more Negroid ethnic groups to the northern Islamic groups, such as the Fulani and the Hausa, which had adopted Islam. It was these groups, often operating under the call of *jihad* or holy war, that conquered and dominated the West African interior, although subsequent conversion of the rural population to Islam did not always succeed. Attacks were made against French traders at the mouths of the Senegal and Gambia rivers in the mid-nineteenth century, but these were unsuccessful.

In the latter part of the nineteenth century the mad scramble for colonies and land escalated. The British tried to consolidate their hold in the coastal states and move inland, while the French used the Senegal and Niger river systems to push far into the interior and take over what became the French Sudan and Niger, and to completely surround the British colony along the Gambia River. In 1885 the Berlin conference was convened by the European powers to settle conflicting claims and allocate the remaining interior lands. It was at this conference and the 1898 Niger Convention — with no African representatives present and with disregard for existing ethnic boundaries — that many of the national boundaries were established which persist to this day. As a result of this partitioning, France found itself with a tremendous area of sparsely populated land that presented limited possibilities for development.

In both the British and the French colonies it was a cardinal rule that the colonies should not constitute a financial burden on the homeland. Since colonial income was derived primarily from taxes on foreign trade and direct taxation of the more prosperous coastal population, the colonies soon had to be grouped together administratively, with the richer coastal states supporting the administration in the poorer interior. The French established a governor-general at Dakar, with the long-term goal that the colonies should become part of a greater France. In 1910 French policy towards the colonies was defined as "the greatest administrative, economic and financial independence which is compatible with the greatest political dependence" (Robarts 1974).

In the late 1870s trade in French West Africa totalled $8 million per year, three-quarters of which originated from Senegal. This slowly increased to $14 million by 1897, or less than one dollar per capita. Between 1880 and 1924 a railroad was built from the coast to the upper Niger, but the only profitable portion was the section within Senegal that carried groundnuts for export. Given the distance and environmental conditions in the interior, the French strategy shifted over this period from "opening up" French Sudan (Mali), Upper Volta (Burkina Faso), and Niger to a policy that more closely resembled benign neglect. In the coastal and more productive areas, agricultural production (cash crops) was encouraged (Wade 1974; Franke and Chasin 1980). Both Senegal and Gambia thrived on groundnut exports, and the emerging role of the interior was to provide basic foodstuffs for the Senegalese farmers so that they could concentrate on cash crops for export. One notable exception in the interior was the Office du Niger, which was a large-scale effort begun in 1929 to grow irrigated rice and cotton by tenant farmers. Inspired to a certain extent by the Gezira scheme in the Anglo-Egyptian Sudan, the project required an investment of 340 million French francs and was planned to cover 500,000 hectares. The project, however, rarely turned a profit, and by 1958 the cultivated area had declined to 34,000 ha of rice, 8,800 ha of cotton and 8,700 of "cultures diverses"; 32,500 people were involved, and losses were running at 100–200 million francs per year (Hansson 1960). Overall, outside investment in the French colonies totalled $155 million by 1936, which was only 25 per cent of the amount the British colonies in West Africa had been able to attract. Total trade increased from $58 million in 1912–1913 to $600 million in 1956–1957, and this provided France with as much as $315 million per year in government revenue, or about $17 per capita.

From 1929 the British slowly began to change their policies and provide their colonies with some of the funds needed for economic development. This concept was fully embraced by the French after World War II, when $1,100 million was allocated for investment in the West African colonies over the period 1946–1955. Associated with this economic aid was a general French policy of maintaining tight political and economic control over the colonies, which was accomplished through a variety of means. Only the educated elite were allowed to vote, resulting in only token African representation in the French parliament. Educational opportunities were extremely limited, probably because of both economic and political considerations. The first university in French West Africa was established in 1950, but at this time school enrolment was only 1.7 per cent and concentrated almost entirely in the coastal cities. Thus, by independence in 1960 there were only 1,800 university graduates in all French West Africa, or less than 0.01 per cent of the total population.

In 1958 the French colonies were offered a plebiscite by General de Gaulle to decide between full independence or an association with France in a Franco-African community. While only Guinea voted for full and immediate independence (Bon and Mingst 1980), the other colonies rapidly escalated their demands with regard to self-determination. Mali and Senegal joined together and pushed for full independence before renegotiating any continuing ties with France. They were then joined by each of the other territories, and by 1960 all the former French colonies were suddenly independent. The Mali-Senegal alliance then foundered, and the concept of a greater France was lost to history. Thus, with little preparation and less infrastructure, a series of independent countries were formed. Their leaders then had to cope with the high expectations of newly independent nations in a situation of rapid population growth, often combined with economic stagnation. Political leaders also had to overcome ethnic and religious loyalties that were usually stronger than the nascent concept of nationhood. In view of this background, it should not be surprising that political leadership for most of the period since independence can be characterized as either a rapid succession of coups and governments or the extreme stability of a single, charismatic leader.

Post-independence through the 1968–1973 Drought

Immediately following independence a set of bilateral agreements were established between France and its former colonies, covering the entire spectrum of relations, from economic to cultural to military. These agreements perpetuated an unequal relationship and were therefore increasingly resented (Lateef 1980).

Economically, the countries' dependence on France in the early years was nearly total, and this pattern of dependence has proved very difficult to break. In contrast to the former English colonies, each of which had to establish its own currencies and fiscal policies, France established a "Franc Zone" in West Africa that provided security in exchange for a certain level of dependency. Within the Franc Zone the exchange rate between the French franc and the local currency (West African franc) was fixed and credit guaranteed, thereby stabilizing and ensuring the value of the West African franc. In return, the countries had to accept a variety of fiscal restrictions, including the condition that all government reserves must be held in French francs and all foreign exchange dealings must be handled through Paris. In the mid-1960s Mali, as part of a general move to lessen its dependence on France, withdrew from the collective Franc Zone. Over the next few years the economic disruption was such that Mali eventually had to swallow its national pride and re-enter the Franc Zone, but with its Mali franc, originally at parity, only half the value of the common West African franc. On the other hand, Mauritania broke away from the Franc Zone in 1972 and has succeeded in establishing its own national currency. Robarts (1974) characterized the system as providing some economic stability and reducing the runaway inflation which characterizes so many other developing countries, but at the price of perpetuating French influence.

In short, in the first decade following independence France (and the United Kingdom in the case of the Gambia) was still responsible for virtually all development assistance and budgetary support. Sensitive to the charge of neo-colonialism and economic domination, a 1963 French policy report noted that free trade between the former French colonies and the industrialized countries was essential in order for the developing countries to obtain machinery and other materials necessary for economic growth. Co-operation was the suggested approach, and this was subsequently adopted as the basis for the French foreign aid programme (Lateef 1980).

Although few specific figures are available, France's total foreign aid in 1960 was 1.4 per cent of its gross national product, which is twice the current UN target for aid from the industrialized countries and four times the present US level. Since independence there has been a slow shift of French personnel and support from the educational and administrative infrastructure to more specialized development planning and technical aid (Robarts 1974). Lateef (1980) notes that even in 1975, 72 per cent of all technical assistance personnel supplied by countries of the Organization for Economic Co-operation and Development (OECD) were in the Sahel. Some 20-30 per cent of these OECD personnel in the Sahel were serving in the civil service in ordinary operational posts — a form of assistance normally avoided by both developing countries and donors. Lopez et al. (1980) note that the French emphasis in the 1960s on educational assistance served to preserve and reinforce French cultural influence, as well as compensate for the failure to promote higher education during the colonial period.

As for other donors, in the mid-1960s the United States decided to concentrate its aid efforts on what it identified as ten key, Western-oriented African countries, none of which were in the Sahel. Thus US aid to Chad, Mali, Mauritania, Niger, Senegal, and Upper Volta from 1962 through 1973 totalled $175 million, or somewhat over $7 per capita for the twelve-year period, while aid to the ten emphasis countries totalled more than $3 billion, or approximately $18 per capita (using 1970 population figures). From 1953 to 1972 development support to the Sahelian countries from international organizations (i.e., multilateral aid) added up to $800 million (Sheets and Morris 1974).

The shortcomings of the political and administrative infrastructure made it very difficult for the Sahelian countries to compete with the more "sophisticated" developing countries when applying for aid from multilateral agencies such as the United Nations. (At that time, aid was generally distributed on a competitive bidding arrangement. The resulting inequities led to the present system of allocation as exemplified by the United Nations Development Programme; see chap. 3). Only Senegal, through a combination of factors — more trained personnel, a better infrastructure, a greater capability to provide a counterpart contribution, and, not least, a pleasant climate — was able to attract funding proportional to its size. Otherwise France (and the United Kingdom in the case of the Gambia) was the economic lifeline, the ultimate source of expertise and financial support for the Sahelian countries.

During this transition from colonial status to independence, the Sahel was fortunate in that the period 1956-1965 was, on the whole, the wettest period of this century. Animal herds multiplied because of both better pastures and the provision of veterinary services; sedentary farmers pushed north in search of new and better land (Matlock and Cockrum 1976). Rules to control land use were promulgated, indicating some awareness of the fragility of the Sahel, but these were relatively ineffective (FAO 1965). Several authors (Wade 1974; Franke and Chasin 1980) indicate that the movement of farmers onto drier, more marginal lands was due at least in part to the pressure, often exerted through official channels, to use the best lands for cash crops such as cotton and groundnuts. From 1960 to 1965 agricultural production increased 10-20 per cent in all the Sahelian countries except Chad, thereby more than compensating for population growth.

In 1966 and 1967 the rains across the Sahel were, if not as abundant as in the previous years, at least reasonably well-spaced and sufficient to maintain the existing intensity of land use. In 1968, however, the rains came heavy and early, and then stopped in May. Seedlings withered and died before the rains returned in June, and the late replanting led to below-average crop yields and poor pastures. As noted in the Niger case study (UNCOD 1977a), agrostological studies concluded that over-grazing was not occuring except in localized areas (e.g. in the immediate vicinity of boreholes) as long as the rainfall was plentiful. But once the rains were irregular and did not exceed the annual average, carrying capacity dropped, and by the end of the dry season (early 1969) the first animals were dying of hunger. Mali, Niger, and Senegal asked the US government for food sufficient for a million people, and the US Agency for International Development (USAID) responded with $2.6 million of food aid (Sheets and Morris 1974).

In 1969 rainfall was more evenly distributed in time, but

in some areas it was quite deficient. The Agadez area in Niger received only half its annual mean of 164 mm, with 62 per cent of this coming in August. In contrast, Marnham (undated) reported — without explanation — that rainfall in the Sahel was 99 per cent of the 50-year average. Widespread food deficits were not apparent, and only $600,000 of emergency food aid was provided by the United States. Still a livestock loss of nearly 30 per cent was reported in the Sahara-Sahelian zone of Niger, and losses were approximately 12 per cent in the Sudano-Sahelian zone (UNCOD 1977a).

In 1970 there was a dramatic decline in precipitation, with many stations recording record low rainfall levels. Not only did this drastically reduce forage and crop production, but it also meant that there was very little recharge of lakes, rivers, and soil moisture. Those farmers and pastoralists who had moved further north during the good years were the hardest hit. When the mediocre 1969 harvest was exhausted, many people had little choice but to move their animals and families south. An estimated 3 million people in Chad, Mali, Mauritania, Niger, Senegal, and Upper Volta were in need of emergency food aid. According to Sheets and Morris (1974), the United States was again the major donor. Originally USAID was to "sell" 200,000 tons of grain in Mali, Niger, Senegal, and Upper Volta in order to stabilize prices, and use the proceeds to improve the production, storage, and marketing of crops. However, the situation during the 1970/71 dry season was so severe that most of the grain was simply used for emergency grants. Similarly, as a result of the drought, the UN World Food Programme (WFP) was experiencing difficulties in carrying out its intended food-for-work programme. In some projects it was necessary to distribute the food to a wider segment of the population than originally intended, so the distribution period was shortened accordingly. In other cases the WFP reports indicate that individual rations were reduced as a means of stretching the designated supplies and to achieve the desired goals (cf. WFP reports on individual projects). Altogether by mid-1971 $16 million of emergency aid had been dispatched to the Sahel (Sheets and Morris 1974).

Again in 1971 rainfall was below average. Lake Chad shrank to one-third its normal size. Officially recognizing the cumulative effect of four years of poor rainfall, the Director-General of FAO said that the Sahel required "special treatment" in the provision of emergency aid. Presumably this meant that the requirements for counterpart assistance were reduced and more flexibility was provided to the director of the World Food Programme in order to provide needed food quickly.

Altogether the total crop deficit from the 1971 harvest was estimated at 80,000 metric tons. The United States provided emergency aid for some 500,000 people in 1971, and

the WFP authorized 55,000 tons of grain worth nearly $9 million. Although it is not generally appreciated, this latter grant was in addition to the $3.5 million of emergency assistance already committed to the Sahel, and together these represented over 10 per cent of WFP emergency aid from 1963 to 1972 (FAO 1973).

As in previous years, the people themselves undertook a number of steps to alleviate the situation. Livestock were shifted south, and perhaps more people than usual migrated to the coastal states to look for wage labour. Redistribution of food within countries, ethnic groups, and families helped alleviate local shortages. In short, people utilized a number of social and economic mechanisms to adjust to a more persistent episode of a periodic hazard.

In 1972 the summer monsoon rains were well below average, causing widespread crop failure and poor pasture growth. The poor harvest and meagre fodder resources meant that a substantial amount of food would be required to carry the population through to the next harvest, but food and capital reserves, both formal and informal, were already seriously depleted. At this stage, in the autumn of 1972 the impending calamity was recognized in the field and it could be seen that the Sahelian countries had little choice but to request outside assistance. However, for a variety of reasons, it took six months before the by-then realized tragedy was officially recognized by the governments involved and then the United Nations (Sheets and Morris 1974; Brown 1977). Because of international protocol, the various multilateral and bilateral agencies could act only after the Sahelian governments had declared a disaster and requested help, and this initial declaration was not made until March 1973 — whether because of internal political reasons, a lack of accurate information, or bureaucratic delays, is unclear.

Both Sheets and Morris (1974), reporting on US efforts, and Brown (1977), evaluating the UN response, heavily criticized the concerned agencies for bureaucratic squabbling and a lack of preparedness. Only in the spring of 1973, seven months after the disastrous 1972 harvest, did the administrative machinery, finally having the political will and necessary authorization, begin to take positive action. Then the unavoidable delays in obtaining, shipping, and distributing food resulted in only minimal supplies becoming available until May or even June 1973. Grain then began pouring into the major West African ports, but the combination of an inadequate overland transport system and the first rains of the new rainy season meant that expensive airlifts were required to deliver the food to some outlying areas. In general the infrastructure was simply inadequate to put the right food in the right place at the right time. Furthermore, the traditional enmity between nomads and farmers meant that distribution was biased, causing substantially

TABLE 8. Donor food-aid commitments to the Sahel, crop year 1973 (October 1972–September 1973) (metric tons)

Donor	Mali	Niger	Senegal	Upper Volta	Mauritania	Chad	Total
United States	55,250	68,250	45,000	41,250	33,250	8,000	251,000
EEC	35,000	14,500	17,000	15,000	5,000	6,000	92,500
France	10,000	10,000	8,000	9,500	8,000	9,000	54,500
China	10,000	10,000	10,000	5,000	8,000	4,000	47,000
FRG	5,210	7,420	7,000	3,000	9,000	—	31,630
Canada	5,000	5,500	4,000	4,500	5,000	2,000	26,000
USSR	13,000	2,500	2,000	2,500	3,000	2,000	25,000
Other	—	—	—	—	—	—	74,370
Total	133,460	118,170	93,000	80,750	71,250	31,000	602,000

Source: El-Khawas 1976

higher death rates for nomads than for the rest of the population.

Food distribution to the sedentary population was generally much more satisfactory, with measles probably being the major cause of death. This is especially ironic since a large USAID/WHO vaccination project had been conducted in the late 1960s. The summary of a US Center for Disease Control report stated, "A contributing factor in the current measles epidemic is the large reservoir of susceptible children which accumulated following a decrease in emphasis on measles immunization after the mass vaccination campaigns recently conducted in West Africa" (Sheets and Morris 1974).

The overall food deficit resulting from the disastrous 1972 harvest was estimated at 900,000 tons, but, according to El-Khawas (1976), only 602,000 tons of food were committed in aid (table 8). Since much of this arrived late, it must be assumed that a variety of other mechanisms were operating to cope with the shortage (e.g., commercial imports, migration, accelerated slaughtering of animals). In addition, private relief organizations were soliciting contributions specifically for the Sahel by mid-1973, and these largely undocumented activities may have helped reduce the shortfall. FAO (1975) records show that the WFP contributed 57,000 tons in calendar year 1973, but it is unclear when this was actually dispatched. Table 8 indicates donor *commitments* for the 1973 crop year, but this does not necessarily correspond to the amount of grain actually received and distributed in the Sahelian countries.

In addition to the contributions of food, 63 aircraft were made available from twelve different countries, and these carried some 20,000 tons of emergency food aid between May and October 1973. Trucks, railroads, and even camel caravans carried the remainder. As detailed by Brown

(1977), much of the grain piled up at the West African ports because of the limited road and railroad capacity as well as sporadic shortages of fuel. Total relief aid for 1973 was estimated at $150 million, with 17 per cent of this spent for airlifts and 10 per cent for other means of transportation. On a per ton basis, airlifts were roughly 35 times as expensive as ground transport.

The 1973 rainy season was again well below average, and crop yields were further reduced by a lack of seed for planting and by the large-scale movement of farmers to the cities and refugee camps, where food was generally more abundant. The total deficit between the 1973 and 1974 harvests (crop year 1974) was estimated at 1.12 million metric tons of food grains and cereals, but even this poor harvest provided a temporary supply of food in many rural areas. The new crop of grass also provided some fodder for those who still had animals. Because of this seasonal availability of food, together with the on-going relief effort, fears that millions would die of famine were stilled. However, the nomads in the outlying camps, who had neither crops nor animals, would continue to suffer from malnutrition several more months (Sheets and Morris 1974).

To meet the 1973 deficit of 1.12 million metric tons, 613,337 metric tons were donated and 266,908 metric tons were purchased (using primarily donated funds). Another 239,382 metric tons became available as part of earlier pledges and donations that did not arrive until after October 1973. Table 9 indicates the source and destination of food aid for the crop year 1974.

On the donor side, officials tended to be misinformed or to overstate the problem and their efforts to alleviate the situation. UN Secretary-General Kurt Waldheim was quoted in 1974 as saying, "The encroachment of the desert threatens to wipe four or five African

TABLE 9.   Donor food-aid commitments to the Sahel, crop year 1974 (November 1973–October 1974) (metric tons)

Donor	Mali	Niger	Senegal	Upper Volta	Mauritania	Chad	Non-allocated	Total
United States	69,000	83,804	4,940	17,525	34,734	20,000	—	230,003
EEC	26,000	30,000	15,000	15,000	14,000	10,000	—	110,000
France	10,000	10,000	6,000	9,000	10,000	8,000	21,500	74,500
FRG	10,000	10,000	—	3,000	10,000	—	2,000	35,000
Canada	11,917	8,298	2,458	4,580	6,060	4,878	—	38,191
USSR	10,000	—	—	—	—	—	—	10,000
China	—	—	—	5,000	6,000	—	—	11,000
WFP	8,000	15,946	5,060	2,475	—	—	—	31,481
Denmark	4,000	2,000	10,000	2,000	5,000	—	—	23,000
Belgium	3,000	5,000	1,900	2,000	1,500	—	—	13,400
Others	15,217	4,402	1,927	—	7,250	966	7,000	36,762
Government purchases	101,184	23,000	109,700	20,000	10,000	3,024	—	266,908
Subtotal	268,318	192,450	156,985	80,580	104,544	46,868	30,500	880,245
Pipeline from November 1973	63,524	27,782	52,570	38,877	39,269	17,360	—	239,382
Total	331,842	220,232	209,555	119,457	143,813	64,228	30,500	1,119,627

Source: El-Khawas 1976

countries from the map" (Lateef 1980). A memo to US President Nixon dated 19 August 1973 claimed, ". . . mass famine — which threatened millions some weeks ago — has been averted" (Sheets and Morris 1974). In reality, there was indeed a tremendous amount of food aid committed and in transit, but it had not reached many of the more remote settlements in sufficient quantities to claim that famine had been averted.

While the actual number of deaths due to famine is not known, an American medical team extrapolated from the highest observed death rate in the relief camps to the entire non-sedentary population of Mali, Mauritania, Niger, and Upper Volta. The resulting estimate of 101,200 deaths sets an upper limit well below the levels mentioned in early press reports on the drought (Sheets and Morris 1974). The mortality levels observed by this team were corroborated by an independent survey in Mauritania (Greene 1975). This upper limit of mortality must be taken cautiously, however, as it was obtained by applying the highest death rates measured at a cluster of camps in northern Niger to the entire nomadic population. Not only is this a questionable procedure, but estimates of the nomadic population are themselves very rough. Both surveys recognized tremendous variability in the nutritional status of nomads, and this variability was reflected in mortality rates in the different camps. Current opinion is that between 50,000 and 100,000 deaths occurred as a result of the drought (Club du Sahel/CILSS 1980).

A review of the various emergency relief measures suggests that emergency aid is based not only on humanitarian concerns but also on political will. For example, US relief efforts in 1973 were constrained by the fact that two-thirds of all relief efforts were being directed to Viet Nam. Chad refused food aid from the United States because of criticism in the US press of the handling of relief efforts in Chad, and from the Federal Republic of Germany because of problems with a German hostage. Throughout the drought the Sahelian countries declined to reveal the level of their commercial food imports; this could be attributed either to their desire to maximize contributions or to an unwillingness to define precisely the extent of their agricultural failures. There was also an initial preference on the part of the Sahelian governments for requesting aid on a bilateral basis rather than issuing broad appeals for assistance (Lateef 1980).

By late 1973 the international relief movement had begun to sort itself out and resolve the problems of co-ordination and distribution that plagued initial efforts. Instead of individual surveys and pledges, the major donors began to undertake "multi-donor" missions, in which they would collectively estimate the harvest and food needs of each country and balance their estimates against government requests. In this way the donation process also became more organized, and a spirit of co-operation developed which was to be essential in implementing the forthcoming structural changes in the allocation of international aid.

It is an interesting reflection on previous aid that throughout the drought the primary cause of death for livestock was starvation and not thirst. Losses, as might be expected, were higher in the more arid northern areas. In general cattle populations suffered the most, with up to 100 per cent losses in some areas, while camels and goats fared somewhat better. FAO estimated the overall loss of cattle in 1972–1973 in the Sahelian countries at 3.5 million head, or 25 per cent. Cattle losses were estimated at 20–50 per cent in Mauritania and Niger, 20–40 per cent in Mali and Chad, and 10–20 per cent in Upper Volta. This does not include the accelerated slaughter that probably took place as herders realized their animals might not survive the next dry season (USAID 1980b). Sheep and goat losses were put at an average of 10 per cent (Club du Sahel/CILSS 1980).

As their animals died off, many of the nomads moved south and into the larger towns, where emergency supplies were more readily available. Interviews by Laya (1975) provide fascinating accounts of the drought, with many of the respondents reporting losses of all but one or two animals. Attitudes towards returning north and resuming their traditional life-style were highly variable, with some herders saying they would not return even if they were provided with animals, while others said they would do whatever the government told them. From the 29 interviews it is clear that the farmers and herders went to refugee camps only when they were absolutely destitute and that they accepted the drought without question. Many of them simply ascribed the drought to the will of Allah. Ethnic differences were also expressed; for example, in Niger the Fulani, having fewer ties to a given region and herding more mobile cattle, tended to move quickly into Nigeria or Cameroon, while the Tuareg stayed as long as possible in their traditional homeland.

In 1974, six years after the drought began, the situation began to improve with generally adequate rains (Allen 1974). However, the Sahel-wide 25 per cent loss of livestock, the presence of many farmers in refugee camps, and the lack of farm inputs meant that it would take more than one good year to return to previous production levels. With the procuring, shipping, and distribution of food supplies reasonably well in hand, attention shifted to the recovery and rehabilitation of the Sahel.

One of the first controversies that arose was over the climatic patterns in the Sahel — how often does such a drought occur, and will the drought itself trigger other changes to exacerbate the situation? In regard to the first question, Winstanley (1976) says that six consecutive years of below-median rainfall will occur every 70 years. On the other hand, the Niger study on desertification calculated that the chances of a drought similar to that of 1970–1973 are 1 in 2,400 (UNCOD 1977a). No real evidence was found for substantial climatic change, especially as annual variability is so very large and records relatively short (Seifert and Kamrany 1974). Similarly, fears that changes in albedo occurring as a result of the drought would lead to changing rainfall patterns seemed unjustified, for in 1975 and 1976 above-average rainfall fell in much of the Sahel.

It is clear, however, that for a period of five or six years during the drought the low-rainfall isohyets moved further south, in effect increasing the area of the "desert" (defined as land having less than 100 mm of rain) by an estimated 500,000 km^2. In Niger, for example, the 100-mm isohyet moved approximately 200 km southwards, while the 350-mm isohyet shifted about 150 km. In contrast, the higher rainfall areas ($>$1,000 mm) experienced normal or higher rainfall during the Sahelian drought. Thus the isohyets from 100 to 800 mm not only shifted south but also came closer together, thereby increasing the steepness of the rainfall gradient from north to south (table 10).

This climatic explanation of the drought does not provide a full accounting for the tremendous impact the drought had on the rural population. As suggested earlier, the effects of the drought must be measured in the context of the large increase in human and livestock populations over the previous decade, and the expansion of dryland farming onto normally unproductive lands. If these factors did exacerbate the impact of the short-term decline in rainfall, it needs to be asked what the causes of these trends were — whether a desire to increase cash-crop production, better health care and medical services, a change in farming practices, or economic incentives to increase the export of meat and hides. It is tempting and possible to put forward any number of plausible cause-and-effect hypotheses that apply to this situation, but a definitive analysis is beyond the scope of this and perhaps any report. The institutional response to the drought is a topic that is also fraught with conflicting values and judgements, but it is both more limited in content and more central to the purpose of this report.

Institutional Responses to the Drought

As a result of the 1968–1973 drought a number of institutional changes were made both inside and outside the United Nations. Within the United Nations, the Office of the UN Disaster Relief Co-ordinator (UNDRO) was created and became operational in March 1972. While its constitution was not necessarily a direct response to the crisis in the Sahel, it was given the responsibility of mobilizing, directing, and co-ordinating external aid to disaster-stricken countries, assisting countries in preventing disasters (e.g., through flood-control measures), and assisting countries in preparing and planning for possible

TABLE 10. Areas in various rainfall zones under various climatic conditions, by country (km^2 and percentage of total area of each country)

Rainfall (mm/year)	Mauritania	Senegal	Mali	Niger	Burkina Faso	Chad	Total
Period of average rainfall							
< 100	515,000 (50%)	—	421,600 (34%)	443,450 (35%)	—	539,200 (42%)	1,919,250 (36%)
100–300	432,600 (42%)	11,820 (6%)	347,200 (28%)	532,140 (42%)	—	192,600 (15%)	1,516,360 (28%)
300–650	82,400 (8%)	74,860 (38%)	223,200 (18%)	253,400 (20%)	41,130 (15%)	218,280 (17%)	892,270 (17%)
650–900	—	59,100 (30%)	111,600 (9%)	38,000 (3%)	120,648 (44%)	179,760 (14%)	509,118 (10%)
> 900	—	51,220 (26%)	136,400 (11%)	—	112,422 (41%)	154,080 (12%)	454,122 (9%)
"Little pluvial" period (1962–1964)							
< 100	399,640 (39%)	—	285,200 (23%)	595,490 (47%)	—	462,240 (36%)	1,742,570 (33%)
100–300	556,570 (55%)	3,940 (2%)	409,200 (33%)	202,720 (16%)	—	192,600 (15%)	1,375,030 (26%)
300–650	56,000 (5%)	68,950 (35%)	223,200 (18%)	418,110 (33%)	16,450 (6%)	243,960 (19%)	1,026,670 (19%)
650–900	7,790 (1%)	47,280 (24%)	148,800 (12%)	50,680 (4%)	95,970 (35%)	192,600 (15%)	543,120 (10%)
> 900	—	76,830 (39%)	173,600 (14%)	—	161,780 (59%)	192,600 (15%)	604,810 (11%)
Drought period (1970–1972)							
< 100	710,700 (69%)	—	471,200 (38%)	709,520 (56%)	—	539,280 (42%)	2,430,700 (46%)
100–300	298,700 (29%)	43,340 (22%)	384,400 (31%)	354,760 (28%)	—	218,280 (17%)	1,299,480 (25%)
300–650	20,650 (2%)	87,710 (43%)	193,400 (16%)	190,050 (15%)	76,780 (28%)	282,480 (22%)	853,020 (16%)
650–900	—	41,370 (21%)	99,200 (8%)	12,670 (1%)	90,480 (33%)	115,560 (9%)	359,280 (7%)
> 900	—	27,580 (14%)	86,800 (7%)	—	106,940 (39%)	128,400 (10%)	349,720 (6%)
Total area	1,030,000	197,000	1,240,000	1,267,000	274,200	1,284,000	5,292,200

disasters (p. 53). In view of the organizational rivalries within the United Nations and the initial staff of only three officers, it is not surprising that UNDRO played virtually no role in the Sahel disaster other than providing a token $100,000 contribution.

As the food crisis developed in the Sahel, the first emergency relief was provided by the World Food Programme. However, it was FAO that had the most expertise and best first-hand knowledge of the situation by virtue of its network of field officers and agricultural projects, and

it was the United Nations Development Programme (UNDP) that had the best infrastructure (since it generally provides much of the administrative support for FAO-executed projects). Thus it should not be surprising that FAO had already created an inter-departmental working group in early 1973 to study the drought. As the scope of the crisis became evident, this internal working group was succeeded in May 1973 by the Office of Sahelian Relief Operations (OSRO), which was also under the direction of FAO. By this time it was already very late in the crisis — very little was left of the previous year's harvest and it was the height of the dry season — but at least it was agreed that OSRO would be the focal point for UN activities, and a staff was put together in both Rome and Ouagadougou, Upper Volta. An FAO Sahelian Trust Fund was quickly established, and $4 million was pledged by June. OSRO's initial operations were hindered by the fact that immediate action was required, yet there was a substantial lag between pledges and actual payment. Some UN agencies, such as WHO and UNICEF, diverted project money to relief operations, while WFP initiated new procedures to shorten the time required for the approval and implementation of projects. By the end of February 1974 some $25 million had been contributed to the ongoing relief effort.

Although the Office for Sahelian Relief Operations was responsible for co-ordinating emergency relief, the head of UNDP was designated in May 1973 to be the co-ordinator in New York for long-term relief operations. More importantly, the Special Sahelian Office (SSO) was established to serve as the focal point for programmes concerned with the medium- and long-term recovery of the Sahel. One of the first activities commissioned by SSO was a set of sectoral studies on the Sahel.

During this same period when the United Nations was setting up its machinery for drought relief and long-term rehabilitation, the Sahelian countries were also making an effort to improve co-ordination among themselves. In March 1973, when the full magnitude of the drought was becoming apparent, representatives from Mali, Mauritania, Niger, Senegal, and Upper Volta met and jointly declared the Sahel a disaster area. Their mutual requests for emergency relief then provided the political authorization for both the United Nations and donor governments to act. At the same time these five countries also created CILSS (the Permanent Interstate Committee for Drought Control in the Sahel), which was quickly joined by Chad. As an intergovernmental organization, CILSS was to represent the Sahelian states, particularly with regard to the financing of future rehabilitation and development projects. As such, CILSS is a unique case of developing countries banding together to more effectively put forth their views on what aid should be provided and how.

By September 1973 CILSS was proposing some 300 projects, which would cost an estimated $3,000 million, with $850 million of this for what were identified as priority projects. As a first set of proposals these were admittedly imperfect, and some observers have suggested that many of them sprang from older proposals that had not been funded for one reason or another. In any case, the proposed projects did serve as a basis for discussion and to link the Sahelian countries in their efforts at development. In March 1974 the CILSS states formulated the three objectives that have guided activities since then: (1) to reduce the consequences of future droughts, (2) to ensure self-

sufficiency in staple foods (cereals and meat), and (3) to accelerate economic aid and social development (Club du Sahel/CILSS 1980).

The activities of CILSS and the UN Special Sahelian Office became much more intimately related in October 1974, when the UN Sudano-Sahelian Office (UNSO) was created to supercede the Special Sahelian Office. Originally based in Ouagadougou, UNSO's mandate was enlarged from simply offering advice on development prospects to (1) co-ordinating UN participation in Sahelian rehabilitation programmes and being responsible for contact with CILSS, (2) assisting in the mobilization of resources for CILSS projects, and (3) monitoring UN activities in the Sahel and helping ensure that these are consistent with the goals of CILSS (Brown 1977). UNSO thus assisted CILSS in the formulation of projects and in 1975 helped convene a donors' meeting in Geneva. As mentioned in chapter 3, the first donors' conference, in July 1975, was relatively successful in that the donor countries expressed interest in most of the 56 projects (costing $154 million) that were proposed by CILSS/UNSO and regarded as appropriate for near-term implementation. Shortly thereafter the Gambia joined CILSS, followed somewhat later by Cape Verde, which was also badly affected by the drought.

By mid-1975 the World Bank, FAO, USAID, and the other major donors had had time to analyse the situation and try to develop an overall strategy for the Sahel. Although each agency had independently prepared an overview study, they concurred in their major conclusions: (1) that planning must be done on a regional basis; (2) that development efforts must be pursued in an integrated manner; and (3) that 20–30 years would be necessary to achieve the basic goals of CILSS. Beyond these expected statements, the studies agreed that the goals of CILSS could be attained and that there was no evidence of climatic change (i.e., the 1968–1973 drought, although an infrequent event, was well within the range of normal climatic variability) (USAID 1976a).

In view of the context that these studies provided, the obvious need for a concerted long-term programme, and the criticism directed at the initial CILSS compendium of projects, a need was felt — primarily by the donor countries — for a more informal forum where donors and the Sahelian countries could sit together to work out strategies and co-ordinate their activities. This suggestion was accepted by the CILSS countries in late 1975, and in March 1976 the Club du Sahel was formally constituted (Williams 1977).

The Club du Sahel can be considered a co-ordinating body between CILSS and various donors, a forum for discussion, and a vehicle for increased communication and study. It was hoped by some that the Club du Sahel would also facilitate the provision of additional development assistance to the Sahel. Consistent with its mandate, a concerted effort has been made to keep the Club informal. Membership is open to all, and the Club plays no financial role other than maintaining a small secretariat.

At its first meeting, in March 1976, the Club du Sahel agreed on the broad outlines for defining a development strategy and discussed issues such as the amount of outside assistance that could realistically be absorbed by the Sahelian countries. There was some dissent, however, over the means of achieving these goals. In the case of food self-sufficiency, for example, there was disagreement over the relative importance of dryland farming versus irrigated farming. Finally, it was agreed that dryland farming had to be emphasized initially while the potential of the different rivers for irrigated agriculture was studied more thoroughly (OECD 1976). To prepare a more detailed strategy for economic and social development, a working group of ten teams was established. Four teams dealt with production (rain-fed agriculture, irrigated agriculture, livestock, fisheries), while five other teams dealt with intersectoral issues (human resources, transport, trade/price and storage, ecology, and technology). A final synthesis group was responsible for the coherence of the work of the other nine teams.

The resulting strategy was approved by CILSS in April 1977 and by the Club du Sahel at its second meeting, in Ottawa in May 1977. The strategy represented a major step forward in defining goals and the action that needed to be taken to reach those goals, but the final document had some inevitable shortcomings. For example, it did not provide a guideline for balancing irrigated and rain-fed farming, nor did it outline the future development of the livestock industry.

From this the working group developed a programme of activities which has since become known as the "first-generation programme", consisting of an array of projects designed to cover the period 1978–1982. Some of these were new, while others were a continuation of existing activities or were drawn from the CILSS programme proposed in 1973. Hence it was subject to the same criticism of heterogeneity, but it was a joint effort and it did respond in part to the newly adopted strategy. The total cost was estimated as $3,000 million.

The Club du Sahel working groups have now been replaced by joint CILSS/Club working groups on crop production, livestock, fisheries, ecology and reforestation, transport and infrastructure, and human resources. The successful presentation of national reviews of irrigated agriculture at the fourth meeting of the Club du Sahel, in 1980, has led to more emphasis on studies at the national level, as presumably the policy impact is greater at this level. National reviews have now been or are being prepared in most of the areas covered by the working groups.

Thus the first-generation programme has served as the framework for development efforts in the Sahel since 1977, but it has not — despite suggestions to the contrary — been an authoritative and uncompromising blueprint for assistance. The identification and funding of projects is an ongoing process, and although CILSS and the Club du Sahel have been remarkably effective in bringing order to what could have been a chaotic situation, CILSS has not put the Sahelian countries in a situation of full control over the development process. Each donor still picks and chooses projects from the CILSS/Club du Sahel smorgasbord depending on the donor's own interests and expertise, and then goes off to negotiate a specific project document. The details of project formulation, planning, and execution are discussed in more detail in the first half of chapter 5.

As for the effectiveness of the CILSS proposals, it is difficult to assess the average extent to which a final project document resembles the original proposal. Certainly in some cases the original concept is nearly unrecognizable. The Sahelian states have also requested assistance for sectors not included in the first-generation programme, and projects that were already scheduled or ongoing have continued. In short, the first-generation programme has helped to guide the orientation of new activities, but it is not possible to separate first-generation projects from development assistance in general (Club du Sahel/CILSS 1980). The shift over time of priorities for development assistance will be discussed in quantitative terms in later sections of this report.

The wide range of development agencies operating in the Sahel means that donors can finance particular activities without making long-term financial commitments or having to set up an infrastructure of field offices. As described in chapter 3, UNSO is designed both to be a middleman and to manage projects for donors. Alternatively, donors can provide funds-in-trust to the relevant UN agency, and in this way the donor can control the type of project but not be bothered with many of the administrative problems and political pitfalls. Outside the UN system there are a number of other multilateral and private agencies that can serve as channels for development assistance. Often, however, these agencies are not willing to accept restricted or "tied" funds (i.e., aid of which a certain proportion has to be spent on goods and services from the donor country). The existence of all these avenues for development assistance means that while all projects should relate to the CILSS/Club du Sahel–approved programme, both the CILSS/Club programme and the process of project formulation are sufficiently flexible to allow the development of a variety of mutually agreeable activities, some of which may not necessarily be part of the overall development plan.

Not only are donor countries responsible for the selection of projects to be implemented, but the very close co-operation between the Club du Sahel and CILSS means that the donor countries also have considerable input into the setting of priorities. Hence the CILSS/Club objectives — which are often quite broad — are likely to be in line with overall donor goals and almost any project the donors are interested in proposing.

In the years from the "end" of the drought in 1974 until 1976, adequate rains allowed a slow recovery of animal herds and a return of many of the migrants to the country-side (WFP 1975). In 1977, however, the rains were late and very irregular. In mid-September, at the end of the harvest, the Director-General of FAO warned that at least 200,000 tons of cereals were required beyond the normal level of food imports. Towards the end of October 1977 CILSS estimated a deficit of 500,000 tons. Multi-donor assessment missions were sent to each country, and the emergency food needs of the Sahelian countries — including Cape Verde — were estimated at 457,000 tons. Further appeals for assistance were made, and by October 1978 — one year after the original appeals — 380,246 metric tons, or 83 per cent of the required aid, had been delivered. An additional 16,000 tons were in West African ports, and 41,000 tons were pledged but not yet delivered (UNDRO 1979). Despite these shortcomings there was no famine, indicating again that the Sahelian people have their own alternatives for coping with drought-induced shortages. These data also suggest that the international community, while much better able to anticipate shortages and take timely action, is still not able to overcome some more basic problems, including unpredictable delays between pledges of assistance and the actual transfer of funds and materials, the problem of unpaid pledges, and the difficulties of transporting bulky foodstuffs to remote areas.

In 1977 there also occurred an illustration of the import-ance of national policies in exacerbating or alleviating the problems of poor harvests. In Upper Volta the government established relatively low cereal prices, presumably to allow the purchase of food by people with low incomes. However, the low domestic price encouraged illegal grain exports to neighbouring countries such as Ghana and discouraged the sale of surplus grain by the farmers, and thereby contri-buted to the country's estimated grain shortage of 114,000 tons (*New African* 1977).

It should be recognized that drought need not be a Sahel-wide phenomenon. From 1977 to 1981 the rains didn't fail to the extent they did in 1973, but localized, short-term food deficits have been caused by low rainfall and pest outbreaks. The World Food Programme has been providing emergency assistance over this period, indicating that as long as people are dependent on grazing and rain-fed agri-culture, in almost every year there will at least be local shortages of basic foodstuffs.

In order to provide an early warning of food shortages in the Sahel, the United Nations has tried to establish a number of monitoring systems. WHO has an extensive network of weather stations providing rainfall data on a regular basis, and FAO is supposed to monitor crop pro-duction; WFP provides a weekly report on "pledges, ship-ments and other relevant developments" (WFP 1978c). Nevertheless, there are still serious questions about the ability of the United Nations system to respond quickly and adequately.

To alleviate some of the problems associated with emergency aid, attempts are being made to keep food stocks in major centres so that they are readily available when emergency assistance is approved. Distribution in the rural areas may still pose severe administrative and practical problems, especially during the rainy season when most roads are impassable. The provision of food stocks also will not solve the problem of a time lag between a government's request for assistance and official approval of aid by a donor.

Usually before substantial aid can be provided, a group of officials from the major donors must be sent to survey the situation at first hand. Pledges are then made based on their recommendations. The two main problems asso-ciated with this procedure are the extensive time delay and the lack of data on which to base a recommendation. For example, the Gambia made an official request in March 1976 for 7,200 tons of food aid to feed 160,000 persons for 150 days (after which the new harvest should have been available), but "it took some time to assess the real needs, and after a careful analysis of the crop situation the request was approved on 10 August for only 3,000 tons" (WFP 1977). Despite the Gambia's location on the Atlantic coast, food was then not available until October, when the rainy season was nearly over and the new crop was already in the storehouses or in the process of being harvested. In addition to illustrating the first problem, this example also indicates the second: the uncertainty inherent in any assessment of crop yields and food needs. A multi-donor mission to Mauritania in 1976, for example, estimated the harvest at 26,000 tons, when it actually turned out to be 50,000 tons (UNDP 1979a). In develop-ment projects these problems may not be so critical, but when one is talking about emergency relief, lives are literally at stake and errors can't be tolerated unless they are on the side of oversupply. A review of project reports indicated that differences between government requests and mission recommendations were the rule rather than the exception, with the tendency for the mission to have a lower estimate of needs than the respective govern-ments.

In the early 1980s another series of poor-rainfall years struck most of Africa. In contrast to 1968-1973, the worst of the drought appeared to be in eastern and southern Africa, and attention focused initially on Ethiopia. By 1984 some 22 countries were in need of assistance, including all the CILSS countries except the Gambia. Total food-aid requirements for the 22 countries were estimated at 6.6 million tons.

Although it is too early to evaluate the response of the donor community fully, at least some of the lessons from the 1968-1973 drought appear to be remembered. Official awareness of the deteriorating food situation seemed to be quite high, and early attempts were made to collect pledges and transport food. However, the internal political situation — particularly in Ethiopia — made it very difficult to transport and distribute supplies to all those in need. From the timing of the donors' response it seemed that the political will to make substantial contributions was as dependent on public support (largely in response to media presentations) as on the humanitarian instincts of the various offical aid organizations.

It can only be concluded that mass famine will not reappear as long as the donor community does not lapse into an attitude of complacency. It is less clear, however, that development efforts in the Sahel will meet the CILSS objectives and obviate the need for future emergency relief. The following chapters will provide a detailed look at agencies of the United Nations system and analyse their efforts to remove the shadow of famine from the Sahel and improve the quality of life of its inhabitants.

3. THE AGENCIES OF THE UNITED NATIONS SYSTEM AND THEIR PROGRAMMES

Introduction

Established in 1945, the United Nations has as its primary concern the maintenance of peace and security. Provisions were made in its Charter for it "to co-operate internationally in solving international economic, social, cultural and humanitarian problems and in promoting respect for rights and fundamental freedoms" (UN 1980). To co-ordinate the economic and social work of the United Nations, the Economic and Social Council (ECOSOC) was created. A number of specialized agencies such as Unesco, FAO, and WHO were set up to co-ordinate work and establish international links in their specific fields of expertise, but initially technical assistance programmes were relatively limited.

Over the years the number of specialized agencies and other subsidiary bodies has grown tremendously in response to the needs of global co-operation and development as perceived by the General Assembly, and there has been a concomitant expansion of activities in the older agencies. There are now 17 specialized agencies and other autonomous bodies within the system and more than 12 subsidiary bodies (fig. 5). The purpose of this chapter is to provide an overview of the UN system and a brief review of how each body is involved in natural resources development in the Sahel.

In theory there are distinctions between the specialized agencies and the subsidiary bodies with the UN family, but in practice the primary difference is that the subsidiary bodies report directly to the General Assembly as well as to the Economic and Social Council, while the specialized agencies report through the Economic and Social Council to the General Assembly. This distinction is not particularly useful, for within both groups there is a tremendous diversity in terms of size and programmes. The UN family tree is further complicated by the fact that ECOSOC has also created regional subsidiary bodies (e.g., the Economic Commission for Africa) as well as a number of standing committees on topics such as natural resources, science and technology for development, etc. (fig. 5).

ECOSOC is attempting to put some order into relations among the eternally feuding agencies and co-ordinate their respective activities, but this has, for the most part, been in vain. Several approaches have been taken as a means of alleviating jurisdictional conflicts. At the highest level there is an Administrative Committee on Co-ordination, which consists of the heads of each of the agencies, but these contacts appear to be largely a formality. More useful are exchanges among the heads of divisions within agencies, as in UNEP's focal-points network. Agencies often sign mutual memoranda of understanding to facilitate co-ordination and perhaps define their respective roles, but these are so general in nature as to play little part in the planning and execution of specific programmes.

The Secretariat and System-wide Activities

The UN Secretariat's main functions are providing the necessary system-wide administrative support and servicing the policy-making bodies such as the General Assembly and the Security Council. The Secretariat also includes a Department of Technical Co-operation for Development (DTCD), which was established in 1978 as part of a wider reorganization and then restructured in 1983. The DTCD's main function is to manage and provide support for technical co-operation activities that are carried out by the United Nations itself rather than one of the specialized agencies; in effect, it could be considered a specialized agency within the Secretariat. In 1983 DTCD was responsible for spending some $112 million on various technical co-operation projects, with just 6 per cent of this amount originating from the regular UN budget. Seventy-one and 10 per cent came from UNDP and the UN Fund for Population Activities respectively; so these technical co-operation activities will be discussed in more detail in the sections on the funding agencies. The remaining technical assistance funds came from a variety of sources, with most of the activities directed towards southern Africa and Namibia.

Natural resources and energy are the two most important sectors of DTCD's programme, accounting for nearly half its total expenditures. Development planning is the next most important sector with 22 per cent of the expenditures, followed by statistics (11 per cent) and public administration and finance (10 per cent). Population was a very important sector, but UNFPA's shift from basic data

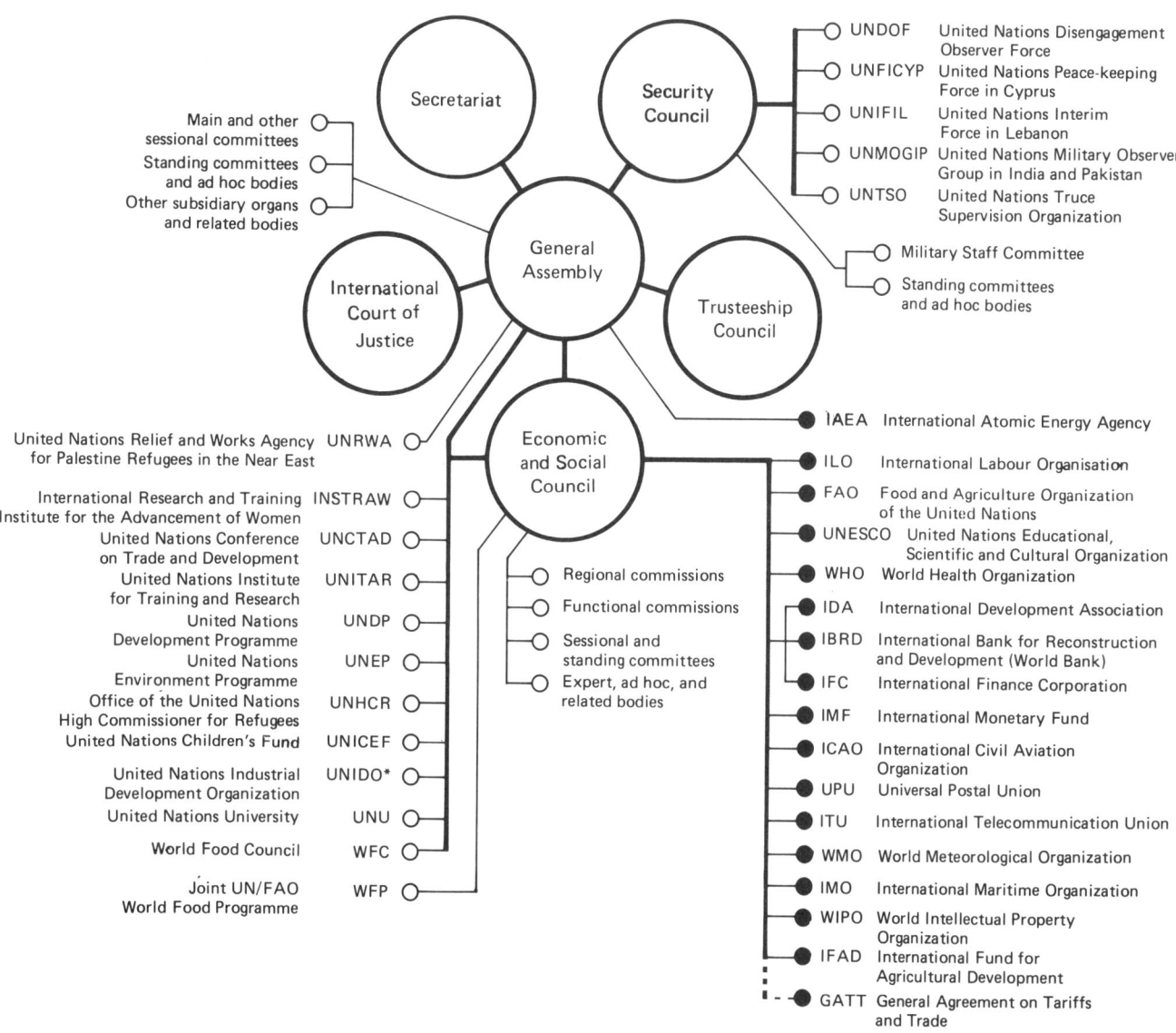

FIG. 5. The United Nations system. The large circles represent the principal organs of the United Nations. The small open circles represent other United Nations programmes and organs, whose governing bodies report directly to the principal organs (representative list only). The small solid circles represent specialized agencies and other autonomous organizations within the system. (*UNIDO is in the process of becoming a specialized agency.)

collection and analysis to emphasizing maternal and child health has substantially reduced DTCD's technical assistance operations in that area (UNDP 1984e).

The work of DTCD's Division of Natural Resources and Energy consists of sectoral research, technical co-operation, technical assistance, and the facilitation of co-operation. Often it works closely with the regional commissions under ECOSOC. Its activities are grouped under the sub-programmes of energy; minerals; water; and surveying, mapping, and cartography. The sub-programme on energy has been increasingly important, particularly since it is responsible for following up the UN Conference on New and Renewable Sources of Energy in addition to its earlier

work on energy exploration, energy planning, etc. Water has traditionally been one of the strongest areas within the Secretariat, and the focus here has been on shared water resources. In particular the division has been active in regional planning studies for the Senegal, Logone, and Gambia river basins. The sub-programme on minerals has been concerned with various aspects of mineral-resource development. Activities relating to surveying, mapping, and cartography constitute a much smaller part of the division's work and consist primarily of organizing conferences, providing limited technical assistance, and doing some printing of maps. In the future the unit hopes to strengthen its capability in remote sensing and provide assistance as needed to governments.

A second unit within the Secretariat concerned with the Sahel is the Economic Commission for Africa (ECA), which is one of five regional commissions directly under ECOSOC. ECA, with some 200 professional staff members, is involved in almost every aspect of development, from agriculture to heavy industry, from education to international trade. The overall aim of ECA with regard to natural resources can best be described as giving African countries the capability, either through training or through the provision of experts, to make the best possible use of their resources. In general, however, ECA is not concerned with the technical assistance necessary to exploit a given resource, except on a supervisory basis. Thus, most of the projects concentrate on the development of national policies, resource surveys, the organization of seminars and training courses, and the publication of a variety of materials. The natural resources and energy programme represents only about 5 per cent of ECA's budget, and it includes sections on mineral resources, water resources, energy, and cartography/remote sensing and a small project in marine resources. Outside funds for the natural resources and energy activities are on the same order of magnitude as the core budget (approximately $1.5 million). On a sectoral basis, the planned allocation for funds in 1982/83 was 30 per cent for mineral resources, 20 per cent for water resources, 18 per cent for energy, 25 per cent for cartography/remote sensing, and 7 per cent for marine resources. Most of the extra-budgetary funds are directed towards water resources, with UNDP and the UN Fund for Population Activities accounting for 42 and 24 per cent of all the extra-budgetary funds respectively (UNGA 1981a).

Although the Department of Technical Co-operation for Development and the Economic Commission for Africa are the only two bodies within the UN Secretariat that are directly and significantly involved in resource development in the Sahel, there are a number of other UN bodies that do have an effect on the Sahelian countries by stimulating change on the global or international level. For example, the Law of the Sea conference has helped to trigger the establishment of 200-mile exclusive economic zones, and this has greatly benefited both Mauritania and Senegal. Mauritania in particular has rich fishing areas just off its coast, and in recent years substantial outside investment has been directed into the exploitation of these fisheries and the processing of fish.

Another body whose activities may have repercussions in the Sahel is the UN Conference on Trade and Development (UNCTAD). UNCTAD was established in 1964 with its primary purpose being the promotion of international trade, especially for the benefit of developing countries. In addition to being heavily involved in the negotiations on the General Agreement on Tariffs and Trade (GATT), UNCTAD has introduced the generalized system of pref-

erences, which is supposed to enhance the export possibilities of manufactured and semi-manufactured goods from developing countries. UNCTAD is also concerned with the burden of debt of developing countries. In this context it is trying to enhance the transfer of resources (i.e., development aid) to developing countries and make other changes in the monetary system in order to reflect the goals of the New International Economic Order. It has also attempted to stabilize the prices of basic commodities, such as tin and rubber, through the financing of buffer stocks, but UNCTAD's recommendations have tended not to be implemented because of a lack of financial support. This type of impasse is often used to argue that the major industrialized countries are not willing to back up their words (or UN resolutions) with action. Further to this economic and political work, UNCTAD occasionally serves as an executing agency for UNDP when projects involve the enhancement of foreign trade.

Another system-wide activity that affects the Sahel is the organizing of special conferences, which seem to have proliferated in the last decade. The results of the Conference on Science and Technology for Development held in Vienna in 1979 have already been mentioned, and the 1977 Conference on Desertification is described later in this chapter. Other relevant conferences include those on the human environment (1972), population (1974 and 1984), human settlements (1976), water (1977), and new and renewable sources of energy (1981). Typically, each conference develops a plan of action, and for the first couple of conferences this resulted in the setting up of a new UN body. In the mid-1970s, however, there was a major shift in the willingness of the traditional major donors to set up new UN bodies or to pledge new funds. The lack of support for the approved action plans suggests that the conferences since 1977 have been financial failures. It can be argued, however, that the primary benefit of these conferences is not the funding pledged but the generation of a political awareness, with each country then following up as it sees fit. While the United Nations is continuing to schedule conferences in response to topical issues, as long as the present economic and political climate continues it is unlikely that any significant new initiatives will develop.

In the following sections the work of each of the UN agencies directly involved in natural-resources development in the Sahel will be summarized. A project-by-project listing for each agency would take several volumes, but a brief synopsis will be made of their fields of specialization, type and scale of activity, mode of operation, and current trends. The discussion begins with UNDP, as it is the primary funding body for development assistance, and then goes on to UNEP and UNCOD, followed by the other agencies in alphabetical order.

The United Nations Development Programme (UNDP)

The United Nations Development Programme is the driving force in the United Nations for improving social and economic conditions. As the largest organization for multi-lateral technical co-operation, it is currently responsible for approximately 5,000 projects of technical co-operation throughout the world. Operating on five-year cycles, using estimates of available funds called "indicative planning figures", UNDP's total expenditures are around $670 million per year. In addition, UNDP is responsible for a number of special funds and organizations, including:
— the Capital Development Fund,
— the Revolving Fund for Natural Resources Exploration,
— United Nations Volunteers,
— the United Nations Sudano-Sahelian Office,
— the Trust Fund for Assistance to Colonial Countries and Peoples,
— the Special Fund for Landlocked Developing Countries,
— the Fund for Population Activities,
— the United Nations Financing System for Science and Technology for Development, and
— the Energy Account.
Each of these, except the Trust Fund for Assistance to Colonial Countries and Peoples, is involved to some extent in activities affecting the countries of the Sahel and is discussed individually below.

UNDP plays a key role in the implementation of UN activities. In almost every country in which it operates, UNDP has a field office that serves as the administrative base for all UNDP projects. In general, the UNDP office also serves as an umbrella for the field activities of all the other agencies of the UN system. Even if the larger agencies such as FAO or Unesco have a sufficient number of field activities to justify their own country offices, the head of the UNDP office ("Resident Co-ordinator") is supposed to be the leader among equals and ensure co-operation among agencies.

Project execution is covered in detail in chapter 5, but at this point it is worth noting that most of UNDP's country projects are not executed by UNDP itself but are con-tracted out to the UN agency deemed to have the relevant technical expertise and experience. Only a relatively small proportion of UNDP projects are executed in-house by the Office of Project Execution. This in large part explains why UNDP can be regarded as the driving force for technical assistance activities in the United Nations and why its funding levels have repercussions throughout the entire UN system.

UNDP was not the original channel for technical assistance; in the earliest years of the United Nations the Expanded Programme of Technical Assistance was the main channel for development aid. In 1959 a Special Fund was created to carry out projects that would lead to (1) further capital investment (e.g. natural resource surveys and feasibility studies), (2) strengthening educational institutions, (3) strengthening applied research centres, and (4) providing assistance in development planning and for programme execution. By 1966 a total of $583 million had been committed by the Special Fund, while the Expanded Programme for Technical Assistance was carrying out 2,500 projects at a total annual cost of $50 million (UN 1968). In 1965 the General Assembly decided to combine these two agencies into the United Nations Development Programme, and that integration took place over the next few years as the old projects were phased out.

UNDP, now carrying out both technical assistance and pre-investment work, continued the past policies of simply approving projects on an *ad hoc* basis as they were proposed. In 1968 UNDP commissioned a major study by Sir Robert Jackson on the capacity of the UN development system (Jackson 1969). Many of his conclusions are reviewed in chapter 5, where development projects are discussed in a more general way, but in short he strongly criticized UNDP for being slow and unwieldy, for not making best use of its resources, for not properly evaluating and following-up its projects, and for a lack of co-ordina-tion and general principles on which to base operations. In large part because of these criticisms, a number of important changes were instituted.

The most important of these was an effort to allocate UNDP funds more fairly, both among sectors and among countries. To do this, UNDP began in 1972 to draw up five-year plans for each country, detailing how UNDP funds were to be used by sector. Even though contributions are made on an annual basis, efforts also began to be made to estimate the amount that should be available for a given five-year period for each country: the indicative planning figure (IPF). Initially the IPF was closely related to the aid received in previous years, but it was realized that the least-developed countries weren't as able to prepare competitive project proposals, so UNDP's resources tended to be directed towards the middle or even upper tier of developing countries. Hence, additional funds were made available to those countries designated least-developed, most seriously affected, and subject to drought. For the second programme cycle (1977–1981) the expected programme funds were allocated on the basis of a complex formula including such variables as income and population. For the third cycle (1982–1986) there was a further shift towards emphasizing low-income and otherwise dis-advantaged developing countries (UNDP 1981).

Initial plans for the third cycle called for 14 per cent annual growth in funding, which would have resulted in some $6,700 million being available over the period 1982–1986.

This seemed feasible since contributions increased 16 per cent in 1979. In 1980, however, growth slowed to 3 per cent, which represented a decline in real terms. Consultations with governments indicated that a more realistic target for 1982–1986 would be $5,100 million (UNDP 1981), which would still represent an annual growth rate of 8 per cent. Then, in 1981, for the first time in UNDP's history, there was a decline in contributions of 6 per cent, from $821 million to $804 million. (Exchange rate fluctuations were said to have caused a drop of $77 million in voluntary contributions [UNDP 1982h].) However, at the same time the momentum of programme implementation continued, resulting in a 10 per cent increase in expenditure in 1981 and a net deficit of $133 million. This shortfall, which was much larger than expected, reduced UNDP's reserve to $71 million, with nearly 60 per cent of this being in non-convertible currencies (UNDP 1982g).

Income in 1982 recovered to approximately $825 million, but expenditures are still predicted to exceed income by over $20 million. Since then income has remained at a relatively stable $670 million to $680 million. Thus, total resources over the period 1982–1986 are more likely to fall in the range of $4,000 million. Programme expenditures under the indicative planning figures are being held to an annual level of $550 million, a reduction of nearly 40 per cent in project activities. In view of the weakness of the world economy, the deficit of most national governments, and the strength of the US dollar, pledges to UNDP are remaining relatively static. This results in a decline in real terms in technical assistance to developing countries. Expenditures are currently being held to 55 per cent of the original planned IPF figures for 1982–1986.

UNDP Activities in the Sahel

Before discussing the individual country programmes, we should note a few common aspects of UNDP's activities in the Sahel. First, planning for the third cycle was based on an "illustrative IPF" that assumed that the total resources of UNDP would be $6,500 million instead of $4,000 million. Second, UNDP has learned from experience that a substantial amount of each country's IPF should be left as unprogrammed reserve, to be used for new activities in the latter part of the programming cycle. The minimum amount to be withheld for this reserve is 20 per cent, but, given the current status of contributions, none of this will become available. Another 15–25 per cent of the IPF is earmarked by sector, with the detailed projects to be worked out at a later stage. Again, most of these funds will be withheld. Finally, the third-cycle country programmes for the Sahelian countries were delayed for one year so that UNDP's efforts could be tied in with the medium-term plans of CILSS and the individual countries. Hence the third cycle for the Sahelian countries covers only 1983–

1986, with 1982 treated more as an extension of the second programming cycle.

Along with UNDP's rationalization of funding have come efforts to better co-ordinate activities. Given the overall direction provided by CILSS and the Club du Sahel, and the similarity of problems among the seven countries covered in this report, one might expect UNDP's country programmes in the Sahel to bear more resemblance to each other than any comparable group of developing countries. In fact, these tendencies of convergence have been consciously pushed through meetings of the UNDP Resident Co-ordinators in the Sahel. In January 1981, for example, it was agreed that five topics selected by the countries of the Sahel would form the framework for the country programmes: (1) food self-sufficiency, (2) water management, (3) development of the Sahelian region, including environmental protection, development of wooded areas, desertification control, and human settlements, (4) diversification of the Sahelian economies, and (5) human resources/training. It may be noted that these categories actually exclude very little, although they may be somewhat indicative of priorities. These categories are also impractical for comparative or statistical purposes, for UNDP projects are classified according to a UN-wide classification system agreed on by the Administrative Committee for Co-ordination. Unfortunately this system has been subject to various modifications, and so direct comparisons by sector between years or UNDP programming cycles are usually misleading.

Burkina Faso (Upper Volta)

In 1972 Upper Volta approved a five-year plan calling for investments of $270 million by 1976. Three-quarters of this $270 million was to be financed by public or external credits. A number of projects within the plan were earmarked for UNDP support and became the 1972–1976 country programme (UNDP 1973g). Of the $10.7 million IPF, 38 per cent was to be used for rural development, 23 per cent for natural resources (mainly mineral exploration and secondarily water resources management), 22 per cent for human resources (primarily education and training), and 15 per cent for industry. Overall, the country programme was significant for the large number of projects (46), over half of which cost less than $50,000, and for the heavy emphasis on expenditures in the first three years (UNDP 1973g).

The implementation of these activities encountered more than the usual share of problems, partially because of the large number of projects. The problems were fairly typical — delays in both the approval of projects and their execution, lack of supporting infrastructure, and occasionally a lack of data. Small projects, such as fellowships and consultancies, seemed to suffer more (UNDP 1977g).

Presumably this was because they required nearly as much administrative work as the larger projects but internally were given lower priority.

The second programme cycle (1977–1981) also was designed to coincide with Upper Volta's next five-year plan. First priority was given to the development of water supplies in the rural sector, with education and training also being emphasized. In general, UNDP funds were to be used for activities that would stimulate further investments (UNDP 1977g).

The IPF for 1977–1981 more than doubled, to $23.75 million, while $1.1 million was subtracted for previous over-spending and $836,000 was added from the fund for least-developed countries. Almost 13 per cent of the IPF was held as a reserve, with the remainder being allocated among rural development (29 per cent), human resources (24 per cent), industry (22 per cent), and infrastructure (13 per cent). Major projects in the rural-development sector included assistance to the relevant government departments, an integrated rural-development project, support for an irrigated-crops experimental centre, and a forestry project involving training and reforestation. Large-scale mining surveys constituted half of the planned expenditures in the industry sector.

The second country programme for Upper Volta was unusual in that fellowship and short-term consultancies were grouped, with funds to be drawn as needed. The allocation for fellowships was $1 million, for miscellaneous consultancies $290,000, and for UN Volunteers $465,000. This procedure was designed to simplify the administrative work and maximize flexibility. The soundness of this approach is indicated by a similar procedure being adopted for the third cycle (UNDP 1982h).

The illustrative IPF for the third country programme was set at $55 million. After subtracting 20 per cent as a reserve and $7.5 million for 1982, $36.5 million was left. A positive balance of $373,000 from 1977–1981 and an addition of $486,000 from the fund for least-developed countries meant that a total of $37.4 million was available for programming. Of this, nearly half was to be used for ongoing projects and 10 per cent was to be held for future projects, leaving only $15 million available for "new" activities.

The emphasis for 1983–1986 is heavily on agriculture, forestry, and fisheries. Together these are allocated 40 per cent of the funds available. Most of the projects are ongoing, including work on a soils institute, an animal-traction project, agricultural extension, etc. Natural resource development accounts for 18 per cent of the third-cycle funds, with most of the money being used for

water development and the Sahel-wide strengthening of agro-meteorology and hydrology. Primary health care will account for about 10 per cent of the UNDP programme, while education, employment, industry, and general development issues are each allocated less than 7 per cent (UNDP 1982h).

Chad

The first country programme for Chad allocated $7.5 million for 1972–1976. Another $2.6 million became available because of Chad's status as a least-developed country (LDC) and its susceptibility to drought. The UNDP country programme was formulated in concordance with Chad's 1971–1980 development plan, but this plan was subsequently modified and then rejected. As might be expected, agriculture was the dominant sector in the first UNDP country programme, accounting for 42 per cent of the IPF, with the ongoing rural development project in the Ouaddai requiring nearly half of the funds for this sector. Another 28 per cent of the funds for agriculture have been used for well-drilling activities, since only one-fifth of an estimated 10,000 needed wells have been drilled to date. The remaining funds for agriculture were divided among a miscellaneous collection of projects concerned with livestock development, market gardening, wildlife, price policy, reforestation, etc. Major projects in other sectors included retraining of primary-school teachers, support of an economic planning team, and industry/mining projects (UNDP 1971).

The IPF for 1977–1981 was increased to $19 million, with an additional $860,000 being carried over from 1972–1976 and $322,000 available from the fund for LDCs. In introducing the country programme, UNDP emphasized the lack of trained manpower, the inability of the government to provide anything but the most minimal of counterpart assistance, and the lack of infrastructure. UNDP also noted that it has proved extremely difficult to recruit experts and consultants, with some posts remaining vacant for over two years (UNDP 1977a).

The country programme called for about one-fourth of the UNDP funds to be used for agriculture and about 10 per cent each for industrial promotion, health, geological services, planning, education, a rural water supply project, and programme reserve. Civil unrest, however, caused a complete cessation of activities and a drastic restructuring of assistance when the UNDP office was reopened in 1981. Substitute projects included repair of the airport, a ferry to provide an essential transport link, support of the central electricity generating plant, as well as the distribution of foodstuffs and control of animal diseases. However, continuing civil war forced many of these projects to be abandoned or delayed. Altogether only 40 per cent of the funds allocated for 1977–1981 were actually spent.

For 1982-1986 the illustrative IPF for Chad was $52 million. After the $8 million left over from the second cycle was added in and adjustment was made for the required reserve and the shortened cycle, nearly $47 million was to have been available. Noting the exceptional need for infrastructure and basic food production, UNDP has adjusted its projects to provide more support costs and require less in terms of counterpart assistance. Six million dollars was to be devoted to ongoing projects, with most of this for emergency relief, administrative support for relief operations, and continuing support of Chadians studying overseas who have been unable to return. New projects cover nearly all aspects of the development spectrum but are essentially oriented towards putting Chad back on its feet. In recognition of the political and climatic fluctuations in Chad, a full $15 million (32 per cent) was set aside as an unprogrammed reserve, as well as $11 million (25 per cent) allocated by sector for projects to be formulated later (UNDP 1983). The sporadic political unrest in Chad suggests that UNDP will have to maintain a flexible approach, and that some funds will be diverted to short-term or emergency relief.

The Gambia

The IPF for the Gambia was set at $500,000 per year for 1972-1976, but the first country programme was established only in time to cover the last three years of this period. At the time the country programme was formulated, the Gambia had not yet developed a comprehensive national plan; instead investments were guided by the third capital expenditure programme. Agriculture and fisheries projects, together with infrastructure, development planning, and administration, accounted for 80 per cent of the funds allocated (UNDP 1973a). With regard to infrastructure, the two main projects were (1) to develop inshore fisheries and (2) to experiment with fodder crops and establish a pilot irrigated farm to fatten livestock.

The second country programme, which was to guide expenditures for 1977-1981, included severe criticism of the first country programme. The development efforts were characterized as fragmented, and it was noted that all but one of the projects were concentrated in the area around Banjul, the capital. Project design was not very satisfactory, with unrealistic targets and timing leading to extensive revisions. Expenditures exceeded the IPF by 28 per cent. This over-expenditure, combined with UNDP's financial crisis in 1975, made it necessary for the Gambia to lend UNDP $300,000 in order to continue a number of the UNDP projects (UNDP 1977b).

Hence, the country programme for 1977-1981, after the subtraction of $618,000 for the over-expenditure in 1972-1976 and the addition of special allocations for Gambia's least-developed-country status, totalled $6.74 million.

Increased awareness of the possibilities of drought and a desire for greater flexibility resulted in $1.25 million (18.5 per cent) of the IPF being set aside as a reserve, compared with just $54,000 in the previous programme. As in Chad, the lack of trained manpower rather than the unavailability of funds is seen as the major constraint to development. This shortage is exacerbated by the fact that some individuals trained with UNDP assistance either have not returned to the Gambia or have been assigned functions unrelated to their training (UNDP 1977b).

Of the projects planned for 1977-1981, 16 were ongoing and only 6 were new. Agriculture, forestry, and fisheries were allocated only 22 per cent of the IPF, although rural development was supposed to be emphasized. The primary projects in the agricultural sector were concerned with inshore fisheries and agricultural marketing/farm management. General economic and social planning was considered of primary importance and was allocated more than a quarter of the budget, while 18 per cent was set aside as a reserve and the remaining 34 per cent was scattered over eight different sectors. Overall the programme was consistent with the general trend in UNDP towards fewer and larger projects (chap. 5).

For 1982-1986 the illustrative planning figure was doubled to $14.25 million. However, more than $1 million had to be subtracted to cover a 17 per cent overrun in the second planning cycle, and 20 per cent was designated as a reserve. Since the 1977-1981 programme was extended for an additional year in order to put UNDP's third planning cycle in phase with the government's planning cycles, the total amount available for programming was $10.7 million. UNDP planning was also influenced by the Gambian government's shift in emphasis from building up infrastructure to investment in directly productive ventures. As in the other Sahelian countries, 85 per cent of the investment capital required in the government's development plan was expected to come from outside.

In keeping with these considerations, one-third of the immediately available UNDP resources will be devoted to agriculture, forestry, and fisheries. Projects include the development of sheep and goat husbandry, reduction of post-harvest losses, and the development of a planning, programming, and monitoring unit within the ministry of agriculture. In the natural resources sector, 19 per cent of UNDP's contribution will be allocated to an ongoing well-drilling project and a long-term effort to develop the Gambia's hydrological and meteorological capabilities. A similar amount is being devoted to development planning, including a joint project with the World Bank to establish a management development institute. Just 5 per cent ($470,000) is being devoted directly to education, while assistance to vocational training and the provision of business services is 8 per cent of the IPF. Eighteen per cent of the IPF is being held for activities that will be formulated later (UNDP 1982c).

Mali

The IPF was set at $10 million for 1972–1976, but, as in the case of the Gambia, a country programme was available only for the last three years of this period. Since $6 million had already been spent in the first two years (1972–1973) and there were some thirty projects underway, the country programme was basically just a continuation of existing activities. Plans were made to reduce expenditures from over $2 million in 1974 to $300,000 in 1976, but this was not achieved, resulting in a total overspending of $2.19 million. Although the very high rate of expenditure in the first two years should never have occurred, once that had happened, the resultant overspending was justified by the need to keep the major long-term projects operating (UNDP 1977c). Some additional funds were provided because of Mali's status as both an LDC and a drought-stricken country, but these were used to initiate new projects.

In sectoral terms the 1974–1976 programme concentrated on education and training, especially at the post-secondary level. Agricultural projects received 24 per cent of the IPF, but efforts were concentrated on improving the national body responsible for marketing livestock and meat (UNDP 1973c).

Nearly 10 per cent of the 1977–1981 IPF of $24 million had to be subtracted to cover the $2.1 million debt incurred in 1975–1976. In addition, the large number of ongoing projects absorbed virtually all the resources available in the first two years of the second cycle. Thus, new activities could begin only in 1979, and these accounted for just about 20 per cent of the IPF. This meant that only $375,000, or less than 2 per cent of the IPF, could be set aside as a token reserve.

Agriculture was dominant in the 1977–1981 plan, with two livestock production and marketing projects totalling $3.2 million, a $2.3 million project to support seed-producing centres, and two studies costing $1.2 million each to prepare rural development plans. The largest single project in the programme was for the drilling of 2,000 wells and associated activities. Altogether, the agricultural projects accounted for 60 per cent of the IPF. The remainder of the IPF was to be used for assistance to various training programmes and institutes, and a variety of projects on administrative reform, feasibility studies, and establishing a central project office in the ministry of planning. Thus, the Mali country programme carried the tendency towards consolidation quite far, with only 17 projects planned for the five-year period, the majority of these being continued from the previous country programme.

The illustrative IPF for 1982–1986 was set at $65 million. After subtraction of the usual 20 per cent reserve, the $9 million authorized for 1982, and the small over-expenditure for 1977–1981 ($362,000), $42 million was available for programming. Of this amount, 16 per cent is reserved for future projects in agriculture, forestry, and fisheries.

Overall, the third country programme for Mali is much more diverse than the 1977–1981 plan. Agriculture, forestry, and fisheries account for just over 30 per cent of the IPF, with half of this to be used for projects that will be formulated later. Nearly 20 per cent of the IPF will be devoted to natural resources, with the emphasis on drilling additional wells. Thirteen per cent will be devoted to general development issues, most of which are ongoing projects. As in the other Sahelian countries, many of the "projects" in this sector are simply allocations to provide the necessary administrative support for non-UNDP activities. For example, one project executed by UNDP was to administer UNCDF activities, another was to administer other UN projects, and a third was to cover the costs of organizing round-table meetings of all the development assistance agencies active in Mali. There is also an attempt to design projects that will attract additional funds from other donors. Other general development projects include such standard items as assistance to the ministry of planning, funds for administrative reform, etc. Industry, transport and communications, international trade and development financing, health, and education are each to receive 5–7.5 per cent of the IPF (UNDP 1982d).

Mauritania

Mauritania is unique among the Sahelian countries in that no country programme for UNDP assistance was formulated until 1977. Efforts had been made in 1973, but the lack of a national planning framework, together with the drought, made it impossible to design even a three-year programme. The IPF for 1972–1976 was $5 million, but expenditures were approximately $6.65 million, and this debt reduced the 1977–1981 IPF of $9.75 million by 17 per cent (UNDP 1977d).

For the period 1972–1976 UNDP funds were allocated as follows: 47.5 per cent for strengthening government institutions (including some fellowships), 36.5 per cent for training and education, and 16 per cent for increasing agricultural production. Management problems arose for a number of reasons, the primary one being simply that 42 different projects were undertaken, two-thirds of which were either technical assistance or fellowships. Since these required a considerable amount of administrative work and the shortage of trained manpower was probably more severe in Mauritania than in some of the other Sahelian countries, it should not be surprising that considerable difficulties were encountered in executing these projects. Furthermore, the need to continue existing activities as well as cover previous over-expenditures meant that relatively few new projects were initiated until the latter part of the cycle.

In the 1977–1981 IPF, rural development accounted for 43 per cent, mineral exploration 14 per cent, education and training 20 per cent, and miscellaneous activities 15 per cent. Within the rural development sector, $1.31 million was allocated for the agricultural extension and training centre at Kaedi, $389,000 for water projects, $420,000 for marine fisheries, and $236,000 for agricultural meteorology (UNDP 1977d). (The characterization by UNDP of a marine fisheries project as "rural development" demonstrates the more general problems in classifying projects, particularly when there are administrative constraints or managerial pressures to demonstrate a particular trend.)

For 1982–1986 the IPF was set at $24.5 million. Subtracting the 20 per cent reserve, a $1.4 million deficit from 1977–1981, and the $3 million authorized for 1982 left $15.2 million to be programmed. Of this, 37 per cent is to be devoted to agriculture, forestry, and fisheries. Projects include poultry raising, small-scale marine fisheries, seed research, and $2 million for Mauritania's activities in relation to the Organization for the Development of the Senegal River (OMVS). Water management is another key area, and planned activities include the construction of earth dams, drilling of boreholes, repair and maintenance of existing wells, etc. Nearly one-fourth of the IPF is allocated to infrastructure, while less than 9 per cent is devoted to human resources and training (UNDP 1982e).

Niger

The original IPF for 1972–1976 was $10 million, and the first country programme covered the entire five-year period. Activities were planned in conjunction with the government's "Ten Year Targets", but there was not a clear strategy behind the UNDP programme (UNDP 1977e). The obvious need for trained nationals led to 54 per cent of the IPF being committed to human resources, mostly for training various groups (teachers, managers, etc.). The remainder was divided between infrastructure, rural development, and natural resources. About two-thirds of the funds in the natural-resources sector was for mineral prospecting and one-third for well-drilling activities. In contrast, the 16 per cent for rural development was for a single project that included various components — research, demonstration, training, and extension (UNDP 1973d). The additional funds that became available as a result of the drought and Niger's status as an LDC were used for rural development and water resources projects (UNDP 1977e).

The country programme for 1977–1981 was drawn up under the guidelines of the 1976–1978 three-year programme, which was basically an outline for recovery from the drought. The IPF for 1977–1981 was $19.75 million, but this became $20.1 million when adjusted for over-expenditure in 1972–1976 and the extra LDC and drought funds. Nearly 30 per cent of the IPF was devoted to rural production, and the two largest projects in this sector were concerned with training agricultural technicians and soil mapping. Another project was to draw up a plan for the development of the zones freed from onchocerciasis, even though the disease-vector control programme had not yet begun. Other major projects included assistance to planning agencies, training managers, improvement of meteorological and hydrological services, mineral exploration, and the improvement of agricultural statistics (UNDP 1977e).

The illustrative IPF for 1982–1986 was set at $45 million. Following the allocation of the standard 20 per cent reserve and corrections for overspending and activities in 1982, $29.5 million was available for programming. This was roughly broken into thirds, with one-third directed towards ongoing projects, one-third for new projects (or new phases of ongoing projects), and one-third allocated by sector but not yet assigned to projects.

In keeping with the goals of the CILSS countries, 35 per cent of the IPF was to be used for agriculture, forestry, and fisheries. A wide variety of projects were planned, including soil mapping, assistance with agricultural statistics, seed technology training, research on irrigated rice, etc. Another 19 per cent was devoted to natural resources, which, in this case, meant primarily water development and secondarily mineral assessment. Ten per cent of the IPF was designed to help strengthen a variety of industrial enterprises (e.g., brickworks, tourism, a foundry/forge), with much smaller amounts assigned to other sectors (UNDP 1982f).

Senegal

The IPF for 1972–1976 was set at $10 million, but, since the fourth development plan was made public only in mid-1973, the UNDP programming exercise covered just 1974–1976. Moreover, such heavy commitments were made in 1972–1973 that only 39 per cent of the IPF was available for the next three years, and 83 per cent of this was already committed for ongoing projects. Thus the planning exercise was close to an exercise in futility, as only 6 per cent of the total IPF could be devoted to new projects. In general the UNDP programme concentrated on strengthening the governmental infrastructure, developing tourism, and improving/diversifying agriculture (UNDP 1973e). As a special relief measure, nearly a million dollars was made available for drilling wells, reforestation, and improving the national meteorological service. In addition to the country programme, there were a number of UNDP regional projects concerned with the development of the Senegal River basin (UNDP 1973f).

The 1977–1981 IPF did not allow any basic change in this situation, as it was only 17 per cent higher and two-thirds of this increase had to be used to cover the over-commitments made in 1976. Thus, 65 per cent of the IPF was used to continue ongoing projects and 14 per cent was designated as an unprogrammed reserve, leaving only 20 per cent to be allocated to new projects. As in 1972–1976, UNDP efforts were concentrated on improving the government's administrative capability (41 per cent), industrial development (25 per cent), and rural development (27 per cent). In this latter category there were eight projects on topics such as grain improvement, forest utilization, sand-dune stabilization, small-scale fishing, and water resources. The continuing integrated rural development projects in the Senegal and Gambia river basins were regional projects and so did not come under the country IPF (UNDP 1977f).

For 1982–1986 the illustrative IPF was set at $33 million. The over-expenditure in 1977–1981 was $831,000, and, after subtraction of the 20 per cent reserve and 1982 expenditures, $21.2 million was left for 1983–1986. In contrast to the previous programmes, ongoing projects required a relatively small 28 per cent. In fact, however, much of the remaining 72 per cent was devoted to new phases of older projects. The deteriorating economic situation of most of the Sahelian countries also has forced UNDP to pick up more of the counterpart contributions than expected, and this has slightly reduced the funds available for programming.

The sectoral pattern of assistance planned for 1983–1986 is similar to that for the countries previously considered. Twenty-eight per cent of the IPF is to be devoted to agriculture, forestry, and fisheries, 25 per cent to natural resources (mostly for activities as yet unspecified), 13 per cent to general development (i.e., administration and planning), and smaller amounts for health, industry, employment, science and technology, etc. Overall, Senegal also illustrates the general trend towards fewer and larger projects. In the third country programme there was also a greater emphasis on water resources development, including assistance to irrigation projects, groundwater development, possible uses of sewage effluent, and activities supporting the work of the Organization for the Development of the Senegal River (UNDP 1982g).

Regional and Global Projects

In addition to the country programmes already described,

UNDP supports a variety of regional (e.g., for Africa or for Europe) and interregional projects. As these projects are generally organized by UNDP and do not require much in the way of negotiating and counterpart contributions, the tendency has been to increase the proportion of UNDP funds allocated for them, from 15 per cent in the first cycle to an estimated 22 per cent in the third cycle (UNDP 1982n). Given the concentration of developing countries in Africa, the regional programme for Africa generally receives about 30 per cent of the total allocation for regional and interregional funds. For 1972–1976 the regional IPF for Africa was set at $71.2 million, but this was overspent by $9.9 million. As a result the second cycle had its IPF reduced from $109.4 million to $99.5 million (UNDP 1982r).

During the second cycle (1977–1981) 308 regional projects were implemented. Those projects which facilitated regional and sub-regional integration had the highest priority, and these generally involved supporting a variety of intergovernmental organizations. While not all of these were necessarily relevant to the Sahel, assistance was provided to key organizations such as the Organization for the Development of the Senegal River, the Lake Chad Basin Commission, the West African Economic Community, the West African Rice Association, CILSS, and the Organization of African Unity. Selected meetings were also sponsored with funds from this sector (UNDP 1982o).

By sector, human resources development — including health, training, and employment projects — accounted for one-quarter of the regional IPF. Some of the activities directly relevant to the Sahel were the control of diseases such as onchocerciasis, trypanosomiasis, and schistosomiasis. Regional training courses were conducted on a variety of topics. Another 22 per cent of the regional activities were concerned with food production and crop protection. Projects in this sector included river basin development and irrigated agriculture, locust control, and support for regional institutions. Projects in the category of development administration accounted for 17 per cent of the regional IPF; for the most part these involved support for regional centres. Only 7.5 per cent of the regional funds were spent directly on science and technology, with the Sahel benefiting from a project to strengthen meteorological sciences and assistance in the fields of energy and mineral development.

For the third cycle, 1982–1986, the regional IPF was originally set at $283 million. The decline in UNDP pledges, plus 20 per cent overspending in the second cycle, resulted in an actual planning figure of $206 million (UNDP 1982r). In consultation with governments the three top priorities were identified as food self-sufficiency, regional and subregional co-operation, and transport and communications. However, over two-thirds of the available funds will be used for continuing projects, so there is limited potential for shifts in funding to meet these priorities. For the Sahel, this results in continuing support for projects such as regional pest and disease control, river basin development, agro-meteorology, village water supplies, a variety of regional organizations, transportation links such as the trans-Saharan highway, and a solar energy centre.

Interregional and global projects together account for about one-fifth of the overall IPF for regional and intercountry programmes (UNDP 1982i). Since projects in this category generally involve many countries from different regions, the direct impact on the Sahel is relatively small. Most of the activities in the interregional and global programme are training courses and meetings, ranging in topic from geothermal energy to financial co-operation, from electronic assembly plants to international trade. As a rule these types of projects are not as subject to delay, resulting in a fuller utilization of the funds available. Since this relative ease of execution has led to regional, interregional, and global projects receiving an increasing share of UNDP resources, UNDP's governing council has put a ceiling on the proportion of funding that can be devoted to these activities. In general, developing countries prefer to see projects in their own countries rather than more diffuse regional and global activities.

Synthesis

Table 11 presents a summary of UNDP's assistance to the African region and the Sahelian countries since 1972. This indicates that UNDP country assistance has generally increased by a factor of 2 to 4 from the first to the third country programme. Only Senegal, which is the most developed of the seven countries, experienced a smaller increase. This can be ascribed primarily to its initial ability to compete in obtaining projects and hence a relatively high starting point, and secondarily to its higher standard of living resulting in a lower per capita allocation. The table also shows the extent to which actual expenditures matched the available funds in 1972-1976 and 1977-1981. The available expenditures for 1982-1986 were obtained simply by multiplying the illustrative IPF by a factor of 0.55. In the case of Chad, actual expenditures may lag even further because of the periodic civil unrest.

From the country summaries and table 11, several general points emerge. First, UNDP is increasingly able to match expenditures to available resources. Obviously there will be some discrepancies, but the gross overspending that triggered UNDP's fiscal crisis in the mid-1970s is not likely to recur. Borrowing from future IPFs may well continue, but on a much smaller scale. On the other hand, the

TABLE 11.   UNDP allocations and expenditures by country, 1972-1986 ($000)

	1972-1976	1977-1981	1982-1986
Burkina Faso (Upper Volta)			
IPF	10,700	23,750	55,000
available	12,074	23,462	30,250
expenditures	13,198	23,774	—
Chad			
IPF	7,500	19,000	52,000
available	10,100	20,182	28,600
expenditures	8,687	12,409	—
Gambia			
IPF	2,500	7,000	14,250
available	2,500	6,743	7,838
expenditures	3,170	8,288	—
Mali			
IPF	10,000	24,000	65,000
available	12,510	21,919	35,750
expenditures	14,704	20,412	—
Mauritania			
IPF	5,000	9,750	24,500
available	5,736	8,100	13,475
expenditures	7,386	10,364	—
Niger			
IPF	10,000	19,750	45,000
available	11,475	20,093	24,750
expenditures	11,770	21,049	—
Senegal			
IPF	10,700	23,750	55,000
available	12,074	23,462	30,250
expenditures	13,198	23,774	—
Africa region			
IPF	71,200	109,400	283,400
available	71,200	99,500	155,870
expenditures	81,136	120,164	—

"Available" represents the amounts actually available for programme activities after adjusting for previous spending and the addition of LDC and other funds. The "available" figures for 1982-1986 were obtained by multiplying the original IPF by 0.55.

difficulty of matching resources and expenditures is compounded by the uncertainty of contributions. In the late 1970s nobody predicted that contributions to UNDP would remain constant in absolute terms for four years, although the optimistic character of the 1982-1986 IPF figures (i.e., a 14 per cent annual increase) was recognized. The increasing fluctuations in the value of the dollar have also made it much more difficult to predict costs accurately.

The second main tendency is the growing gap between the postulated budget and the actual budget. As indicated earlier, UNDP predicts a specific growth rate in contributions, based on consultations with member states and a

TABLE 12. Planned expenditures by UNDP for 1982–1986 by sector and country ($000)

Sector	Burkina Faso	Chad	Gambia	Mali	Mauri- tania	Niger	Senegal	Total	%
General development	1,177	2,610	1,765	5,305	1,236	1,488	2,833	16,414	8.2
Natural resources	6,570	767	1,654	8,688	1,560	5,634	5,273	30,146	15.0
Agriculture, forestry, and fisheries	14,165	2,361	2,285	13,177	5,612	10,338	6,124	54,062	26.9
Industry	2,120	1,500	—	2,493	819	3,016	1,235	11,183	5.6
Transport and communications	—	2,822	30	2,158	501	643	560	6,714	3.3
International trade	—	627	—	2,370	—	144	42	31,813	1.6
Human settlements	—	1,134	—	—	1,044	1,800	650	4,628	2.3
Health	3,592	1,138	—	3,186	—	—	854	8,770	4.4
Education	2,504	2,828	470	2,212	1,000	645	106	9,765	4.9
Employment	2,111	700	791	—	1,420	1,114	1,730	7,866	3.9
Humanitarian aid and emergency relief	—	2,014	—	—	—	—	—	2,014	1.0
Social conditions and equity	1,374	40	—	—	509	—	183	2,106	1.0
Culture	—	100	—	180	—	—	—	280	0.1
Science and technology	—	—	—	—	—	—	148	148	0.1
Other	1,947	26,499[a]	1,578	1,763	1,157	3,882	390	37,216	18.5
Total[b]	37,359	46,778	8,573	42,338	15,178	29,544	21,177	200,947	99.7
Percentage in ongoing projects	45.3	12.2	13.7	43.3	23.8	32.9	27.5	30.5	

[a] This includes $11.5 million which is allocated by sector but for which specific projects have yet to be formulated.
[b] These totals, obtained by simply adding up the allocated funds, are not equivalent to the IPF figures shown in table 11 because of the many adjustments to the latter.

dose of optimism. In previous years contributions more or less matched expectations, but this changed drastically in 1979–1980. For tactical/political reasons UNDP has maintained the existing, optimistic IPF figures as a target but operates on a much more prudent and realistic basis.

Another trend, which is not so apparent, is the increasing degree of co-ordination between UNDP and the CILSS countries, and among donors. In particular UNDP has made a strong and conscious effort to synchronize its planning cycle with the planning cycles of the Sahelian countries and to integrate its projects with national development plans. Considerable assistance has also been provided to strengthen the planning process.

UNDP has also tried to build more flexibility into the planning process by holding more funds in reserve — not only because of the financial uncertainties already mentioned but also because of the realization that in such a variable environment one cannot plan in detail on even a medium-term basis. In hindsight, UNDP has not taken this policy far enough, as contributions have lagged much more than initially predicted.

Finally, and particularly in the Sahel, UNDP has tried to lessen the burden of development assistance. It is now absorbing more of the local costs, including local manpower and materials. It has also tended to programme fewer and larger projects in order to lighten the administrative burden both for itself and for the recipient organization. In some cases fellowships or expert missions are grouped under one umbrella project, thereby simplifying the administrative procedures.

Table 12 summarizes planned UNDP assistance to the Sahel by sector for the third cycle. Agriculture, forestry, and fisheries account for over one-fourth of planned UNDP assistance, in line with the CILSS goal of food self-sufficiency by the year 2000. Fifteen per cent of UNDP's assistance is devoted to the development of natural resources, and most often this involves the further exploitation of water resources through boreholes and dams.

Other sectors are much smaller — general development activities are targeted for 8.2 per cent of expenditures and industrial development for only 5.6 per cent. This de-emphasizing of industrial development is in strong contrast

TABLE 13.   UN Capital Development Fund: voluntary contributions, commitments, and disbursements (million $)

	Voluntary contributions	Interest and other income	Project commitments	Disbursements (voluntary contributions only)	Disbursements as % of voluntary contributions
1975	7.7[a]	0.3	15.5	0.3	4
1976	13.5	1.7	13.5	5.9	44
1977	16.7[a]	2.2	14.8	8.5	51
1978	17.8	4.2	27.2	10.2	57
1979	23.9	NA	40.0	8.9	37
1980	29.5	NA	52.2	19.3	65
1981	29.7	NA	71.1	48.6	164
1982	26.2	NA	60.0	27.7	106
1983	24.3	NA	23.9	24.8	102
1984	21.0	NA	20.6	30.0	143

Sources: UNDP 1982j; UNCDF (personal communication)

[a] Includes receipt of some contributions pledged in previous years.

NA = not available

to the past efforts of many other developing countries. Education expenditures average just under 5 per cent for all the Sahelian countries, despite the low literacy rate and lack of trained manpower. Health, employment, science and technology, and human settlements account for the bulk of the remaining project funds.

An average of 30 per cent of planned UNDP expenditures is devoted to ongoing projects, varying from under 15 per cent in Chad and the Gambia to over 40 per cent in Mali and Burkina Faso. This relatively high percentage is due in part to the long-term nature of building up the infrastructure. It can be argued that building a strong technical and administrative base is a prerequisite to all other activities and that UNDP's capabilities are much more suited to the former than the latter.

Care must be taken in interpreting tables such as this, as the assignment of projects to a specific sector is a somewhat arbitrary process. Many projects are multi-sectoral, and the categories themselves tend to change periodically in accordance with current development phraseology. Conventional activities may receive new names in order to satisfy some broader institutional goals of resource allocation.

Bodies Operating under UNDP Jurisdiction

As was noted earlier, there are at least eight semi-autonomous bodies that operate to some extent under the jurisdiction of UNDP and are involved in activities affecting the Sahel. In view of the variety of their origins and the vast differences in the scale of their activities, it is not surprising that they vary widely in their degree of independence. Brief descriptions of each of these bodies follow.

Capital Development Fund (CDF)

The UN Capital Development Fund was originally approved by the General Assembly in 1966 to provide financing to grass-roots projects sponsored by low-income groups that could not meet normal credit standards. In 1975 it metamorphosed to its present form, in which it concentrates on a wide variety of community self-help projects that benefit the poorest segment of the population in the least-developed countries. CDF grew quite rapidly until 1980, but the weakening world economy and stronger US dollar then caused a substantial decline in resources (table 13). Contributions are voluntary, and in 1984 they were supplemented by an estimated $9 million in joint financing arrangements (trust funds and cost-sharing). In this way CDF has remained a significant channel for capital assistance on concessional terms.

Table 13 also indicates that, like many new agencies, CDF was not able to design and implement new projects at the same rate that contributions were increasing. An average of 12 to 18 months was required just to develop and finalize project plans, so CDF's expenditures often lagged more than two years behind income. As contributions levelled off and the project approval procedure was streamlined, disbursements were ahead of contributions for the first time in 1981. Since then disbursements have matched or exceeded contributions, and this has helped to reduce the accumulated capital. By the end of 1984 over $184 million had been disbursed to more than 200 projects.

Funds are provided either as grants or as loan guarantees. CDF works only in the 31 countries designated by the General Assembly as least developed and eleven others that are sufficiently disadvantaged to warrant similar treatment. Often the projects also receive supporting technical assistance from UNDP, FAO, UNICEF, or bilateral agencies (UNDP 1979e).

In sectoral terms, from 1975 to 1984 22 per cent of CDF's resources were devoted to agriculture, 20 per cent to potable water and sanitation, 15 per cent to transport and communications, 10 per cent to water resources development, 9 per cent to industrial development, 8 per cent to primary health care facilities, 8 per cent to energy development (particularly rural electrification), 5 per cent to education and training, and 5 per cent to low-cost housing. A number of projects have been established in Chad, the Gambia, Mali, Niger, and Burkina Faso. A review of sixteen of these projects in 1978 (UNDP 1978a) indicated that five projects had no major problems, two had severe problems, in one the government decided to seek bilateral rather than multilateral aid, and eight others were more or less satisfactory although often incomplete. In one of the two problem projects only 43 per cent of the anticipated credit had been extended during the first three years of a four-year project, with such difficulties in accounting and reporting that CDF could not reimburse the local executing organization. In the other problem project CDF was to extend credit to local entrepreneurs in Chad, but the continuing civil strife had limited the loan guarantees to only 5 per cent of the targeted amount.

As for the eight projects that were generally satisfactory, it is an open question whether the facilities will be used and maintained. For example, in a major school-construction project, the original target has already been cut from 36 schools to 15; the first three were constructed in a non-traditional style, and "this reduced the villagers' interest in constructing the schools." A project in Upper Volta to construct 40 small dams was delayed by administrative and transport problems. A project in Niger to provide credit for the reconstitution of sheep flocks was delayed because of the "underestimated organizational and logistical requirements, as well as the complexities of establishing a viable co-operative structure, particularly among nomads" (UNDP 1978a). In summary, it appears that the category "generally successful" includes, at least in the Sahel, approximately equal numbers of projects that are reasonably successful in the short term and others that diverge considerably from their intended timetables and goals. Simple construction of the physical facilities is an important step, but this alone is not a sufficient criterion for success. These problems are quite typical, as will be seen in chapter 5.

Revolving Fund for Natural Resources Exploration

As approved by the General Assembly in 1973, the UN Revolving Fund for Natural Resources Exploration has a mandate to carry out all phases of exploration for mineral, water, and energy resources. However, when the fund began operating in 1975, the UNDP Governing Council decided that its initial activities should be concentrated on exploration for solid minerals (UNDP 1975a). The revolving character of the fund comes from the requirement that, if a project discovers reserves that are subsequently developed, 2 per cent of the gross value of production should be paid back for 15 years.

Contributions are voluntary and have been rather disappointing. Cumulative contributions through 1981 totalled just $37.5 million (UNDP 1982k), with contributions since then averaging around $2.5 million per year. Japan has been the major donor to date, although Belgium, Canada, Norway, and the Netherlands have also made significant contributions. The time lag between funding and expenditures as well as the uncertainties of project planning resulted in over $6 million being available for projects in 1982; this is well short of the target of $10 million per year for solid mineral exploration (UNDP 1982k).

In accordance with the original legislation, a full review of the fund was conducted after six years. Some changes were deemed necessary because of several incidents in which projects were cancelled very late in the formulation process because of resistance to the 2 per cent replenishment clause (UNDP 1979d). Hence the replenishment rule was modified to include a ceiling of ten times the original investment, and the 2 per cent replenishment rate was reduced to 1 per cent for projects in the least-developed countries. UNDP also recommended that the Revolving Fund's mandate be expanded to include geothermal energy, and in this area the fund is working closely with the Department of Technical Co-operation for Development. It was predicted that these changes would result in the fund's encountering less resistance on the part of governments and having more scope for possible activities, thereby increasing its viability (UNGA 1979).

The Revolving Fund's long-term success, however, depends on a sufficient number of projects reaching the stage of commercial exploitation, thereby causing the fund to "revolve". So far only a few projects have been completed and none of these are particularly promising. With regard to the Sahelian countries, general mineral surveys have been conducted in Mali and Burkina Faso, and another project evaluated nickel deposits in Niger, but these have generated no significant commercial interest. Since the Sahelian countries also appear to have little or no geothermal energy reserves, it is unlikely that the Revolving Fund will play a significant role in the development of the Sahel.

United Nations Volunteers (UNV)

The United Nations Volunteer Programme might be considered a type of UN Peace Corps, in which volunteers serve in developing countries, usually at a "middle level" of expertise. UNV began operations in 1971, and by mid-1981 the target of 1,000 volunteers in service had been reached. Volunteers are supposed to be drawn from both the developing and the industrialized countries, but the proportion of volunteers from the industrialized countries has declined to less than 25 per cent. The shortage of volunteers from the industrialized countries is probably due to the existence of national volunteer services and the fact that UNV must recruit through intermediary volunteer organizations. Thus most of the volunteers probably end up in the intermediary organization rather than in UNV. In addition, volunteers from the industrialized countries must be "co-sponsored". This means that the sponsoring country or organization must pay the external costs, and UNV is responsible only for placing the volunteer and providing local costs. UNV's apparent concern with maintaining a reasonable proportion of volunteers from the industrialized countries is noteworthy because of the marked contrast to the United Nations' usual emphasis on technical co-operation among developing countries. In most cases the volunteer works in association with a larger UN project (including UNHCR, UNICEF, and WFP projects), and the project budget provides the necessary funding (UNDP 1982l). In keeping with the United Nations' increasing emphasis on the least-developed countries, over 50 per cent of the volunteers are found in the 31 least-developed countries (UNDP 1984c).

UNV's operating costs are supposed to be met from contributions to its Special Voluntary Fund, but donations are averaging only $1.2 million per year. Since this and other income doesn't cover all of UNV's administrative costs, UNDP typically makes up the difference. In 1981 the estimated annual cost of a volunteer was only $14,000, which was one-sixth of the estimated average cost of a UN expert. Thus — assuming the volunteers have the necessary skills — UNV would seem to be a relatively cost-effective means of providing development assistance.

At the end of 1983 there were 57 volunteers serving in the seven Sahelian countries covered in this report, including 5 in Chad, 7 in Mali, 10 in Mauritania, 11 in Niger, 1 in Senegal, and 8 in Upper Volta. Surprisingly, 25 volunteers from these same countries were serving elsewhere, including 7 from Chad, 9 from Mali, 3 from Senegal, and 7 from Upper Volta (UNDP 1984c).

United Nations Sudano-Sahelian Office (UNSO)

As the magnitude of the 1968–1973 drought became

apparent, the Secretary-General of the United Nations created a Special Sahelian Office to co-ordinate plans for the medium- and long-term recovery of the Sahel. As a first step the Special Sahelian Office commissioned a set of over twenty studies on different aspects of the Sahel — forestry, transport, education, etc. In 1974 the UN Sudano-Sahelian Office was formally established, with three main functions: (1) to co-ordinate UN activities related to the rehabilitation of the Sahel, (2) to assist in finding support for projects identified by CILSS, and (3) to manage the UN Trust Fund for Sudano-Sahelian Activities. In 1976 UNSO was transferred from the Secretary-General's office to UNDP. Two years later, following the UN Conference on Desertification, UNSO was given the additional responsibility of implementing — together with the United Nations Environment Programme (UNEP) — the Plan of Action to Combat Desertification (pp. 46–47). UNSO's original functions concerned only the 8 CILSS countries, but its anti-desertification responsibilities now cover 21 sub-Saharan countries.

In response to its first broad task, the rehabilitation of the Sahel, UNSO began by assisting both CILSS and the respective governments in formulating 31 national and 21 regional projects with an estimated cost of $153 million. UNSO then helped convene a meeting in mid-1975 at which bilateral and other donors expressed interest in, or agreed to support, specific projects. UNSO thus began to play its role as a middleman between CILSS and the donor countries, helping in the formulation (or reformulation) of projects, drawing up project documents, and supplying needed information. UNSO also solicited contributions to its own trust fund, most of which came from donors who did not wish to set up their own bilateral aid programmes.

The success of this first donors' meeting encouraged UNSO to continue to help formulate and propose a variety of national and regional development projects. By January 1982 an additional 7 regional and 60 national projects had been formulated, with the total cost of all 119 projects estimated at just over $700 million. Some $450 million has been provided for these projects, but only about 13 per cent of this amount has come from the Trust Fund for Sudano-Sahelian Activities. In general, countries such as the United States and France that have the infrastructure and the resources to execute projects in the Sahelian countries tend to do so directly, while countries which don't have an elaborate aid mechanism must work through multilateral channels such as the United Nations. The desire for closer control results in new channels being created for funds from OPEC, the EEC, etc. This tendency, together with the receding urgency of the 1968–1973 drought, tends to diminish contributions to items such as UNSO's trust fund. Thus UNSO has had to set up a variety of arrangements to cover its basic administrative and programming costs.

The projects sponsored directly or indirectly by UNSO can generally be classified as either agricultural development (e.g. food storage, use of improved seeds) or strengthening of the national infrastructure in terms of feeder roads, telecommunications systems, and agro-meteorological and hydrological services. The feeder-road project has been one of the main focuses for UNSO, and a large portion of the early trust-fund contributions was devoted to this project. The basic goal is to construct some 39,900 kilometres of secondary or feeder roads as a stimulus to the whole development process and a means for providing food and supplies to the outlying rural areas. By the end of 1981 some $105 million had been committed by multilateral, bilateral, and other agencies — enough for 2,100 kilometres (UNSO 1982).

UNSO has also conducted major well-drilling projects in the Gambia and Senegal. Other work has included improving the water supply to Dakar, building irrigation canals in Niger, and crop protection and/or animal health activities in the Gambia, Mali, Mauritania, and Senegal. In addition to these types of technical assistance activities, UNSO also has projects that just provide the local or counterpart contribution necessary for a country to receive a particular loan or other credits.

As a result of its mandate and the limited amount of unrestricted funds available to it, UNSO generally tries to supply only seed money. In other words, it concentrates on feasibility studies, planning and programming missions, and pilot projects, all the while looking for other donors to take over the financing of the main project. Thus UNSO has generally avoided setting up the extensive administrative structure necessary to carry out technical assistance activities. When a contract is drawn with an agency to execute an UNSO project, UNSO negotiates the overhead with the agency rather than paying a flat rate of 14 per cent as UNDP used to do. UNSO also has the option of letting the UNDP Office for Projects Execution (OPE) execute a given project; in 1979 it channelled $8.9 million through OPE (UNDP 1980). UNSO also has tried to set a precedent by having the local government act as the executing agency whenever possible.

UNSO's other major responsibility is to help implement the Plan of Action to Combat Desertification in most of arid Africa south of the Sahara. Originally this mandate covered Cameroon, Ethiopia, Kenya, Nigeria, Somalia, Sudan, and Uganda as well as the CILSS countries; in the past few years Benin, Djibouti, Ghana, Guinea, Guinea-Bissau, and Togo have been added, making a total of 21 countries. This second mandate is to be carried out in close conjunction with UNEP, which has the overall responsibility for implementing the Plan of Action. For this reason UNEP has joined with UNDP in providing nearly $2 million per year for institutional and programme support; this has been used primarily for staff at UNSO's field headquarters in Ouagadougou, Burkina Faso.

UNSO's mode of operation in trying to meet this second mandate is not significantly different from that which it uses in the Sahel. Generally UNSO concentrates on assisting national governments in formulating and presenting a wide variety of projects and then tries to facilitate their funding, sometimes by making counterpart or other contributions. UNSO attempts also to play a co-ordinating role and relies on UNDP and the other specialized agencies for technical advice and detailed project execution in cases where either UNSO funds the project or the donor wishes UNSO to be responsible for the overall execution of a particular project.

Since the Plan of Action was extremely comprehensive, UNSO's activities are equally broad. By the end of 1981 planning and programming missions had identified some 229 projects consistent with the Plan of Action, with a total estimated cost of $689 million. Approximately $372 million has been made available for these projects from different sources, with less than 4 per cent of this coming from the UNSO trust fund. In general, afforestation has been heavily emphasized, with water resource management and range/livestock management also constituting more than 10 per cent of the projects (UNSO 1982). UNSO has also been active in implementing soil conservation techniques and developing national plans of action to combat desertification (UNSO 1985b).

It should be recognized, however, that the labelling of projects as "anti-desertification" can be misleading. The Plan of Action to Combat Desertification is so encyclopaedic in its coverage that virtually any development activity in an arid or semi-arid environment could be considered to be responding to the needs identified in the Plan of Action. Thus, existing activities can often be termed anti-desertification projects, and this has probably already happened (e.g., a project in the Casamance woodland in Senegal — see UNDP 1978b and UNDP 1979b). If just the desertification control measures are considered, UNSO has mobilized $78 million over the period 1979–1984, with 71 per cent of this being funnelled through its trust fund (UNEP 1985b).

The critical question, however, is whether donors increase the total amount of aid funds available in response to a new concern such as the Plan of Action to Combat Desertification or whether they simply reallocate existing development funds. To date the response of the donor countries does not suggest that there has been a significant increase in development aid as a result of the Plan of Action. In all likelihood there has been a minor shift in funds to support some of UNSO's additional anti-desertification projects, but these are not "new" funds but funds that probably would have been used for other types of development projects. As noted earlier, the advantage for donors in funding UNSO's projects is that they save the time and trouble of formulating and implementing their own projects. But, as the political will generated by the Conference on Desertification and the most recent drought recedes into the past, even the present modest level of funding is likely to be reduced in favour of more immediate concerns. This is not to say that anti-desertification projects will be completely eliminated but rather that they will be funded because they fit into the overall development strategy and priorities developed by donor and recipient countries. Subsequent droughts are likely to cause a renewed surge of interest, which will again taper off. The fact that contributions to UNSO's trust fund for anti-desertification measures jumped to $19 million in 1984 (UNEP 1985b) tends to support this viewpoint.

Given this uncertainty in donor motivation and project content, it is very difficult to evaluate UNSO's effectiveness in carrying out its two mandates. Would donor countries have supported CILSS projects if UNSO hadn't been playing the role of marriage broker? Has the effectiveness of UNSO resulted in a net increase in aid to the Sahel or in anti-desertification measures in sub-Saharan Africa? While these questions may be impossible to answer, it seems at least that UNSO has not satisfied its own ambitious goals. Co-operation between UNSO and the other UN agencies has been improving but still seems rather limited given the emphasis initially placed on its co-ordinating role.

Special-Fund for Landlocked Developing Countries

The Special Fund for Landlocked Developing Countries was created in late 1976 under the supervision of UNDP, although the responsibility of defining and executing projects is to be shared with the United Nations Conference on Trade and Development. Contributions are voluntary and pledged in conjunction with the UN Pledging Conference for Development Activities. By the end of 1981 cumulative contributions were approximately one million dollars, with over half of this from a single donor (UNDP 1982k). From 1982 to 1984 contributions averaged $70,000 per year, making the Special Fund insignificant in development terms. Altogether 21 projects have been approved, with 13 of these already completed.

In view of the very limited resources available, the main function of the fund has been to conduct studies and provide small-scale assistance — primarily in the fields of transportation and trade — relevant to the 19 landlocked developing countries. Although four of these — Burkina Faso, Chad, Mali, and Niger — are in the Sahel, the only project in this region has been the provision of a special advisor in trade planning to Mali. Since the projects are all so small in scale, no approval is needed from UNDP's Governing Council.

The repeated refusal of the major donors to contribute to the Special Fund for Landlocked Developing Countries reflects their belief that groups of developing countries should not be singled out for special treatment. Since this attitude has not changed in the eight years of the fund's existence, and most of the current contributions are coming from the landlocked developing countries themselves, UNDP is willing to dissolve the fund. This pragmatic attitude is not shared by UNCTAD and is not likely to be welcomed by the majority of members in UNDP. Hence the fund is likely to continue at its current level, with its administrative and bookkeeping costs (which are absorbed by UNDP) just about balancing its annual income (UNDP 1985).

United Nations Fund for Population Activities (UNFPA)

In response to the growing concern of some countries that rapid population growth can negatively affect social and economic development, a trust fund was created in mid-1967 to finance activities in the field of population. From 1967 to 1969 $5 million was raised, but only 19 per cent of this was used, primarily for improving the statistical and demographic work of the United Nations itself. In early 1969 responsibility for the trust fund was transferred from the Secretary-General's office to UNDP, and it was renamed the UN Fund for Population Activities. Its mandate was broadened to include the support of work on population-related activities by all UN and non-governmental organizations. It was also given greater freedom to cover costs that would normally be considered appropriate for a counterpart contribution from the recipient government. With the United States initially providing matching funds, voluntary pledges rose steadily to $125 million in 1980 (UNFPA 1982). From 1980 to 1984 contributions have risen only to an expected $134 million in 1984. In contrast to some other UN agencies, problems with non-payment of pledges or payment in non-convertible currencies have been minimal. Since 1973 up to 9 per cent of the pledges to UNFPA have been expressly designated for other agencies, primarily the International Planned Parenthood Foundation.

Until 1976 funds were provided in response to requests received, but it was recognized that this system did not necessarily provide funds to the countries with the greatest need. To rectify this, UNFPA, following in the footsteps of UNDP, established a system of priority countries based on indicators such as the infant mortality rate, population growth rate, and density of agricultural population on arable land. Certain thresholds were established, resulting in the identification of 40 priority countries and 14 borderline countries. The goal is for two-thirds of UNFPA's resources to be spent in priority and borderline countries, and the proportion so used has increased from 39 per cent in 1969–1976 to 69 per cent in 1982 (UNDP 1982m; UNFPA 1983).

UNFPA works essentially like a small UNDP concentrating on population-related activities. Projects are formulated and often farmed out to other UN agencies for execution. In 1981 the UN Secretariat was the executing body for 25 per cent of the projects, followed by WHO (15 per cent), ILO (5 per cent), regional commissions such as the Economic Commission for Africa (5 per cent), Unesco (5 per cent), UNICEF (3 per cent), etc. UNFPA, either for practical reasons or to avoid paying the usual 13 per cent overhead costs, implemented 21 per cent of its own projects.

In addition to the country allocations, 30 per cent of the project funds has been devoted to regional, interregional, and global projects. There is a general feeling in UNFPA's governing body that this percentage is much too high, as the benefits to the priority countries are less direct. As with UNDP, a reduction in this figure has proved difficult because the activities undertaken (seminars, studies, training courses, etc.) are not as subject to delays and disruptions as the country programmes, and a reduction in these activities is more difficult when there is no real growth in the overall budget. To a large extent the increase in intercountry activities was one way to cope with the rapidly growing budgets of the 1970s when the country programmes could not be expanded fast enough.

Consistent with UNFPA's emphasis on the priority countries, the proportion of project resources devoted to sub-Saharan Africa increased to 17 per cent in 1982. Basic data collection still accounted for nearly one-third of all expenditures in this region, while family planning and regional activities each took over 20 per cent of expenditures. In future years UNFPA expects to emphasize maternal and child health and to reduce its role in collecting and analysing census data.

Each of the Sahelian countries has UNFPA-funded projects except Chad, where the combination of political unrest and the government's satisfaction with present trends has resulted in no projects being submitted to UNFPA for funding. In the Gambia the government adopted an explicit family planning policy in 1979; the major projects are concerned with improving family planning and maternal and child health services in rural areas. In Mali the emphasis is on the development of a maternal and child health/family planning programme and a variety of educational activities. Mauritania has placed priority on collecting and analysing census data as well as providing family services. Niger concluded its census in 1981 and was planning for new assistance in fields such as demography, health, and population policy. In contrast, Senegal had ten projects operating in 1981, with the two main activities being, first, the support of a UNFPA co-ordinator in Senegal and, second, data collection and analysis as the basis for establishing a population distribution policy. Senegal is

also in the early stages of initiating a major family health project. Finally, in Upper Volta development of a data bank, support for a UNFPA representative, development planning, and a project to integrate traditional beliefs into population policy made up the bulk of the expenditures (UNDP 1982n; UNFPA 1983).

Regional activities include projects to develop selected research and training centres, support for regional offices and population experts (e.g., at ECA), and sponsoring fellowships, publications, conferences, etc. (UNFPA 1982). Thus, most of the regional activities are devoted to the development of an infrastructure outside the Sahel, with some of the funds trickling back through participation in seminars, regional studies, and "sectoral programmes". One notable exception was the provision of over $400,000 in 1981 to the Institut du Sahel for its socio-economic and demographic unit.

It can be seen that basic data collection and analysis made up the bulk of initial activities in the Gambia, Mali, Mauritania, Niger, Senegal, and Upper Volta. UNFPA resources have now shifted from this first step to a variety of family health and family planning projects, as well as an effort to build up the national infrastructure with regard to population. As is indicated in table 14, there has been wide variation in UNFPA expenditures among the seven Sahelian countries. Senegal can be considered to have received more than its share of UNFPA funds, but over time the priority-country system should help even these figures out (though there will always be some annual variation). The other key factor in determining activities in a given country is the political will at the national level. As evidenced by Chad, UNFPA can be involved only if the government believes that population is an important issue. UNFPA's project-identification missions can be help generate the necessary awareness, but the recipient government must ultimately make a formal request before any assistance can be provided.

UNFPA has been relatively forthright in evaluating it own activities. For example, a review of UNFPA's census programme in eight African countries noted a number of problems, including a high turnover of expatriate expert staff, delays in providing equipment, and dissatisfaction with some of the experts provided and the executing agency in general. Training possibilities were not fully utilized, so it was felt that only three of the eight countries could conduct their next census without substantial technical assistance (UNDP 1982o).

A review of four country and five inter-country projects indicated that the results were generally good, but both project design and the management of some projects was weak. Often there were delays in obtaining equipment and recruiting experts, and the results were not adequately

TABLE 14.   UNFPA expenditures in the Sahel ($)

	1969–1980	1981	1982 allocation
Chad	480,517	0	0
Gambia	197,512	219,079	264,540
Mali	2,611,556	260,321	349,929
Mauritania	1,755,395	819,039	632,746
Niger	1,626,856	70,496	100,000
Senegal	3,607,718	601,816	610,330
Upper Volta	1,385,195	612,421	635,713
Total	11,664,389	2,583,172	2,593,258

disseminated and applied. Such problems are hardly unique to UNFPA, and at times they almost seem to inevitably accompany technical assistance efforts (chap. 5).

United Nations Financing System for Science and Technology for Development (UNFSSTD)

In August 1979 a UN conference was convened on the topic of science and technology for development. The recommendations of the conference basically called for greater efforts to strengthen the scientific and technological capability of developing countries, and a fund-raising target of $200 million was set. Contributions were voluntary, and after much wrangling between donor and developing countries, an Interim Fund for Science and Technology for Development was established under UNDP's management. However, pledges totalled only about $35 million, while over 900 project proposals were received. Only 65 projects were approved for funding (UNDP 1982k).

In the meantime the General Assembly, recognizing that contributions would likely fall far short of the initial target, decided that the Interim Fund would be supplanted on a longer-term basis by a UN Financing System for Science and Technology for Development, which would also fall under UNDP's direction and rely heavily on UNDP's existing infrastructure for planning and administration.

By the end of 1982, 84 projects had been approved at a total estimated cost of $38 million. Another 78 projects valued at $83 million were rated as ready for implementation when funds permitted. Contributions, however, have declined from $23 million in 1980–1981 to $8 million in 1982, and $0.5 million in 1983. Another $2.7 million has been pledged but not yet paid (UNDP 1984a). Given current fiscal conditions and political attitudes among donor countries, it would be unrealistic to expect a resurgence in funding. UNFSSTD seems destined, therefore, to slowly disappear as the initial set of activities winds down.

Current UNFSSTD projects span a wide range of technological levels and goals, and a variety of financing arrangements. Efforts in the Sahel have concentrated on building up scientific or administrative capability in a given field (e.g., technology planning in Niger, energy technology in Mauritania, rural energy technologies in Niger). Other activities include the establishment of a national centre for agricultural machinery in Niger and the development of optimal technological packages for farming in the different ecological regions of Niger. Small energy devices are being donor countries, it would be unrealistic to expect a resurgence in funding. UNFSSTD seems destined, therefore, to slowly disappear as the initial set of activities winds down.

Energy Account

In 1980 UNDP set up a special Energy Account to provide assistance to developing countries in the energy sector. This was basically in response to the rapidly increasing prices for petroleum and the growing shortage of fuelwood in many rural areas.

Contributions through mid-1984 totalled $18 million, with one-third coming from the OPEC Fund for International Development, one-third from the Netherlands and Sweden, and the balance from a variety of other sources (UNDP 1984).

Two major, world-wide projects have been undertaken to date. The first was a joint World Bank/UNDP assessment of the energy situation in 70 developing countries, with the twin goals of aiding decision-makers and stimulating future activities. The second was to follow up on the assessment, and activities have included a variety of seminars, demonstration facilities, etc. A number of in-country activities have been supported by the Energy Account, including the preparation of an energy master plan for Niger.

The future of the Energy Account remains somewhat uncertain at this point. UNDP is trying to emphasize the role of Energy Account projects to provide "seed money" and stimulate additional, more substantial contributions. It is still too early to determine what the average level of contributions to the account will be, or the extent to which the projects can attract supplemental funding. Even if there is not a substantial increase in petroleum prices, the ongoing rural energy crisis in developing countries should continue to stimulate interest on the part of donors.

The United Nations Environment Programme (UNEP) and the UN Conference on Desertification (UNCOD)

In the latter part of the 1960s the United Nations and its Member States began to recognize that environmental

TABLE 15. UNEP fund allocations for 1973–1977 and 1980–1983 (million $)

Programme area	Expenditures 1973–1977	Commitments	
		1980–1981	1982–1985
Human settlements and human health	15.0	5.6	5.5
Support	17.3	11.5	11.2
Environment and development	4.7	4.0	4.2
Oceans	8.7	6.3	6.3
Energy	1.6	0.8	1.3
Environmental management, including environmental law	1.5	1.2	1.4
Terrestrial ecosystems	16.9	8.9	7.7
Natural disasters	0.3	0.2	0.2
Earthwatch, including the International Register of Potentially Toxic Chemicals	7.8	11.8	11.0
United Nations Habitat and Human Settlements Foundation	4.0	0	0
Environmental data	1.4	1.2	0.5
Arid lands, including desertification	NA[a]	5.5	4.8
Other	0.9	0.6	0.8
Total	80.1	57.6	54.7

Sources: UNEP 1978b, 1982a, 1984

[a] Included with terrestrial ecosystems.

quality was important not only for aesthetic reasons but also because environmental quality could pose very real limitations to health, food production, and the general standard of living. As a result of these concerns the UN Conference on the Human Environment was convened in June 1972 in Stockholm. The main outcome of the conference was a recommendation for a new specialized agency and, equally important, a commitment of financial support from the major donor countries. Later that same year the General Assembly, realizing that many UN activities were already related to the broad theme of the environment, carefully crafted the United Nations Environment Programme to have a strong co-ordinating, catalysing, and financing function. Thus, each existing UN organization was still to retain responsibility for the environmental aspects of its own programme, while UNEP was to provide a mechanism for co-ordination and appropriate scientific input.

Operating from a voluntary Environment Fund, UNEP began life with contributions of just under $100 million for 1973–1977. As a new agency, UNEP required a few years to establish a structure and initiate projects, so it spent only $400,000 in 1973 and $5.5 million in 1974 (UNEP 1975). It thus had 94 per cent of its five-year budget available for the final three years, and built its financial commitments up to a peak of $34 million in 1977.

Contributions, however, did not increase to match UNEP's ambitious plans but peaked in 1979 and 1980 at just under $32 million. Since 1980, contributions have generally shown a slight decrease in absolute values. When combined with the effects of inflation, this has forced a continuing reappraisal of UNEP's activities and objectives. Further disruptions in planning and programming have been caused by uncertainties over the precise amount of contributions that could be expected. This was particularly true in the case of contributions from the United States, which was providing one-third of UNEP's budget yet delayed both pledges and payments until the last minute. This uncertainty over funding is still a serious problem. For example, the target budget for 1984–1985 was tentatively set at $35 million per year, while an alternative budget of $25 million was prepared in case donations were further reduced (*UN Chronicle* 1983). Actual contributions are running about $29 million per year (UNEP 1985a).

Thus UNEP has occasionally been forced to dip into the programme reserve established in the first couple of years of operation. In 1981 this reserve contained $25 million, with just half of this in readily convertible currencies (UNEP 1982a). Since an average of 13 per cent of UNEP's annual contributions are in non-convertible currencies and it can't spend these quickly enough, it appears that UNEP will maintain a substantial cash reserve consisting of an ever higher percentage of non-convertible currencies.

Table 15 indicates UNEP's expenditures by programme area for 1973–1977 and its commitments for 1980–1981 and 1982–1983. Given the pattern of past contributions, one would expect these latter figures to be revised downward by about 10 per cent. (The political solution to budget controversies seems to be to set high targets and then let contributions fall short.)

Each of UNEP's programme areas is relevant to one or more of the Sahelian countries, but activities designed specifically for the CILSS countries appear to be relatively few. Presumably this is because UNSO's dual mandate for the rehabilitation of the Sahel and anti-desertification activities leaves little room for UNEP. Since UNEP by definition is not an operational agency, field projects are actually implemented by agencies such as ECA, Unesco, and a variety of local institutions. As suggested above, UNEP's own diversity means that there are any number of projects directly or indirectly relevant to the Sahel. Some examples are the regional seas programme for West Africa, feasibility studies for the protection of wildlife, and rural energy in Senegal. Many of UNEP's other projects are different types of seminars and training courses, which typically involve one or more participants from each country in a particular region.

Initially activities relevant to arid lands and desertification were based in the general programme of terrestrial ecosystems. However, as a result of the heightened interest in arid lands resulting from the UN Conference on Desertification and the creation of UNEP's Desertification Branch, a separate programme area was established about 1979. Since then a wide variety of projects have been undertaken, ranging from ecological research to conferences on training needs and preparation of state-of-knowledge reports. Various groups are involved as collaborators or executing agencies, although FAO and Unesco tend to handle most of the field activities.

As mentioned before, responsibility for anti-desertification activities is shared with UNSO. UNEP has set up a small desertification unit to help co-ordinate, formulate, and implement national and regional projects, but UNSO is responsible for the Sahel and most of sub-Saharan Africa. For this reason UNEP is not very active in anti-desertification activities in the Sahel. In fact, UNEP contributes about $1 million per year to UNSO to help it strengthen its anti-desertification efforts (UNDP 1984d).

In addition to its catalytic functions, UNEP is supposed to co-ordinate all environmental activities within the UN system. The Environment Co-ordination Board (ECB), the main mechanism set up by UNEP to carry out this function, consists of the heads of all relevant UN agencies. However, each agency also designates a "focal point", usually the person in charge of the most relevant division. It is at meetings of these "focal points" that the most useful exchanges take place. As another attempt at co-ordination, UNEP regularly requests other agencies to provide information on their activities in a given field, which UNEP then collates to produce extensive documents of dubious value. The demands by UNEP for information and co-ordination meetings have become so great that some agencies are complaining to the ECB's parent body, the Advisory Committee on Co-ordination (UNEP 1980).

To cope with the increased interest and activities in desertification since 1977, the ECB created a separate body, the Inter-agency Working Group on Desertification, to co-ordinate anti-desertification activities within the UN system. The working group utilizes the Desertification Unit in UNEP as its secretariat (UNEP 1978a). Completing the picture is a body called the Consultative Group on Desertification Control, a broad-based group whose two main functions are to discuss ways to mobilize funds, and to act as a forum where government agencies, UN agencies, and non-governmental organizations can get together to discuss desertification control measures. To a large extent the effectiveness of this entire mechanism has been limited by staff and funding problems. UNEP has been unable to provide much support, and the staff members contributed by UNDP and UNFPA have been withdrawn as funding within those agencies became more limiting, leaving the Desertification Unit short-staffed (UNEP 1982b). Project proposals put forth by the Consultative Group have generated little interest among donors. In fact, very few countries are even approaching UNEP to request assistance in preparing national plans to combat desertification (UNEP 1985b). The absence of a specific programme of activities, independent of other agencies, has also made it difficult for the Desertification Unit to carve out a distinctive niche.

In summary, UNEP seems destined — at least for the medium term — to languish at its present level of funding or slowly decline in real terms. Staff and other support costs will remain, thereby taking an increasing proportion of its budget. Efforts to establish trust funds and open other windows of funding have been only moderately successful. To a large extent UNEP is dependent on the contributions of the United States and Japan, who have been the major donors, but the United States has fluctuated in its attitude towards UNEP. Many of the developing countries favour an increased role and increased contributions for UNEP, but there is certain to be continued resistance to this even as the world economy recovers (*Nature* 1982). The system-wide medium-term environmental programme was a major undertaking, but its general nature failed to ignite much interest. The entire anti-desertification mechanism seems ponderous and unable to generate much support. UNEP must look to the future instead of the fading beacon of Stockholm 1972 and somehow convince the industrialized world that its efforts are essential to achieving the broad goals of environmental quality.

United Nations Conference on Desertification (UNCOD)

The 1977 UN Conference on Desertification was another in

the series of specialized conferences that followed the 1972 UN Conference on the Human Environment. In line with the format used for the conferences on food, population, water, and habitat and human settlements, a series of background papers were prepared together with a Plan of Action. Since many governments, especially the traditional major contributors to the United Nations, have become leery of setting up new and costly agencies, UNCOD proposed a small but permanent co-ordinating secretariat on desertification within UNEP, while the follow-up activities would be carried out by the existing agencies according to their respective spheres of competence. This was generally accepted and UNEP was given the lead role, but the necessary financial support was not as simple to arrange. Knowing the difficulties in obtaining new donations, UNEP proposed a small tax on certain international business transactions, such as the export of selected non-renewable raw materials. Since many countries did not want to set such a precedent, this proposal was rejected and UNEP was left with its Plan of Action but no real support to execute it with.

The Plan of Action, as it was finally approved, contained 28 recommendations. These covered, explicitly or implicitly, nearly all the physical and social aspects of desertification as well as the questions of implementation, co-ordination, and financing. The intergovernmental nature of the conference forced the recommendations to be encyclopaedic in content and lacking in specific priorities, but the conference did contribute to a wider recognition of the problem. As an example of the work of the conference, Recommendation 5 is reproduced in full (except for the introductory paragraphs) as follows:

It is recommended that comprehensive measures for soil improvement, soil and water conservation and soil moisture management be introduced to combat desertification in rainfed farming.

To implement this recommendation national action would be required to:
(a) Survey affected areas to determine land capability, degradation hazards and climatic risk, and put forward proposals for conservational land use.
(b) Assist the introduction of improved, appropriate crop systems, including cover crops, rotational systems with legumes, rational use of organic and chemical fertilizers, careful soil cultivation and tillage and proper use of plant remains, to reduce exposure of soil and maintain fertility and soil structure.
(c) Assist with the reconstruction and introduction of works such as terracing for soil conservation and water spreading.
(d) Encourage the adoption of measures to counter erosion, such as strip cropping, shelter belts, protective forest belts, structures for water control, use of soil conditioners, etc.
(e) Reclaim degraded lands by such actions as stabilizing sand surfaces, levelling dunes and checking gully systems.
(f) Assist the revegetation of watersheds and the protection of upland pastures from excessive grazing or cutting for fuel.
(g) Encourage diversification in farming systems, with appropriate inclusion of livestock and arboriculture.
(h) Encourage changes in land tenure systems which are incompatible with introduction of improved agriculture.

The recommendation implies regional action to develop through national and regional institutions such as universities and research establishments, improved agricultural techniques which resist desertification, and drought-resistant crop varieties. [UN 1978]

From this recommendation it should be clear that any concrete results will come not as a result of the recommendations but as a result of individual governments or international agencies making a specific commitment. Thus the ongoing series of UN conferences may serve as a useful stimulus and create a mandate to deal with a given set of problems, but the inherently political nature of these conferences tends to limit their practical results. Israel, for example, has had considerable experience in making arid and semi-arid lands productive, but during the presentation of its case study at UNCOD all the Arab and most of the African countries walked out as a political protest.

In addition to the general recommendations of the Plan of Action, six more specific transnational projects were formulated: (1) management of the major regional aquifers in north-east Africa and the Arabian peninsula, (2) establishment of a transnational green belt in North Africa, (3) management of livestock and rangelands to combat desertification in the Sudano-Sahelian region (SOLAR), (4) monitoring desertification processes and related natural resources in arid and semi-arid areas of South America, (5) monitoring desertification processes and related natural resources in arid and semi-arid areas of south-west Asia, and (6) establishment of a Sahelian green belt to combat desertification. While each of these projects may have a scientific basis, the political difficulties in getting countries to co-operate has prevented any significant collective action. For example, the SOLAR project would set up a series of zones whereby cattle and other animals would be slowly moved south to allow final fattening close to the major markets of Abidjan, Lagos, and other West African coastal cities. However, this would require not only substantial changes in the traditional patterns of animal husbandry but also a degree of co-operation and freedom of movement of animals across international boundaries that is presently impossible. Only in the case of the transnational green belt in North Africa has there been much progress. In this case a subregional training programme has been organized together with a variety of national projects (UNEP 1982c).

As implied above, one positive result of UNCOD was the collection and synthesis of knowledge about desertification. The general background paper "Desertification: An Overview" (UNCOD 1977c) was widely regarded as an excellent synopsis of the problem. On the other hand, the overview maps prepared for the conference were on such a large and generalized scale that their usefulness is rather limited (Mabbutt 1978). Other, more detailed maps of different regions and case studies were prepared, which may not point out the global dimensions of the problem but are more useful for planning and administrative purposes.

The other significant event stimulated by UNCOD, although not formally a part of the conference, was the meeting sponsored by six national academies of science on the indicators of desertification. At this purely scientific meeting held before the conference, it was decided to investigate a number of physical, biological, and social variables for use as indices of desertification. Working groups were set up, and, even though projects are on a voluntary basis, their joint efforts may eventually result in a more practical set of standards for measuring certain features or processes of desertification (AAAS 1977).

As discussed previously, UNEP was given the responsibility of overseeing the implementation of the Plan of Action but no funds to work with. An account was established for voluntary contributions, but after five years only three countries had donated a total of $25,000. Similar problems have afflicted the Desertification Unit in Nairobi, which is supposed to co-ordinate and stimulate UNCOD-related activities. These problems have not significantly affected the Sahel, as UNSO was given the responsibility for following up the Plan of Action in the Sahel. The advantage of UNSO is that it may well have better contracts with governments, but, on the other hand, its expertise is more in the field of technical assistance than desertification. As mentioned in an earlier context, there is often a tendency to identify a project as "anti-desertification" because that is a politically desirable label, when in reality the project is not substantially different from many other technical assistance projects. This then makes it impossible to assess the real impact of a conference such as UNCOD, and the effectiveness of UNSO in implementing the Plan of Action.

Other Agencies of the UN System

Food and Agriculture Organization (FAO)

The Food and Agriculture Organization was one of the first specialized agencies created by the United Nations, as it was established concurrently with the United Nations itself. Its purposes are to raise levels of nutrition and standards of living; to secure improvements in the efficiency of the production and distribution of all food and agricultural products from farms, forests, and fisheries; to better the conditions of rural populations; and, by these means, to contribute to an expanding world economy and ensure humanity's freedom from hunger (UN 1980). Thus FAO's main thrust is improving agricultural production (e.g., food, fibre, wood, and fish) as a means of raising the standard of living, especially in rural areas. It is involved to a lesser degree in accessory activities such as data collection, population planning, and food contamination standards.

In budgetary terms FAO is one of the largest specialized agencies of the UN system. In 1982–1983 its working budget was $367 million, and another $683 million was expected to be provided from outside sources (FAO 1981a). Traditionally UNDP has been the major source of outside funds, but the proportion of funds from other sources has increased from 14 per cent in 1970 to more than 50 per cent in 1982–1983. A variety of trust funds account for the bulk of these extra-budgetary funds. Generally, these trust funds are received for support of specific programmes such as emergency relief, food security, and tree-planting. Another major source of extra-budgetary funds is government contributions for FAO projects. A summary of the estimated expenditures by programme for the bienniums 1980–1981 and 1982–1983 is given in table 16.

As can be seen from the table, the technical and economic programmes are at the heart of FAO, for they include agriculture, forestry, and fisheries. Together these account for nearly half the regular budget, but, more importantly, 91 per cent of the extra-budgetary funds are directed towards this division. The emphasis is on agriculture, with fisheries and forestry each accounting for less than 10 per cent of FAO's total funding.

FAO's technical and economic programme is organized into a series of programmatic areas, which are presented together with their respective financing in table 17. FAO dwarfs the expenditures of other agencies, such as Unesco, in most fields relating to land use and productivity. In selected areas (e.g., desertification) UNSO may play a major role, but FAO's size and long-standing presence gives it a pre-eminence that it is loathe to surrender. Still the creation of agencies such as UNSO, IFAD, and UNEP have all chipped away at FAO's responsibilities. One indication of this overall trend is that FAO's share of UNDP funds has dropped to about 25 per cent, as compared with 31 per cent in 1972 (FAO 1981a).

TABLE 16.   FAO programme and budget, 1980–1983

| Major programme | Regular programme | | | | Extra-budgetary funds (estimated), $000 | Total funds 1982–1983 | |
| | 1980–1981 approved budget | | 1982–1983 budget | | | | |
	$000	%	$000	%		$000	%
General Policy and Direction							
Governing bodies	8,827	3.2	11,206	3.0	–	11,206	1.1
Policy, direction, and planning	5,858	2.1	7,235	2.0	3,387	10,622	1 0
Legal	2,498	0.9	3,153	0.9	267	3,420	0.3
Liaison	5,889	2.1	7,162	1.9	626	7,788	0.7
Subtotal	23,072	8.3	28,756	7.8	4,280	33,036	3.1
Technical and Economic Programmes							
Agriculture	97,132	34.9	127,929	34.8	475,806	603,735	57.4
Fisheries	16,784	6.0	21,651	5.9	80,081	101,732	9.7
Forestry	11,340	4.1	14,701	4.0	66,085	80,786	7.7
Subtotal	125,256	45.0	164,281	44.7	621,972	786,253	74.8
Development Support Programmes							
Field programme planning and liaison	3,319	1.2	4,502	1.2	7,694	12,196	1.2
Investment	13,608	4.9	18,539	5.0	16,976	35,515	3.4
Special programmes	1,767	0.6	2,182	0.6	350	2,532	0.2
FAO representatives	20,866	7.5	34,483	9.4	1,325	35,808	3.4
Programme management	608	0.2	714	0.2	800	1,514	0.1
Subtotal	40,168	14.4	60,420	16.4	27,145	87,565	8.3
Technical Co-operation Programme	32,638	11.7	47,387	12.9	–	47,387	4.5
Support Services							
Information and documentation	13,122	4.7	17,157	4.6	4,771	21,928	2.1
Administration	30,196	10.8	33,569	9.1	14,666	48,235	4.6
Programme management	1,154	0.4	1,361	0.4	5,015	6,376	0.6
Subtotal	44,472	15.9	52,087	14.1	24,452	76,539	7.3
Common Services	12,534	4.5	14,485	3.9	5,198	19,683	1.9
Contingencies	600	0.2	600	0.2	–	600	0.1
Grand Total	278,740	100.0	368,016	100.0	683,047	1,051,063	100.0

Source: FAO 1981b

Overall, 22 per cent of the regular budget and 35 per cent of the extra-budgetary funds are devoted to Africa. Excluding headquarters costs, the percentage of funds allocated to Africa has increased from 31 per cent in 1976–1977 to 39 per cent in 1981 (FAO 1981b). This high level of assistance is due to the facts that per capita food production in Africa has declined nearly 10 per cent between 1969 and 1981, one-quarter to one-third of the population are malnourished or undernourished, the majority of the least-developed countries are in Africa, and food production must be increased while trying to maintain the export earnings of cash crops.

FAO projects in the Sahel include the control of livestock diseases — such as trypanosomiasis, tsetse fly infestation, and bovine pleuropneumonia — control of crop pests and post-harvest losses, training and technology development, grazing-lands management, gathering and evaluation of information and statistics, developing food and nutrition policies, utilization of marine resources in the exclusive economic zones, meeting fuelwood demand, and strengthening national agricultural and forestry institutions.

In its overall policies FAO has followed the general trend within the UN system of decentralizing its activities and

TABLE 17.   Proposed FAO technical and economic programmes for 1982–1983 ($000)

Programme	Budget	Extra budgetary funds (estimated)	Total funds
Agriculture			
Natural resources	14,167	91,591	105,758
Crops	19,225	159,410	178,635
Livestock	11,986	116,976	128,962
Research support	5,055	2,325	7,380
Rural development	21,182	65,987	87,169
Nutrition	10,254	8,113	18,367
Information and analysis	13,848	457	14,305
Policy	25,708	30,617	56,325
Programme management	6,504	330	6,834
Subtotal	127,929	475,806	603,735
Fisheries			
Fisheries information	2,828	963	3,791
Exploitation and utilization	9,536	75,447	84,983
Fisheries policy	5,795	3,671	9,466
Programme management	3,492	–	3,492
Subtotal	21,651	80,081	101,732
Forestry			
Forest resources and environment	2,381	34,311	36,692
Forest industries and trade	2,706	12,497	15,203
Forest investment and institutions	4,009	16,232	20,241
Forestry for rural development	2,495	3,045	5,540
Programme management	3,110	–	3,110
Subtotal	14,701	66,085	80,786
Grand total	164,281	621,972	786,253

Source: FAO 1981a

concentrating on the poorest of the poor. Specifically it claims to be emphasizing food crops rather than export crops, although it recognizes the need to earn foreign exchange. It also recognizes the need for land reform, and it took the relatively progressive step of sponsoring the World Conference on Agrarian Reform and Rural Development in 1979. As with the other UN conferences, any follow-up activities are dependent on the political will in a given country or region, and in this area changes — no matter what FAO's position is — will be slow. FAO is also placing a continuing emphasis on "integrated rural development" and pushing "forestry for community development", although again it is difficult to fully evaluate the effects of these concepts at the field level.

FAO has also been relatively successful in its efforts to co-operate with a variety of funding agencies besides UNDP. For example, it often participates in "multi-donor missions" to develop projects, and then becomes the executing agency for those projects in its sphere of expertise. It also established a special investment centre in 1966 to help formulate projects for donors, and from 1977 through 1980 this centre played a role in formulating 137 projects worth $8,500 million (FAO 1981b). Many of these projects have been developed by the FAO/World Bank Co-operative Programme, and similar links have been or are being built with multilateral funding organizations such as the International Fund for Agricultural Development, the regional development banks, the Arab Bank for Economic Development in Africa, etc. (FAO 1979).

FAO's Technical Co-operation Programme works on a different basis, as it is intended to provide short-term assistance in response to requests from governments. The original emphasis was on training and technical assistance in the case of emergencies caused by drought, agricultural pests, or diseases. Increasingly, however, assistance has been provided to governments (or the Investment Centre) in order to help attract other funds. About 39 per cent of the programme's resources have been devoted to Africa, and the work has tended to concentrate on plant protection, animal health, and seed production.

It is interesting to note that the increase in FAO's budget from 1980-1981 to 1982-1983 was expected to be 32 per cent. This is particularly significant in view of the fact that most of the other UN agencies are experiencing little or no real growth. As might be expected, many of the major donors opposed the scale of the increase while reaffirming their commitment to fight hunger and malnutrition. Many of the objections centred around the fact that just over half the budget will be spent on established posts in Rome (*Overseas Development* 1981). It is doubtful that future budgets will allow increases of a similar scale.

International Atomic Energy Agency (IAEA)

The International Atomic Energy Agency came into existence in 1957 when its charter was ratified by 18 countries. Its two primary purposes are to stimulate the peaceful uses of atomic energy and to help limit and control the military use of atomic energy. Initially its work focused on the development and use of radiation techniques in medicine, agriculture, industry, and water resources development. With the commercial development of nuclear power, IAEA's emphasis has shifted to promoting the use of nuclear power and the economic, safety, and non-proliferation aspects of the nuclear fuel cycle (IAEA 1977).

With an operating budget of over $85 million in 1981 and a staff of 1,600, IAEA is involved in everything from agricultural research using radioisotopes to uranium prospecting and food irradiation. Its technical assistance budget was over $24 million in 1981. Voluntary contributions were the source of over half of the technical assistance budget, while assistance in kind and contributions for particular projects provided another 15 and 11 per cent respectively. Just over 20 per cent ($5 million) originated from UNDP projects that were being executed by IAEA. In general, the level of UNDP-sponsored activities has been relatively constant, but there has been continued rapid growth in technical assistance activities sponsored by other sources.

Of the $21 million actually expended for technical assistance, 47 per cent was used for equipment, 29 per cent for fellowships, and 24 per cent for outside experts (IAEA 1982). Like other agencies, IAEA has been building up a surplus of funds as a result of overestimating the costs of certain projects, the inevitable lags in implementation, and the fact that some expected expenses simply are not

incurred. Another factor contributing to this surplus is the accumulation of non-convertible currencies.

Given the relatively sophisticated nature of IAEA's work, it is not surprising that less than one-quarter of its technical assistance funds are being devoted to Africa. The main area of emphasis in Africa has been on the use of isotopes and radiation in agriculture, and secondarily in biology, medicine, and industry. Mineral development is another major component of IAEA's activities in Africa, and in some of the more developed countries IAEA is assisting with the general development of atomic power. At present only Mali, Niger, and Senegal are members of IAEA, and activities in the CILSS countries in 1981 were limited to a few small projects in each of the three member countries (IAEA 1982). Of course the Sahel benefits from a variety of other research projects being undertaken elsewhere, such as control of the tsetse fly through the sterile-male technique, more effective techniques for applying fertilizers, the use of radiation-induced mutations in plant breeding, and the analysis of trace-element deficiencies and of the presence of pollutants in fish and oils. Much of this research is done in collaboration with FAO or other agencies.

International Fund for Agricultural Development (IFAD)

The newest specialized agency in the UN system is the International Fund for Agricultural Development. Wary of creating yet another agency that would lack sufficient resources to accomplish its intended goals, the General Assembly mandated in 1976 that IFAD could not come into existence until pledges exceeded $1,000 million. That level of commitment was reached in December 1976, and IFAD began operating in late 1977.

IFAD is conceived primarily as a bank giving loans for agricultural development. At present three types of loans are provided: (1) ordinary loans, which carry an interest rate of 8 per cent for 15 years with a grace period of 3 years, (2) intermediate-term loans, which carry an interest rate of 4 per cent for 20 years with a grace period of 5 years, and (3) highly concessional loans, which have only a service charge of 1 per cent, a maturity period of 50 years, and a grace period of 10 years. In addition, up to 12.5 per cent of the funds committed in any financial year can be outright grants (IFAD 1978). So far, 70 per cent of IFAD's lending has been highly concessional loans to low-income countries.

IFAD is concentrating its activities on rural areas and the poorest sector of the population; one criterion is that any project must not have a regressive effect on income distribution (IFAD 1979). In its structure and governing board, IFAD is designed to counterbalance the World Bank, which is often viewed as conservative, interfering, and

Western-dominated. IFAD's governing body is tripartite, with equal representation of OECD countries, OPEC countries, and developing countries. IFAD also claims to be more flexible in its requirements for counterpart contributions from governments, since many of the poorest countries can ill afford to provide items such as counterpart staff and support services, especially when a number of large-scale projects are operating at the same time and competing for scarce counterpart funds and scarcer managerial talent.

The funding of IFAD is also based on a tripartite arrangement, with $1,100 million expected in contributions for 1981-1983. Of this, $620 million was to come from the developed countries, $450 million from the oil-exporting countries, and $30 million from other developing countries. These contributions, plus $240 million in carry-over from the first set of contributions, were expected to allow annual expenditures to rise to $435 million in 1983. However, the general reluctance of the Western donors to increase their contributions, combined with the large drop in oil-derived income in the OPEC countries, resulted in contributions falling short of the 1981-1983 target. Hence IFAD has been forced to reduce its lending to approximately $310 million per year (*UN Chronicle* 1984), roughly 10 per cent below 1980-1981 levels (IFAD 1982). Continuing weakness in oil prices recently led to a proposal to slightly shift the burden of financing from the OPEC countries to the industrialized countries. This met with stiff resistance from the United States, and so IFAD's level of funding will remain constant in the near term.

Between 1977 and the end of 1982 IFAD made over 100 loans worth a total of $1,500 million and provided $60 million in technical assistance grants. Large concessional loans were provided to Niger, Senegal, and Upper Volta for integrated rural development projects. Mauritania obtained a similar loan for an irrigation project, and a $5 million loan was given to the Gambia for a project to assist smallholder agriculture. The loans to both the Gambia and Upper Volta were supplemented by small technical assistance grants. Over half of the technical assistance funds, however, were provided to a variety of established institutions for research purposes. Overall, IFAD is trying to take a more active role in initiating loan requests rather than relying on suggestions made by other agencies (IFAD 1982).

International Labour Organisation (ILO)

The International Labour Organisation was founded in 1919, and in 1946 it became the first specialized agency associated with the United Nations. Its purpose is to contribute to lasting peace by promoting social justice, and to improve labour conditions and living standards through international action. More specifically, ILO tries to serve as the conscience of the world of labour, as a meeting place for governments, employers, and workers, and as an impartial observer of social phenomena and to spearhead action in the service of member states.

This socially relevant mandate has influenced the philosophy of ILO and — in the view of some — made it a very political organization. To protest the work and political stance of ILO, the United States — which contributes 25 per cent of ILO's regular budget — withdrew in November 1977. Since other countries could not take up much of the slack, ILO was forced to slash its budget by 22 per cent and reduce its staff. The United States rejoined ILO two years later, but it took some time to build activities back up to their previous level. This, combined with UNDP's liquidity crisis in 1975-1976, meant that the 1982-1983 budget was the first "normal" budget in six years.

ILO is one of the larger specialized agencies in the UN system, with a regular budget of $245 million for 1982-1983. An additional $288 million of outside funding was expected for a variety of technical assistance and other activities, but this was adjusted to $223 million in 1982 (ILO 1982), while the final figure was only $183 million. This reduction was due primarily to the drop in UNDP-financed activities, which traditionally have constituted more than half of ILO's outside funding (ILO 1984). To a certain extent the decline in UNDP funds has been compensated for by an increase in multilateral, bilateral, and trust funds, but these are not expected to show major increases in the near future.

ILO's 1984-1985 budget was set at $256 million, representing an increase of only 2.6 per cent. Outside funds for technical assistance activities are estimated at $167 million (ILO 1984). As a result of the decline in UNDP funds, ILO will be forced to depend more on its own budget for technical assistance and other programme activities. At present, approximately one-third of the regular budget is devoted to the technical programme. Some of the major topic areas are industrial relations, working conditions and the environment, employment and development, international labour standards and human rights, and training. These topics are furthered by means of research, publications, international meetings, the drafting of international covenants, etc. (ILO 1980).

ILO has been attempting to decentralize its field activities. A network of regional offices has been established in Africa, with an office in Dakar responsible for the Sahelian countries. The extra-budgetary activities tend to concentrate on either training or employment and development. Training projects vary considerably in terms of the level of training, target audience, and length of training. Employment and development often involve labour-intensive development activities. UNDP-supported projects, discussed earlier, include vocational training, establishing special management institutes, and assistance to small-scale artisans and entrepreneurs. Other types of projects may be concerned with technical advice, social security, health and safety of workers, etc. In summary, ILO is very active in the Sahel, but its effect on natural resource use is primarily through the long-term and indirect processes of education, training, and improving management capability.

Office of the United Nations Disaster Relief Co-ordinator (UNDRO)

UNDRO began operations in March 1972 with a dual mandate. Its first responsibility is to co-ordinate relief in response to natural disasters and civil disorders. In this connection UNDRO attempts to maintain information on the location, type, and amount of emergency supplies available and on the emergency needs of countries. In all these functions UNDRO's ability to respond and co-ordinate is dependent on information provided to it by donor countries and organizations. Hence the UNDP Resident Co-ordinators must be regarded as playing a key role in UNDRO's efforts. The second part of UNDRO's mandate is to provide technical assistance in the fields of planning and pre-disaster preparedness (UNGA 1981b).

From the beginning UNDRO has been hampered by very limited financial resources and uncertainty regarding its precise task and priorities. In general, 60 per cent of its resources are devoted to co-ordination, 30 per cent to preparedness, and 10 per cent to disaster prevention, but there is a paucity of actual project funding. For 1980–1981 salaries consumed 78 per cent of the $4.8 million budget. Three trust funds have been set up, but in 1980 contributions for disaster prevention and pre-disaster planning totalled $46,820; for emergency relief, $4,484; and for strengthening UNDRO, $550,937 (UNGA 1981c). Furthermore, the amount of emergency relief channelled through UNDRO has dropped from an annual average of $1.7 million in 1973-1976 to an average of $430,000 from 1977 to 1980. Since UNDRO has essentially no emergency funds, the United Nations provided $360,000 as emergency relief funds for 1981, with a $30,000 ceiling on assistance to any one disaster. From 1972 until mid-1980 UNDRO made 114 emergency allocations, totalling $1.8 million, which was slightly more than 1 per cent of all UN emergency aid for that period.

In the Sahel UNDRO has provided emergency flood relief to Senegal and Upper Volta, flown in generators to the Gambia, and provided assistance in Chad. In terms of technical assistance, a pre-disaster planning project has taken place in Senegal, and funds were given to Upper Volta for a fellowship (UNGA 1978, 1981b). As explained in chapter 2, UNDRO's assistance to the Sahel during the drought was very limited.

In 1980 the UN Joint Inspection Unit, which conducts in-depth reviews of the performance of various UN bodies, issued a report which severely criticized UNDRO. Specifically it described UNDRO's activities as haphazard and erratic, and recommended that its staff should be cut in half and its mandate be reduced to co-ordination in the case of sudden natural disasters. Apparently political considerations have dominated staff selection and promotion, leading to a further decline in morale and effectiveness (Guest 1980).

In summary, UNDRO appears to be increasingly dependent on the United Nations for its core support, and contributions for both emergency aid and technical assistance are dropping. UNDRO's capacity to carry out its mandate, therefore, is dependent on the generosity of larger bodies. At present there doesn't appear to be the political will to resolve the situation, but if budgets continue to tighten, the General Assembly may be forced to take some precedent-setting action.

United Nations Educational, Scientific and Cultural Organization (Unesco)

Unesco, established in 1946 and based in Paris, is one of the largest specialized agencies within the UN system. Its broad responsibilities cover education, science, and culture, and its activities fall into two main areas, reflecting a dual mandate. In the first area — facilitating international intellectual co-operation — it is concerned with everything from copyrights to the support of a wide variety of scientific organizations and cultural affairs. The second area is more development-oriented and could be termed technical assistance in a broad sense. In this latter category most of the operating funds are obtained from the World Bank, UNDP, or other organizations which use Unesco as an executing agency. Although these technical-assistance activities also cover a broad spectrum of topics, there is a concentration in education and culture, particularly since UNEP, FAO, WHO, WMO, etc. can claim greater expertise in their respective scientific fields. Nevertheless, Unesco tries to maintain a presence in important areas such as ecology, energy, and the basic sciences, and it provides a small amount of seed money for research and training. It has been reasonably successful in raising additional funds to further most of these activities, even though these more topical areas generate the most competition from other UN agencies. In the basic sciences and areas such as curriculum development other agencies are less active, for Unesco is regarded as the dominant agency within the UN system in the field of education.

For the 1981–1983 triennium Unesco's regular budget was set at $625 million. Another $379 million is expected in outside funds, with two-thirds of this coming from other

TABLE 18.   Unesco natural science budget, 1981–1983 ($)

Theme	Regular programme	UN sources	Other sources	Total
Science and society/science and technology education	2,387,000	—	—	2,387,100
Science and technology policies	6,552,600	3,000,000	190,000	9,742,600
Scientific and technological research and training	24,800,400	62,400,000	6,400,000	93,600,400
Integrated rural development	211,000	—	150,000	361,000
Mineral and energy resources	6,745,200	9,200,000	400,000	16,345,200
Man and the biosphere	8,218,300	9,300,000	5,000,000	22,518,300
Water resources	6,824,300	10,000,000	1,185,000	18,009,300
Ocean and coastal marine systems	12,146,700	16,880,000	6,250,000	35,276,700
Information systems and services	1,333,000	1,000,000	1,000,000	3,333,000
Total	69,218,600	111,780,000	20,575,000	201,573,600

Source: Unesco 1979

UN agencies. If we exclude the amount reserved for currency fluctuations, the two largest programmes in Unesco are education and the natural sciences, with 17 and 11 per cent of the regular budget respectively. More important, these two sectors attract 46 and 35 per cent of the outside funds. The next largest programme is culture and communication, which is allocated 8 per cent of both the regular and outside funds (Unesco 1981).

As with most of the other specialized agencies, UNDP traditionally has been the main source of outside funds. In 1979–1980, for example, UNDP provided about 50 per cent of the extra-budgetary funds. Altogether UN sources were responsible for more than 80 per cent of Unesco's outside funding, with UNFPA, the World Bank Co-operative Programme, and UNEP the other major UN sources. For 1984–1985 UN sources were expected to provide just 64 per cent of the outside funds, and UNDP's share was considerably less than half (Unesco 1984).

To give some idea of the breadth of activities relevant to natural resources, the key elements of the natural-science programme are presented in table 18. Within the division of natural sciences, "scientific and technological research and training" attracts over 50 per cent of the outside funds. In fact, almost all these funds are for training, indicating again that it is in education and training that Unesco is able to dominate, and this is where most of the outside funds are directed.

Africa receives at least a third of all project funds. Typically, over half of the project funds are devoted to providing outside expertise, with the balance being divided among equipment, training, and subcontracts. In 1979–1980 there were 36 operational field projects in the seven countries that are the main concern of this report, ranging from solar energy to curriculum development.

Activities financed by Unesco's regular budget tend to be much smaller in scale. Generally these are grants ("seed money") for seminars, research projects, and fellowships. Of particular interest is the Man and the Biosphere programme, which consists of a matrix of over a dozen different projects from the humid tropics to arid lands, and from biosphere reserves to urban ecosystems. While there are a number of activities of some relevance, the limited funding prevents a major contribution. Unesco basically provides a framework into which national governments can put projects, which must largely be financed either by the respective government or by another agency. As examples of this *modus operandi,* there are two large "integrated" arid-lands projects with Unesco's label, but almost all the funding comes from UNEP and other agencies (Unesco 1979).

In summary, Unesco's major projects in the Sahel tend to be financed by UNDP and are typically concerned with such things as the establishment of an engineering school in Mali or the reform of elementary education in Chad. A wide range of studies are being carried out in the Sahel and fellowships and small-scale grants are being provided, but the total of these in financial terms is quite small. Of course, over the long term the cumulative benefits of such activities may be considerable, but the direct impact of Unesco's efforts on the natural resources base is rather small. It should be remembered, however, that Unesco did have a rather large research programme on arid lands in the 1950s and 1960s, and this helped lead to the realization that the problem of arid lands management is not the amount of information but the effective utilization of this knowledge (see, e.g., Mabbutt 1979).

In the last several years Unesco has come under increasing criticism. One major cause was a proposal to license foreign journalists, as this was viewed in most Western countries as a violation of the freedom of the press. Critics have then gone on to note the increasing politicization of Unesco and its ponderous bureaucracy. (For 1984–1985, 61 per cent of the regular budget is for headquarters and field-staff salaries and benefits [Unesco 1984]). In late 1983 the United States gave official notice that it intended to withdraw from Unesco because of policy and budget questions, and the United Kingdom and Singapore later followed suit.

Because the United States and the United Kingdom respectively provided 25 and 5 per cent of Unesco's regular contributions, their withdrawal will force a major reduction in the 1985–1986 budget. Since discretionary funds are easier to cut than fixed costs, there is likely to be a larger reduction in programmatic activities than in staff costs. Although Unesco has shown some ability over the past few years to generate outside funds to replace the declining UN contributions, realistically only a small proportion of the lost funds can be expected to be replaced by increased donations.

As a result of these developments the future course of Unesco is uncertain. The combined withdrawal of the three countries tends to suggest that they may stay out of the organization for longer than the two years that the United States was out of ILO. It is not clear whether such actions will indeed force Unesco to make significant shifts in its policy and programmes. In any case, the idealistic glue which bound countries together in Unesco, despite dis-agreements over policy and specific activities, has clearly dissolved. The shattering of this unity will have repercus-sions throughout the UN system, and the political orientation of the observer will be critical in determining whether these are positive or negative. The situation at Unesco should also help expose the fallacy that a political body, such as the governing bodies of most UN organiza-tions, can be expected to be "impartial" and can satisfy all members.

United Nations High Commissioner for Refugees (UNHCR)

The Office of the United Nations High Commissioner for Refugees was established in 1951 with the intention of providing assistance — upon governmental request — to persons outside their country of origin because of persecu-tion for reasons of race, religion, nationality, or political opinion. In the last decade, however, UNHCR has taken a broader view of refugees and provided assistance accordingly. In general, activities have been concentrated

in Pakistan, South-East Asia, southern and eastern Africa, Latin America, and the Middle East.

UNHCR expenditures peaked at $500 million in 1980, when there were major political problems in Asia and the Horn of Africa. As the refugee situation has improved, expenditures have stabilized at $350 million to $400 million per year (UNHCR 1984). To the extent possible, UNHCR's activities are guided by the principle of developing "durable solutions". This generally means that UNHCR tries to assist refugees through repatriation or resettlement rather than the long-term provision of basic living expenses.

During the Sahel drought UNHCR provided only limited assistance, as natural disasters are handled by other UN agencies (e.g., WFP, UNDRO). However, in the early 1980s UNHCR assisted some 200,000 people who were displaced as a result of the civil unrest in Chad. This programme ended in 1983, although UNHCR is continuing to provide support for Chadian refugees in countries such as Benin, Nigeria, and the Sudan. Financial assistance is also being provided to small groups of refugees of mixed origins in Niger and Burkina Faso. The largest ongoing programme in the Sahel is in Senegal, where $1.5 million annually is used to support UNHCR's regional office and a variety of services to 5,200 refugees, most of whom are from Guinea-Bissau (UNHCR 1985).

United Nations Children's Fund (UNICEF)

Founded in 1946 as the United Nations International Children's Emergency Fund (hence the acronym UNICEF), UNICEF's initial efforts were directed towards relief operations in Europe. In the early 1950s the Fund's focus shifted to children in developing countries, and in accordance with this it was renamed in 1953. Its primary activities are in the fields of disease control, health services, malnutrition, and education.

Operating primarily from voluntary annual contributions, in 1981 UNICEF received $223 million from governments, $65 million from non-governmental sources, and $3 million from the UN system (mainly from UNHCR). Twenty-five per cent of this income was earmarked for specific projects. Total expenditures in 1981 were $293 million (including donations in kind). By sector, 21 per cent of this was spent on basic health and nutrition, 16 per cent for water supply and sanitation, 13 per cent for emergency relief (primarily for Kampuchea), 11 per cent for education, 33 per cent for administration and programme support, and 6 per cent for social services for children (UNICEF 1982).

In the Sahel, UNICEF has followed UNDP's example in establishing multi-year country programmes. The amount allocated is based on a combination of gross national product per capita, child population, and infant mortality. Typically these programmes involve a wide variety of projects which are often executed in conjunction with other agencies. Average annual expenditures range from a few hundred thousand dollars in the Gambia and Mauritania to $1.5 million in the larger countries such as Burkina Faso and Mali (ECOSOC 1981b, 1981c, 1981d, 1981e, 1981f). In most of the CILSS countries UNICEF is concentrating on child and maternal health, so there are projects to establish rural health centres, train midwives and nurses, provide medicines, etc. Since water supply is closely linked to sanitation and health, UNICEF is often involved in water resource projects. In most cases this involves digging wells and installing simple hand pumps, although occasionally motor-driven pumps are required. Another area of emphasis is education, and there are projects in most of the Sahelian countries to provide and improve both formal and non-formal training. Social welfare projects involve the provision of day care centres, machines to help grind millet and sorghum, nutrition education, fertilizers, etc. Thus UNICEF is very active in the Sahel, but its projects generally have more of an indirect than a direct effect on the natural resource base. Only the occasional, large-scale water supply projects will substantially alter the patterns of settlement and livestock management.

United Nations Industrial Development Organization (UNIDO)

The United Nations Industrial Development Organization was created in 1967 with the mandate to promote industrial development in developing countries. It does this through direct technical assistance, research and training programmes, and promotion/information activities. Historically, UNIDO is unusual in that it evolved as a unit under the aegis of the General Assembly but it is not a specialized agency. Hence, its research and administrative costs are part of the regular budget of the United Nations, while its technical assistance operations are supported by UNDP, the UN Industrial Development Fund, and other funds in trust. A constitution making UNIDO a separate, independent agency has been agreed to and is in the process of being ratified by the requisite 90 states (UNIDO 1982).

UNIDO is one of the larger technical assistance agencies, having expended $88 million for this purpose in 1984. Only 4 per cent of this amount came from its regular budget, while 70 per cent came from UNDP (making UNIDO the third largest executing agency for UNDP). UNIDO's Industrial Development Fund, established in the late 1970s, is currently supporting about $14 million of technical assistance programmes annually. Trust funds account for most of the balance ($8 million), and are primarily in the form of providing associate experts to UNIDO projects. In comparison, UNIDO's regular budget averages only $37 million per year for 1984–1985 (UNIDO 1985).

TABLE 19. UNIDO technical co-operation programme, 1974–1984 (million $)

	Approvals	Expenditures
1974	44.2	24.1
1975	54.0	36.5
1976	25.2	40.0
1977	54.1	43.9
1978	84.0	55.1
1979	77.3	70.5
1980	94.3	76.4
1981	89.1	88.6
1982	109.2	91.9
1983	89.8	78.0
1984	103.4	87.2

Sources: UNIDO 1982, 1985

The problems of matching technical assistance appropriations and expenditures are illustrated by UNIDO's record for the last decade. Initially, approved expenditures far exceeeded actual expenditures, but this was reversed when UNDP had its fiscal crisis in the mid-1970s. UNDP resumed growth in 1977–1978, thereby increasing UNIDO's technical assistance budget, but actual expenditures again lagged behind authorized expenditures (table 19). In view of the length of time required to finalize and implement projects, a one-year lag between approvals and disbursements should not be surprising. As there has been little change in the level of contributions to the Industrial Development Fund, despite the drop in UNDP activities, it may be that only the long-term shift from agriculture to industry will result in a substantial increase in UNIDO's technical assistance programme.

Like many of the other UN bodies, UNIDO is paying increasing attention to Africa. Particularly relevant to UNIDO is the recently declared Industrial Development Decade for Africa.

The level of UNIDO's technical assistance in a given country in the Sahel varies considerably from year to year, depending on whether any large industrial projects are operational. In 1981, for example, UNIDO had no activities in Chad or the Gambia, while expenditures in the other countries ranged from $364,000 (Mali) to $716,000 (Upper Volta). The larger projects tend to be directed towards the establishment of an industrial management infrastructure. More specific projects are generally smaller in scale and aimed at the industrial processing of local raw materials, such as fish-drying in Senegal, a cement plant in Upper Volta, and gypsum produts in Mauritania.

In general, half of the technical co-operation funds are used to bring in experts, and another fifth for equipment.

The balance is used for subcontracts, training, and miscellaneous other expenses. In Africa nearly two-thirds of UNIDO's technical co-operation funds are used to provide experts, while the percentage devoted to training drops from a world-wide average of 13.4 per cent to 7.6 per cent in Africa. In contrast to UNDP, UNIDO tends to execute a large number of small projects, particularly when its own funds are being utilized (UNIDO 1978, 1985).

United Nations Institute for Training and Research (UNITAR)

The United Nations Institute for Training and Research was organized in 1975 with a broad mandate to carry out training and research that will enhance the effectiveness of the United Nations in achieving its major objectives. Since 1966 it has conducted a variety of training courses, mostly short-term, to prepare government officials from developing countries to work with the United Nations and other international organizations. In this connection UNITAR familiarizes new delegates, employees, and other officials with the UN system, its modes of operation, and some of the issues confronting it (e.g. the New International Economic Order). The annual enrolment in such training courses is now close to 1,000. Altogether from 1966 until mid-1981 over 7,000 people participated in UNITAR training courses, with approximately 180 of them coming from the Sahelian countries (UNGA 1981d). If requested, UNITAR can also organize training courses within a particular country; it has recently organized two such courses on public administration for officials from the French-speaking Sahelian countries.

Research, UNITAR's other main sphere of activity, is almost totally dependent on outside funding. Topics have included development strategy, the United Nations, NIEO, etc. Of particular relevance to this study are reviews of the role of the public sector in African development, and a collection of papers on prospects for the future. This latter project included a review of agricultural and mineral development in the Sahel. Altogether, about a dozen studies are published each year as well as a bulletin on energy and natural resources. Some publications also result from the occasional seminar or meeting organized by UNITAR.

In recent years UNITAR has had difficulty in obtaining the basic funding necessary for its work. Its annual income, already low, has not kept up with inflation and other costs, resulting in a deficit of nearly $200,000 (10 per cent) in 1979 and $490,000 (23 per cent) in 1980. The United Nations has provided special grants from its regular budget to cover the deficits, and UNITAR recently has cut back severely on space and staff in order to attempt to balance its budget (UNGA 1981d).

UNITAR also has a special-purpose fund to support its projects and other activities, and contributions to this were $2.5 million in 1980, or just about equal to the core budget. By the end of 1981 a reserve of $2.6 million had been built up, although nearly one-third of this was in non-convertible currencies (UNGA 1981d).

It is not clear that UNITAR can continue to function effectively in the face of a very limiting core budget. For 1985 it is estimated that $1.8 million of the $2.5 million core budget will come from voluntary contributions; the balance wil be provided from the United Nations' regular budget. Grants from the UN Secretariat are not a long-term solution, but there is likely to be considerable resistance from the donor countries if UNITAR attempts to become part of the regular UN system, where contributions are mandatory. However, as in the case of UNDRO, it may prove even more difficult to set a precedent by eliminating UNITAR or incorporating its functions into a larger body. Any such action would be viewed as a dangerous first attack on the UN system, and so the only politically feasible solution will be to continue the present stalemate.

United Nations Centre for Human Settlements (Habitat, UNCHS)

The UN Centre for Human Settlements was created in 1978 by combining several existing units with the UN system. Foremost among these was the UN Habitat and Human Settlements Foundation, which was founded in 1974 with some initial financial and logistical assistance from UNEP. In 1976 the role of Habitat (as the Foundation is often referred to) was considerably enhanced, as it was given primary responsibility for implementing the action plan resulting from the UN Conference on Human Settlements. In 1978 the Centre for Housing and Building, which was part of the UN Secretariat, was joined to Habitat to establish the Centre for Human Settlements.

At present UNCHS has six main programme areas: (1) settlement policies and strategies, (2) settlement planning, (3) shelter, infrastructure, and services, (4) land-use policy, (5) public participation, and (6) institutions and management. As indicated above, the modes of operation are technical co-operation, research and development (including training), and information exchange. Activities in the Sahel have included the making of films in Senegal and Upper Volta, and work on building materials in Chad and transportation in Mauritania. UNCHS is also responsible for implementing selected UNDP projects in the Sahel, which have included the establishment of a centre for appropriate technology in Mali, work on renewable energy in Mauritania, a study relating to the effects of a dam in Niger, habitat improvement in Senegal, and rural housing in Upper Volta (UNDP 1982p). Regional projects in Africa have included a training course in Dakar on human settlements management, consultancy studies, and the exchange of information.

In 1983 UNCHS was responsible for executing projects worth over $15 million, with 80 per cent of this coming from UNDP. Trust funds, primarily in the form of associate experts, accounted for another 18 per cent. The limited regular programme funds were used primarily for special advisory services and training. Similarly, the Habitat and Human Settlements Foundation funded a number of project-design missions and small-scale projects (UNDP 1984e).

Habitat/UNCHS is a relatively small organization, with a total staff of just over 30. The regular income of the Habitat and Human Settlements Foundation for 1982–1983 was expected to be approximately $4 million, but there was a carry-over of $4.4 million. Support for the Foundation has been limited, as the United States and many of the other traditional large donors have yet to contribute. UNCHS thus seems destined to continue as a relatively minor UN organization, with its principle function being to implement UNDP and other technical assistance projects relating to human settlements.

United Nations University (UNU)

Approved in December 1973 by the UN General Assembly, the United Nations University is one of the newer organizations within the UN system. In contrast to other UN organizations, its governing body is not composed of representatives of governments but is rather a council of scholars, acting in their individual capacities, together with several representatives from other UN organizations. As a rule, project agreements are made directly with academic institutions and do not require approval by local and national governments. Financing is also unique in that the UNU is attempting to build up an endowment fund of US$500 million, with the income from this being used to support all the activities and administrative costs. This would insulate it from the uncertainties of annual contributions. The intent of this unusual design is to provide a certain independence from the political pressures and concerns which can affect the work of other UN agencies.

The UNU began operations in mid-1975 with a mandate to build a community of scholars and, in particular, to strengthen the research and training capability of developing countries. It operates primarily through networks of collaborating institutions and scholars. At present there are nine programme areas, including peace and conflict resolution; the global economy, energy systems and policy; resource policy and management; food, nutrition, biotechnology, and poverty; and science, technology, and the information society. From 1976 through 1982 the UNU provided 355 fellowships and published (or

co-published) some 54 books or proceedings (UNU 1983).

While each of the nine programme areas is relevant to the Sahel, only a few activities actually have taken place in the region. This is at least partly due to the very limited scientific infrastructure in the Sahel, which makes it difficult to set up collaborative research and training programmes. As a result, the main activity of direct benefit to the Sahel has been the award of about 15 fellowships for study overseas. The fields of study have ranged from solar energy to arid lands management to the post-harvest conservation of food. Other relevant activities have included Sahelian participation in scientific workshops and a limited amount of sponsored research, primarily in Dakar.

The UNU has also been attempting to set up specialized academic units to analyse particular problems, but these efforts are dependent on additional voluntary contributions. In late 1983 Finland agreed to provide US$30 million for an institute on development economics research, and discussions are under way for establishing an institute for natural resources in Africa. While the latter could be relevant to the interests of the Sahel, it will be difficult for such an institute to match the expertise now present in CILSS/Club du Sahel, and the sectoral analysis and development being conducted through ECA. It may be that governments will prefer to work with their own national institutions.

Excluding these semi-autonomous entities, the UNU presently has an annual budget of approximately $17 million per year. Most of this income is derived from interest from the $117 million in the basic endowment fund, although some countries have made smaller operating contributions. Given the present reluctance to provide general financing for UN agencies, it is doubtful that the UNU can make substantial progress in increasing its basic endowment. Thus the UNU — in contrast to agencies such as UNITAR — may be relatively secure in terms of its continued existence but uncertain with regard to future growth or the slow erosion due to inflation.

World Food Programme (WFP)

The use of agricultural surpluses to stimulate economic and social development was the basic rationale for the creation of the World Food Programme. Stemming at least in part from the successful experience of the United States in disposing of agricultural surpluses through Public Law 480, the UN General Assembly — together with FAO — created WFP in 1961 to carry out multilateral food aid. WFP was first established on a three-year experimental basis, with initial assets of US$100 million in cash and commodities. Its success in implementing food aid projects and in attracting additional funding resulted in its mandate

TABLE 20. Contributions to WFP (million $)

Biennium	Regular pledges	FAC	IEFR	Total
1975–1976	656	59	12	727
1977–1978	725	61	83	869
1979–1980	801	88	203	1,092
1981–1982	771	12	343	1,126
1983–1984	961	16	322	1,295

being extended in 1966 "to continue in being for as long as multilateral food aid is found to be feasible and desirable" (FAO 1973). The governing body of WFP is the Committee on Food Aid Policies and Programmes (CFA).

Contributions to WFP can be made in the form of commodities, cash, or services. Historically three-fourths of the contributions are in the form of commodities, and another 5 to 10 per cent are in the form of services. (In this context services usually means the transport of commodities, typically by shipping lines of the donor country.) Table 20 indicates the growth in contributions for WFP's regular budget from 1975 to 1984. In commodity terms, however, pledges increased only from 829,000 metric tons in 1969 to 846,000 metric tons in 1979 (WFP 1981a).

Table 20 also shows the contributions channelled through the Food Aid Convention (FAC) and the International Emergency Food Reserve (IEFR). FAC was a 1980 agreement calling for an increase in global food aid to 7.6 million tons per year from its previous level of 4.2 million tons. FAC also included guidelines on the quality and type of foodstuffs. IEFR was established in 1976 as a means of separating emergency food assistance from the food aid used for developmental purposes. Since 1981 IEFR contributions have exceeded the minimum annual target of 500,000 tons, and in 1984 more than 655,000 tons were pledged.

Expenditures in 1980 were $572 million, resulting in a net deficit of $4 million. Since the cumulative surplus at the beginning of the year was $103 million, this deficit did not pose any problem (WFP 1981b). Freight costs represented the bulk of cash expenses, amounting to $122 million, or 22 per cent of all expenditures. Commodities accounted for 73.5 per cent of all "expenditures", but three-quarters of this was donated in kind. Advisory and administrative services accounted for only 5 per cent of total expenditures (WFP 1981a).

In contrast to nearly all other UN agencies, WFP has managed to continue growing despite the general cutbacks in multilateral assistance. For 1985–1986 WFP is aiming at $1,375 million, which would make its budget nearly equivalent to that of UNDP. Such growth is possible as long as the relatively small group of major donors continue to produce such large surpluses of agricultural products.

In 1980 roughly 70 per cent of WFP's assistance went towards development projects. These are either "food-for-work" projects — in which labourers receive up to 50 per cent of their wages in food — or the provision of low-cost meals to school children, infants, pregnant mothers, or refugees. The food-for-work projects are usually directed towards agricultural development and rural infrastructure. Typically the projects are labour-intensive such as road building or the construction of irrigation systems. Over the last 15 years there has been a general trend to carry out larger and longer-term projects, as this minimizes the administrative workload.

Emergency food aid is provided in the case of natural disasters (e.g., hurricanes, drought) and man-made emergencies (war, civil unrest). As might be expected, the proportion of WFP resources used for emergency relief varies considerably from year to year. In 1980 emergency relief absorbed 29 per cent of WFP's resources as compared to 11 per cent in 1979, reflecting greater need in South-East Asia, Africa, and South Asia. Most of this emergency aid was handled through IEFR. As with WFP, 90 per cent of IEFR's resources come from the United States, the European Economic Community and its member countries, Sweden, and Australia (WFP 1981c). Of some concern to WFP is the fact that donations are increasingly earmarked for specific purposes, which limits WFP's flexibility. Donations also have tended to be short in high-protein foodstuffs, but the 1980 Food Aid Convention set guidelines that should help to minimize this imbalance.

Like UNDP, WFP has made a conscious effort to help the least-developed countries. At present it states that 86 per cent of development food aid is directed towards the low-income countries (WFP 1981c). In the case of the seven Sahelian countries, from 1963 to 1972 developmental food aid totalled just $23.6 million, which was less than 2 per cent of all WFP development aid (FAO 1973). Emergency aid over this same period was $12.5 million, or 10 per cent of the total emergency aid provided by WFP. In early 1981 the situation was considerably different, with at least three WFP projects under way in each of the CILSS countries. The total value of these projects ranged from $5 million in the Gambia to over $26 million in Senegal.

Emergency relief to the Sahel has continued on a sporadic basis since the end of the 1968–1973 drought. As a result of the civil unrest and the relatively poor rains in 1980, Chad, the Gambia, Mali, Mauritania, Senegal, and Upper Volta all requested emergency assistance. WFP/FAO then organized multi-donor missions to review the requests and make recommendations on the type and amount of food aid (WFP 1981d). On this basis $20 million of emergency assistance was approved. In 1981 most of the emergency assistance was directed towards Chad, but in 1982 the harvest was again inadequate and substantial amounts of emergency food aid were provided to Chad, Mali, Mauritania, and Senegal. The situation took a major turn for the worse in 1983, and WFP committed over $37 million for emergency relief.

WFP has also been assigned a co-ordinating role for bilateral and multilateral food aid to the Sahel, even though its own contributions have not been dominant. This role as co-ordinator is shared with FAO, WFP's parent body, as well as with such organizations as UNDRO, UNSO, and CILSS/Club du Sahel. Providing food aid to the Sahel is particularly difficult because of the two to four weeks it takes for shipments to travel from the coast to the capitals of Chad, Mali, Niger, and Burkina Faso. Problems of pilferage and spoilage due to poor storage conditions are common, while the lack of infrastructure makes distribution a difficult process. In view of the unpredictable problems involved in distributing perishable commodities, particularly in emergencies, WFP's executive director has been given more flexibility and responsibility than the heads of most other UN agencies. This has helped to lessen the time needed to approve projects and the amount of paperwork involved, but it is not clear that it will reduce the lag in providing emergency aid to acceptable levels.

World Health Organization (WHO)

The World Health Organization was founded in 1946 as a specialized agency of the United Nations, integrating several existing international organizations active in the health field. With a staff of 5,500, WHO is one of the largest UN agencies. Its activities include disease control, establishing standards for food and drugs, work on environmental health, and maintaining health statistics. It is also deeply involved in research as well as technical assistance and the collection, analysis, and dissemination of information. It has been particularly energetic in reducing the high staff costs at headquarters in order to increase the proportion of funds devoted to technical co-operation. In conjunction with this it is attempting — like many other UN agencies — to decentralize its operations. Most of WHO's programmes relevant to the Sahel are now handled through the regional office in Brazzaville.

For 1982–1983 the regular budget was estimated at $484 million, which was a 13 per cent increase from 1980–1981. Just over half of this was designated for country and intercountry activities, with another 6.5 per cent for global and interregional activities. Costs incurred at headquarters, at the regional offices, and by the governing bodies still require over 40 per cent of the budget (WHO 1980a). Another $430 million was expected from outside funds. In contrast to many of the other specialized agencies, WHO receives only a minor portion of its outside funds from UNDP; the Pan American Health Organization, the Voluntary Fund for Health Promotion, and various trust funds are more important sources (WHO 1978).

Given the relatively poor standard of health and health-care activities in Africa, particularly in the Sahel, it is not surprising that WHO has been devoting an increasing proportion of its resources to Africa. Although the development of natural resources is not in WHO's mandate, the utilization of much of the Sahel is dependent on the control of human and animal diseases such as schistosomiasis, onchocerciasis, and sleeping sickness. Thus WHO's activities are of potentially great relevance and must be closely co-ordinated with other development projects.

Approximately $7.2 million was designated for country programmes in the Sahel for 1982–1983, relatively evenly divided among the CILSS countries. Major activities include country health programming, primary health care, epidemiological surveys, immunization programmes, basic sanitary measures, and training. The single largest component is training, usually done through group courses. Outside sources are providing another $3.1 million for the country programmes, with most of this designated for maternal and child health (WHO 1980b).

The largest project of interest in the Sahel is a regional effort, co-ordinated by WHO, to control onchocerciasis in an area of 700,000 square kilometres of the Volta basin. Supported by a special trust fund, this effort encompasses much of Benin, Ghana, Côte d'Ivoire, Mali, Niger, and Burkina Faso. Onchocerciasis ("river blindness") is a disease caused by a parasitic worm transmitted by the female blackfly in the process of feeding on blood. Since the blackfly larvae require oxygen- and nutrient-rich fast-flowing waters to breed, much of the Sahel is free from the disease, but the areas with blackflies are, of course, those with abundant water supplies and hence the highest potential for development. As drugs are relatively ineffective, control measures focus on eliminating the blackfly vector by putting pesticides into the rivers to kill the larvae. Phase II of the project is scheduled from 1980 to 1985 and will cost an estimated $106 million, with the World Bank providing most of the funds. The project has been experiencing some difficulties because the adult flies are found to travel much further than was previously thought, perhaps as much as 500 kilometres. Thus formerly cleared areas are being reinvaded, and without the regular application of pesticides the disease cannot be kept down to tolerable levels (Lamb 1979). Some of the vector species are also evolving strains resistant to the pesticides being used (WHO 1984). These problems may nullify the planning and resettlement processes — already under way — which assume that the disease will be eliminated.

Similar problems of reinfestation are encountered in attempts to eradicate the tsetse fly, which infests much of the more productive, southern part of the Sahel. Transmitting sleeping sickness to both cattle and humans, this fly can effectively exclude people from large areas if uncontrolled. Traditionally, control has been by the widespread application of pesticides and/or destruction of the woody vegetation. This not only is expensive but involves obvious negative side-effects.

Another set of activities of great significance to the development of the Sahel is the work on schistosomiasis. In this case the vector is an aquatic snail, whose preferred aquatic habitat is such that physical instead of chemical control measures can be used. The key question is whether the damming of major rivers and the building of irrigation systems will increase the incidence of the disease. Active control measures will have to be taken concurrently with these development projects and probably continue indefinitely.

World Meteorological Organization (WMO)

Created by the General Assembly in 1951, the World Meteorological Organization is a successor to the International Meteorological Information Organization. The core of WMO's activities are the collection and exchange of meteorological information through programmes such as the World Weather Watch. WMO also carries out major research and training programmes, as well as a variety of technical assistance activities. UNDP is the main source of funding for the latter; it provided approximately $12 million in 1981. Another $5 million was provided through the Voluntary Co-operation Programme, although most of this was actually contributions in kind (e.g. staff and equipment). Generally WMO's technical assistance activities are concerned with strengthening national departments of meteorology and hydrology, setting up various types of training centres, and evaluating water resources. Altogether 271 students began training in 1981, with another 311 continuing or completing their fellowships. Of these fellowships, 11 were from Chad, 7 from the Gambia, 8 from Mali, 4 from Mauritania, 14 from Niger, 1 from Senegal, and 10 from Upper Volta (WMO 1985).

WMO has been responsible for a major, long-term project to strengthen agro-meteorological and hydrological services in the Sahel. Supported by UNDP, CILSS, UNSO, and bilateral sources, this project has developed a network of trained personnel to collect and analyse meteorological and hydrologic data. A telecommunications network has been set up to relay the data to a central institute in Niger. This centre is then responsible for the application of the data and for training activities in the region (WMO 1982).

A related project is concerned with hydrological forecasting in the Niger River basin. Funded by OPEC, UNDP, and the European Economic Community, it also is attempting to link eight countries in the acquisition and analysis of data. Training of local personnel is again a major component of this effort.

Like many of the other specialized agencies, WMO is dependent on outside funds for most of its technical assistance activities. WMO's regular annual budget of approximately $22 million is too small to provide many fellowships and grants, so it tends to use these funds for gathering and publishing data and for research. While this is a very useful function, particularly in the Sahel, where data are so scarce, it is less attractive to donors than the usual development efforts. This may partly explain why WMO has had some trouble collecting its assessed contributions. By the end of 1984, for example, only 89 per cent of 1984 assessed contributions had been collected, with 27 countries having lost their right to vote as a result of being two or more years in arrears (WMO 1985). Since the major donors have not expressed discontent comparable to that directed at ILO or Unesco, WMO is likely to continue with little substantial change in either size or activities.

World Bank (International Bank for Reconstruction and Development, IBRD)

The International Bank for Reconstruction and Development was created in 1945 to assist in the economic development of member countries through long-term loans and technical assistance. While the loans of the Bank are on a commercial basis and must be guaranteed by the recipient country, a subsidiary organization (International Development Association, or IDA) was created in 1960 under pressure from the developing countries to provide loans on a "softer" basis to the poorest countries. The International Finance Corporation (IFC), an allied but legally and financially independent organization, was established in 1956 to provide loans to private enterprise. Together these make up the World Bank group, and they are technically a specialized agency of the United Nations that reports to the Economic and Social Council (fig. 5). In reality, the World Bank has maintained considerable autonomy within the UN system and seems to be little involved in inter-agency politics. Nevertheless, co-operation with many of the other UN agencies is relatively close. For example, IBRD sometimes acts as an executing agency for UNDP projects, and UNDP or FAO projects often serve to prepare proposals for loans from the World Bank group.

The World Bank is also unique in that voting is not on a one-country/one-vote basis but is related to the number of shares held by member governments. Thus, it is dominated by the industrialized countries, with the United States holding about 20 per cent of the votes in both IBRD and IDA. This method of voting has led to a conservative,

Western-oriented lending policy, which has been the basis for considerable criticism. It has also been a major reason why there has been a trend to set up more "progressive" regional banks (Singh 1973).

In financial terms, the activities of the World Bank dwarf even UNDP, with $15,300 million of lending and investment commitments in fiscal 1983 ($9,400 million in disbursements). The International Finance Corporation accounted for only 5.5 per cent of this total, and since its investments to promote growth of the private sector are on a private basis (i.e., without governmental guarantees), we will not consider IFC further.

IBRD accounted for 73 per cent of the 1983 commitments of the World Bank group, or over $11,000 million. Its loans are on a semi-commercial basis, although there is an average grace period of four to five years. The volatile and generally high interest rates of recent years have forced IBRD to make its loans on a variable-interest basis and to charge a front-end fee. By mid-1983 the more favourable economic picture had reduced current interest rates to 10.5 per cent and the front-end fee to 0.25 per cent. IBRD's administrative costs were $322 million in 1983, or nearly 5 per cent of total disbursements. These and other costs are covered by a combination of the 0.5 per cent spread between borrowing costs and the interest rate charged, interest on capital, and the front-end fees.

Whereas World Bank loans can be made to commercial enterprises as long as they are guaranteed by the government, IDA loans (called credits) can only be provided to governments. These credits carry only a 0.75 per cent service charge — no interest — and have a 50-year maturity with a 10-year grace period. Thus IDA requires regular contributions, whereas the World Bank only requires increases in capitalization (90 per cent of which is never actually required but only guaranteed). Credits are extended only to the poorest countries; the eligibility criterion in 1983 was that per capita income had to be less than $796 (in 1981 dollars). In 1983, 44 countries were allocated $3,300 million in credits. This represents an absolute decline from the 1980 high of $3,800 million but is significantly more than the $2,700 million approved in 1982. Plans to increase credit allocations to $4,000 million per year had to be scrapped when the United States — alone among the developed countries — refused to increase its annual contribution. As a result, the funds available for soft loans will remain at $3,000 million per year, which is a decline in absolute terms.

Since 1973 there have been increasing efforts, in line with those of other aid organizations, to stimulate growth in the agricultural sector and to improve the lot of the rural poor. Some of these changes in emphasis and policy can perhaps

TABLE 21.   IBRD and IDA lending by sector, 1983 (%)

Sector	IBRD	IDA	Total
Agriculture and rural development	21.4	39.3	25.5
Development finance companies	10.6	1.8	8.6
Education	2.7	7.5	3.8
Energy	22.5	9.3	19.5
Industry	5.6	2.0	4.8
Non-project	10.5	7.8	9.9
Population, health, and nutrition	0.5	1.7	0.8
Small-scale enterprises	4.6	0.4	3.7
Technical assistance	0.2	0.8	0.4
Telecommunications	0.0	1.7	0.4
Transportation	12.6	15.5	13.3
Urban development	2.9	6.8	3.8
Water supply and sewage	5.7	5.4	5.6
Total	100.0	100.0	100.0
Total (in million $)	11,136.3	3,340.7	14,477.0

Adapted from World Bank 1983b

best be illustrated by reviewing a single sector, namely forestry. In the early years of the World Bank, financing was provided only to industrial-type projects. Pulp and paper mills were financed in 1953 and 1955, and in 1968 funds were provided to assist in the establishment of industrial plantations in Zambia (World Bank 1978). Since 1970 forestry has been an important component of dozens of projects. The initial emphasis was still on highly bankable projects such as industrial plantations, pulp and paper mills, and forest extraction, but there has since been a major shift toward rural development activities. In these latter projects forestry is just one component of varying importance, depending on needs (e.g., fuelwood, timber, windbreaks) and the environment. Forestry projects in the Sahel have included establishing plantations in Niger and Mali, a mixed institution-building/plantation project in Burkina Faso, and community forestry activities in Senegal. Progress and economic return will be much more difficult to measure as the Bank supports these less traditional projects, but the local people are more likely to be the beneficiaries.

Table 21 indicates the percentage of IBRD and IDA loans and credits by sector. Generally agriculture and rural development account for just over one-fifth of all IBRD loans, while IDA credits for this sector have increased to nearly 40 per cent. Considering that IDA credits are limited to the poorest countries, which typically have 80 per cent or more of the work force engaged in agriculture, it is not surprising that this sector is the largest.

TABLE 22.   World Bank loans and credits to the Sahelian countries — cumulative amounts through 30 June 1983

	World Bank Loans		IDA credits	
	Number of projects	Amount $000	Number of projects	Amount $000
Chad	—	—	13[a]	78,500
Gambia	—	—	10	35,400
Mali	1[a]	1,875	24[a]	248,300
Mauritania	2	126,000	15[a]	78,800
Niger	—	—	20[a]	214,600
Senegal	19[a]	164,900	27	286,500
Upper Volta	1[a]	1,875	24[a]	246,200
Total	20	294,550	129	1,188,300

Adapted from World Bank 1983b

[a]   Shared projects (This affects only the number of projects.)

Since the World Bank tends to make large but infrequent loans, the amount of loans and credits extended to a given country can vary greatly from year to year. In 1983 the only IBRD loan extended to the Sahel was to the West African Development Bank; all other assistance to the Sahelian countries was in the form of IDA credits. Projects approved in 1983 included four agriculture and rural development projects in Upper Volta, technical assistance in Mauritania, water/power development and technical assistance in Mali, water supplies and highways in Niger, and rural health, petroleum exploration, and phosphate development in Senegal.

The total value of the eight projects approved in the Sahel in 1983 was $197.6 million. Of this, $119.8 million was to be provided through IDA credits and $19 million as counterpart contributions by the countries themselves. Five of the projects involved other sources of financing, usually multilateral agencies such as UNDP or IFAD. In the case of petroleum exploration in Senegal, however, over half of the total cost was being provided by Petro-Canada (World Bank 1983b). While such an arrangement is rather unusual, this illustrates the broader role of the World Bank in stimulating development.

The other loans approved in 1983 indicate the range of World Bank activities: they included roadwork in Niger, assistance to the Ministry of Planning in Mauritania, improved rural health care in Senegal, and construction of a two-megawatt biomass power plant in Mali. Three separate agricultural development projects, emphasizing agricultural extension services and the provision of technical inputs, were approved for Upper Volta.

Table 22 presents data on the cumulative amount of

IBRD loans and IDA credits to each of the Sahelian countries. From this it is apparent that World Bank assistance has been provided almost exclusively in the form of credits. The major exceptions have been two loans to Mauritania (one of which was to build a railroad to ship iron ore) and a number of loans to Senegal. As noted before, the disproportionately large assistance to Senegal is not unusual, as Senegal has long been identified as having sufficient infrastructure and manpower to absorb and utilize (and thus pay back) larger amounts of development assistance. Many of these loans to Senegal actually date back to the first two decades of the World Bank, when it was more comercially oriented. It is somewhat ironic that Senegal, supposedly the most credit-worthy, has had to reschedule its debt twice in the past few years. As in many other developing countries, a succession of poor harvests, a decline in commodity prices, and an increase in the cost of imports can drastically affect foreign-exchange earnings and hence the ability to pay.

African Development Bank (ADB)

In addition to providing over $1,500 million in loans and credits to the Sahel, the World Bank has also spurred the establishment of a number of regional banks. While these technically are not part of the UN system, they follow the same basic pattern as the World Bank and should be mentioned as another source of multilateral assistance. As noted earlier, the regional banks were created in response to complaints by developing countries that the World Bank was too paternalistic, too capitalistic, and controlled by the industrialized countries and that it financed only the foreign-exchange component of any project. Another stimulus for the creation of the regional banks came when IDA was established by the industrialized countries in lieu of a special UN fund for economic development favoured by the developing countries.

One of the regional banks is the African Development Bank (ADB), which was established in the mid-1960s despite some initial misgivings by the French. Priority is supposed to be given to multi-national projects in order to link the African countries more closely, but political differences have severely interfered with this objective. Initial limitations in capitalization, combined with the need to establish a responsible financial reputation, made it difficult for ADB to establish policies widely divergent from those of the World Bank. At one point it did propose that task forces should be set up in each of the smaller countries to help them develop key economic sectors, co-ordinate decision-making, and obtain additional aid, but this intrusion into technical assistance and financial management was not well received. In 1972 ADB established the African Development Fund (ADF), which essentially is ADB's counterpart to the IDA. In reviewing the progress of ADB, White (1973) concluded that ADB was inadequately endowed and had played only a limited role in providing financial and technical assistance.

The capital available for both ADB and ADF has increased rapidly since the early 1970s, and this has been reflected in the steady increase in loan commitments. From 1974 to 1981 ADB resources increased from $480 million to $2,776 million, and loan commitments increased from $89 million to $323 million. ADF capital increased even more rapidly, from $90 million in 1974 to $1,251 million in 1981, and its loan commitments increased from $47 million to $311 million. At about this time ADB recognized that the Africa-wide decline in per capita food consumption and the generally poor economic situation indicated a need for substantially greater lending. Policies were amended to allow non-African countries to participate. Most of the major Western countries have now joined ADB, and together they represent roughly one-third of the shares of the ADB group. Total capitalization for ADB and ADF at the end of 1983 was $5,500 million and $2,140 million respectively. ADB/ADF also administers the Nigerian Trust Fund, which has total assets of $218 million (ADB 1984).

In 1983 the ADB group made a total of 78 loans, worth $931 million. West Africa received 16 per cent of the ADB funds but 30 per cent of the more concessionary ADF funds. On a cumulative basis, ADB funds in West Africa have been directed towards public utilities and transport, while ADF loans have heavily emphasized agriculture.

In regard to policy, ADB has only recently gained the financial clout to substantially alter the pattern and methods of development finance. However, the need to demonstrate sound lending policies in order to maintain its financial standing and attract Western donors has limited the extent to which it could implement new policies. The soundness of its approach may be indicated by the fact that in 1983 donors contributed another $930 million to ADB-financed projects. ADB has also been important in demonstrating the ability of African countries to work together in generating and providing development assistance. ADB and the other regional banks have also served as catalysts for change by offering an alternative to the World Bank.

The success of ADB and the other regional banks has spurred the development of other institutions, such as the Arab Bank for Economic Development in Africa. While a comprehensive discussion of these other institutions is beyond the scope of this report, one of the more significant and recent developments is the formation of the Special Facility for Sub-Saharan Africa, a special fund administered by the World Bank to provide financing to restructure the agricultural sector in African countries. In particular, the Facility will attempt to increase food production by making this sector more responsive to market forces. A total of $700 million has already been pledged, and this is expected to be fully committed by 1987.

Synthesis

This chapter has described some 35 UN agencies and programmes that are either active or closely related to activities in the Sahel. It has been shown that any specific aspect of natural resource development in the Sahel can be related to several different agencies. Sahel-related funding

TABLE 23.   UN agencies' technical co-operation expenditures in the Sahel, by source and country, 1983 ($000)

	FAO		ILO		Unesco		Other UN agencies		WHO		UNDP	UNDP funds	UNFPA	UNICEF	WFP	Total grant assistance[a]
	A	B	A	B	A	B	A	B	A	B						
Chad	592	7,152	0	0	61	4	86	4	579	122	3,199	266	8	1,901	11,327	25,304
Gambia	275	286	6	254	58	4	5	463	324	258	1,233	1,882	321	112	2,530	8,011
Mali	407	297	12	498	59	334	175	490	603	7	7,411	3,944	440	1,314	13,220	29,211
Mauritania	324	115	18	610	58	112	0	26	625	29	2,048	2,272	672	713	7,304	14,926
Niger	222	991	1	83	12	50	189	74	500	0	4,332	5,501	491	1,029	2,640	16,115
Senegal	0	1,659	4	236	30	254	63	175	458	5	3,366	2,361	862	962	5,559	15,994
Upper Volta	418	1,320	3	418	56	51	31	368	654	91	4,846	2,781	637	1,696	4,317	17,687
Totals	2,238	11,820	44	2,099	334	460	549	1,600	3,743	512	26,435	19,007	3,431	7,727	46,897	127,248
Percentage	1.8	9.3	0.0	1.7	0.3	0.4	0.4	1.3	2.9	0.4	20.8	15.0	2.7	6.1	36.9	100.0

Source: UNDP 1984g

A = regular agency budget; B = external sources other than those listed.

[a] These values vary slightly from the totals in UNDP 1984g because of minor differences in classification and accounting.

in each agency ranges from a few thousand to tens of millions of dollars. Table 23 presents the technical co-operation expenditures in the Sahel of the major UN agencies. It shows that UNDP and the World Food Programme account for well over half of the total activities. If we add in FAO and UNDP-administered funds, all the remaining agencies — Unesco, ILO, WMO, etc. — together provide only 16 per cent of the UN system's technical co-operation assistance to the Sahel. Of course, most of the United Nations' technical assistance is channelled through the various agencies, and this is not shown in the table.

Table 23 also shows that most UN agencies rely largely on extra-budgetary funds for their technical co-operation activities Among the specialized agencies, WHO and IAEA are notable exceptions (table 24), while UNFPA, UNICEF, and WFP have a somewhat different structure and are entirely self-supporting.

Table 24 simply aggregates world-wide data to emphasize the mechanisms by which the UN system carries out its technical co-operation projects. UNDP continues to be the single most important source of funds; it provided 42 per cent of the total funds for 1982–1983. However, the recent lack of growth in UNDP resources means that its relative share has declined from around 50 per cent in the late 1970s. Other extra-budgetary funds, which include a variety of bilateral and multilateral sources, now nearly equal UNDP's expenditures. Overall, the regular programme of the UN agencies provides just 20 per cent of the technical

co-operation funds, and, if WHO is excluded, the percentage drops to a more realistic 8 per cent.

In the last few years UNDP's static financing has forced agencies to look elsewhere for funds for their technical co-operation activities. For many agencies, trust funds have become increasingly important. Donors have also found such arrangements useful because they allow them to channel their funds into a particular activity and/or geographic area. Otherwise there has been relatively little growth in development assistance. As most agencies are simply trying to maintain their core budgets in real terms, one would expect the basic pattern of table 24 to continue.

Since UNDP is the primary source of technical assistance funds within the UN system, the other agencies tend to scramble to be designated the "executing agency" responsible for carrying out a project. It is beneficial to be an executing agency as it improves the agency's image, it gives the agency a chance to operate in the field, and the agency typically receives 13 per cent of the project costs as overhead. UNFPA is a noteworthy exception to this pattern because it operates similarly to UNDP, funding a substantial amount of technical assistance activities while executing relatively few projects in-house. A few agencies such as WHO and WFP carry out sizeable programmes with their own funds but generally do not contract projects out to other specialized agencies. Of course the World Bank also pumps substantial amounts of money into the technical assistance activities of the UN agencies. More surprising is the fact that the World Bank often acts

TABLE 24.   Sources of financing for 1982–1983 technical co-operation activities of UN organizations ($000)

Agency	Regular programme	UNDP	Other extra-budgetary	Total
ECA	2,865	12,954	12,289	28,108
FAO	40,212	269,547	250,873	560,632
IAEA	32,121	8,138	8,157	48,416
ILO	14,368	94,367	88,961	197,696
UNCHS	916	25,017	4,865	30,798
UNCTAD	612	27,460	3,526	31,598
UNDP/OPE	0	84,460	49,257	133,717
Unesco	9,977	86,344	107,377	203,698
UNIDO	7,100	118,400	44,400	169,900
United Nations	13,629	164,720	81,349	259,698
WHO	369,636	36,916	243,175	649,727
WMO	1,374	23,107	9,627	34,108
World Bank	0	78,106	0	78,106
Other agencies[a]	54,908	164,182	103,337	322,327
Total	547,718	1,193,618	1,007,193	2,748,529

[a]   Includes other regional economic commissions, ICAO, ITU, WIPO, etc. (see fig. 5).

as an executing agency for UNDP. Other than UNDP, UNFPA, and the World Bank, only UNICEF and UNEP contract out more technical assistance funds than they receive from other agencies. UNICEF is in this position because of its broad mandate, while UNEP must contract projects out because of its specified role as a catalyst and co-ordinator.

The exchange of funds among organizations within the UN system is extremely common, and frustrates any attempts to analyse expenditures. Agencies such as Unesco often support some activities directed by FAO, for example, as well as accept funds from FAO for other projects. Different agencies may be involved in different components of a large World Bank project, or may jointly support a particular study or conference. This type of exchange usually can be considered "beneficial" to both parties, as the donor agency is demonstrating how closely it co-operates with related agencies while the recipient agency can point out the "attractiveness" of its projects. This practice serves to blur the distinctions between agencies.

Within the UN system each agency has its own particular character, although this is not amenable to objective analysis. The first, and perhaps most important, factor is the type of work, as this tends to determine other features. For example, the degree of politicization seems to be related to the subject matter and often varies within a single agency. The agencies concerned with the natural sciences have a tendency to be more "Western-oriented" in trying to carry out specific field projects, while agencies that are more concerned with social change inevitably become more wrapped up in political considerations. Other important factors include the type of governing council, the source and means of contributions (voluntary or assessed), and the relative emphasis on field activities. In technical co-operation and field activities, the possible modes of operation are rather limited, so the methodological distinctions between agencies in these areas are minimal. Overall, there are very few activities being carried out by one agency that could not be done by a different agency given the funds and specific expertise.

There are, of course, a variety of mechanisms to ensure co-operation between agencies, but most agencies tend to act independently and foster an image of uniqueness. The fact that the older agencies are usually much larger and tend to dominate certain areas makes it more difficult for the smaller, newer agencies to establish an identity and attract the necessary funding. IFAD is the obvious exception, but in its case OPEC funds were instrumental. Otherwise the trend almost seems to be that, while the larger agencies are more or less able to keep up with inflation, the smaller agencies, funded by voluntary contributions, are becoming more and more marginal. Certainly the ratio of activities to administrative support costs tends to be lower in the

smaller agencies, and the small agencies are more limited in both the expertise they can have available and the size of their projects. This negatively affects their image and fund-raising ability and thereby further exacerbates the activities/support-costs ratio.

In general, the traditional Western donors are not nearly as interested in establishing new agencies as the developing countries. This stems partly from the potential lack of control over activities and partly from a general reluctance to increase their total UN contributions at a time when their own economies are burdened with an increasing proportion of public debt. The donors express their scepticism about special funds and the smaller, voluntarily funded agencies by keeping contributions constant in absolute terms or, in some cases, not making any contribution at all. So far only the UN Special Fund, established in 1974, has been stillborn for lack of contributions, but other special-purpose funds exist in name only (e.g., the United Nations Trust Fund for African Development Activities). Similarly, some agencies may be financially weak but just manage to keep the door open and hope for better times or support from the regular UN budget. Those who advocate an expanding role for the United Nations — and this includes most developing countries — would strongly resist any efforts to consolidate or eliminate these marginal agencies and special accounts.

Dissatisfaction with the larger agencies has been more difficult to express, and the donor countries have felt compelled to keep up their end for the agencies which, after all, they were largely responsible for creating. This reluctance to disturb the status quo was shattered by the US withdrawal from ILO and the current outmigration from Unesco. It may be that the larger donors have a certain advantage, for their contribution is significant enough to exert some financial clout. The small contributors can be effective only by banding together. In general, the developing countries have been relatively successful in co-operating to make their views heard, and this has forced the donors to rely on financial means of persuasion.

Some caution should be used in comparing the contributions of the various donors to the United Nations, for a surprising proportion of the funds may be recycled to the donor. For example, in 1981 UNDP ordered nearly $40 million of equipment from the United States and subcontracted work worth over $12 million to US firms; nearly 1,800 UNDP-sponsored fellows were studying in the United States; and over 900 US nationals were serving as UNDP experts. Without even considering the impact of UNDP headquarters in New York, it is quite clear that at least half of the US contribution of $128 million is cycled back through the US economy. Similarly, in 1981 France's pledge of $23.6 million is largely counterbalanced by orders for $8.4 million of French equipment, $5.6 million in subcontracts by French firms, 920 fellows studying in France, and 850 French nationals serving as UNDP experts (UNDP 1982q).

The links between donors and location of expenditures may be even more direct in the case of special-purpose trust funds. In some cases the provision of such funds is tied to the procurement of goods and services from the donor country. While such arrangements are the exception in multilateral assistance, they are much the rule in bilateral assistance.

The review of UN agencies also helps identify certain trends within the UN system — which tend to be more pro- nounced in the larger agencies. For example, both UNDP and WFP have tended towards fewer, larger projects, thereby reducing the administrative workload. Other agencies, such as ILO and FAO, exemplify the tendency to emphasize field offices and decentralize operations, which again should reduce the administrative workload by allowing more local decision-making.

More common is the touting of special themes and the espousing of "new" concepts consistent with current development thinking. One of the most basic changes over the last 15 years has been the move away from trickle- down theories of development to an emphasis on the poorest countries, and a further focusing on the poorest segment of the population. Other controversies still remain. For example, the World Bank's *Accelerated Development in Sub-Saharan Africa: An Agenda for Action,* published in 1981, was immediately criticized by African economic ministers for emphasizing commodity exports as a basis for development and ignoring the role of external factors as constraints. Their development concept, as expressed in the Lagos Plan of Action, emphasized "internally- generated, self-sustaining and self-reliant development".

An important milestone was UNDP's shift in 1971–1972 from a smorgasbord approach of project funding to a national allocation based on population and various indices of the standard of living. Other agencies have followed suit, and this has helped to focus resources on the most needy. Of course, this does not guarantee that development aid will necessarily end up in the desired hands.

Another theme presently being emphasized within the UN system is technical co-operation among developing countries. In other words, there should be a greater exchange of knowledge and experience between developing countries (South-South basis) rather than from developed to developing countries (North-South basis). Countries such as Chad or Mauritania may have relatively little to share, but it should be clear that expertise or experience is much more likely to be relevant to Niger or Burkina Faso if it comes from Senegal rather than from France. Other themes that the UN agencies have taken up include the role of women, integrated rural development, and, in the case of FAO, forestry for community development. Often these concerns are expressed by government representatives within the governing body, and this may be one of the more effective ways in which the resolutions expressed at UN conferences become transmitted into action. While the heads of agencies have considerable latitude in implementing programmes, they are ultimately responsible to the governing body, and, being composed of government representatives (with the exception of the UNU), these bodies are essentially political rather than technical forums. Once this basic point is fully appreciated, agency trends and behaviour are much easier to understand.

In the following chapter an attempt is made to set the UN assistance to the Sahel in the context of all aid, whether multilateral, bilateral, or private. To the extent possible, a contrast will be drawn between the described UN activities and the processes by which non-UN agencies formulate and execute development assistance.

4. AN OVERVIEW OF OTHER AID ORGANIZATIONS

While a full review of the aid being provided to the Sahel is beyond the scope of this or perhaps any study, a brief overview is useful if for no other reason than to put UN aid in perspective. Generally it can be said that the major bilateral and multilateral organizations operate under priorities similar to those of the UN agencies, and they often co-operate with the UN in formulating or executing projects. While these bilateral and multilateral organizations don't have a complex system of technical agencies competing to execute projects, there is often a considerable amount of subcontracting to private enterprise and some funding of non-governmental organizations to carry out development assistance in the broad sense.

It can also be said that much of the present pattern of development assistance can be traced back to the colonial era. The largest difference is simply the number of new multilateral agencies working in the Sahel and the presence of various bilateral programmes from countries that did not provide much development assistance before 1960 (e.g. Saudi Arabia, Kuwait, Japan). France easily remains the largest single donor, contributing over $300 million in 1980, or roughly 20 per cent of all development aid to the Sahel (USAID 1982). Much of this is used for infrastructure (especially expatriate personnel), budget support, and the provision of services rather than development aid per se. Similarly, the United Kingdom maintains close ties to its former colony of the Gambia, and from 1977 to 1979 more than half of its development aid to the Sahel was directed towards the Gambia. Relative newcomers, such as the United States and the OPEC countries, direct their aid on a combination of political and economic criteria.

Table 25 demonstrates that the total contribution of all the UN agencies to the Sahel is significantly less than the individual contributions of the traditional major donors. Since 1975 the proportion of aid derived from the UN system (excluding the World Bank) has remained at just over 5 per cent. Given the recent trends in contributions to both the United Nations and the World Bank, this relative share may well decline over the short term.

Perhaps surprisingly, the multilateral programme of the European Economic Community is the second largest source of aid to the Sahel. Since France, Germany, and

TABLE 25. Commitments of leading donors to the Sahel, 1975–1980

	1975-1977		1978-1980	
	million $	%	million $	%
France	575	19.7	840	18.7
EEC	340	11.3	605	13.4
United States	216	7.4	397	8.8
FRG	306	10.5	342	7.6
World Bank	277	9.5	335	7.4
Saudi Arabia	283	9.7	237	5.3
UN agencies	154	5.3	232	5.2
Netherlands	88	3.0	210	4.7
African Development Fund	95	3.3	132	2.9
Others	586	20.1	1,173	26.0
Total	2,920	99.8	4,503	100.1

Sources: USAID 1979b, 1982

Actual disbursements typically average 75 per cent of commitments, although this can vary considerably (CILSS/Club de Sahel 1981).

the Netherlands are three of the largest donors to the European Development Fund, their respective contributions to the Sahel are actually larger than indicated. US aid to the Sahel has increased tremendously since the early 1970s, making it the third largest donor over the period 1978-1980. (The argument can again be made that since the United States contributes 20 and 25 per cent of the funds for the World Bank and the United Nations respectively, its real contribution is about 50 per cent greater than indicated. This type of accounting, if carried far enough, would be of interest in determining the actual levels of contributions to the Sahel from each country, but it would be extremely difficult to obtain accurate figures.) The Federal Republic of Germany and the World Bank each contribute over $100 million per year to the Sahel. Saudi Arabia and the UN agencies are ranked sixth and seventh, although Saudi Arabia's share has declined while that of the UN agencies has been relatively constant. In addition to the Netherlands, other significant donors include Kuwait, the African Development Bank, Canada, and Japan. Contributions

TABLE 26. Development assistance commitments by country, 1974–1980 (million $)

	1974	1975	1976	1977	1978	1979	1980	Average annual growth (%)
Chad	72.5	71.6	115.7	86.7	182.9	67.9	35.7	−6
Gambia	17.0	12.5	33.3	38.8	40.8	63.1	98.5	36.6
Mali	125.3	163.3	211.8	183.4	198.6	185.7	208.6	6.4
Mauritania	132.8	81.9	234.2	136.0	136.8	417.5	274.7	19.5
Niger	139.7	121.0	191.7	123.1	190.6	166.2	208.9	6.8
Senegal	141.4	155.3	146.3	166.5	248.0	330.8	287.7	16
Upper Volta	107.4	113.8	120.6	151.0	223.3	203.3	250.5	16.7
Regional activities	18.9	78.1	55.3	77.7	93.0	132.8	60.8	20
Total	754.9	797.4	1,108.8	963.2	1,314.0	1,567.4	1,425.4	

Source: CILSS/Club du Sahel 1981

from this latter group tend to be more variable, and in particular the OPEC countries have found it difficult to maintain their level of assistance given the drop in the price of petroleum and their declining trade balance.

The most striking aspects of aid to the Sahel are the very rapid growth since the drought, the relatively high levels of aid as compared to other developing countries, the shifts in aid due to changing political and economic conditions, and the change from individual projects/emergency assistance to an integrated, long-term programme of development.

In many ways USAID is typical: In 1973 its personnel involved in the Sahel consisted of only 20 people in regional in offices in Senegal, Niger, and Cameroon. Of the $42 million it had obligated in 1973 for the Sahel, only one-quarter was for long-term projects. Recognizing the inadequacy of this approach, USAID at this time — along with the UN Special Sahelian Office, the European Development Fund, and others — tried to analyse the problems of the Sahel and devise long-term strategies for development.

It was in this transitional period that CILSS and the Club du Sahel were created, and this air of co-operation helped to forge the political will on the part of the donor countries to double emergency and development aid commitments from about $500 million in 1973 to nearly $1,000 million in 1976. Since this doubling took place as the mechanisms for co-operation were being set up and priorities formulated, many of the initial projects were negotiated and signed before official policies had been established. It was this same sudden burst of political will that triggered the initial surge in contributions to accounts such as UNSO's trust fund.

To a large extent the momentum built up at that time has

been maintained. Annual aid commitments to the Sahel increased to approximately $1,500 million in 1980. This represents an annual growth rate from 1974 to 1980 of 12 per cent, or 3 per cent in real terms. If one excludes Chad, growth rates are substantially higher.

Table 26 indicates the level of development aid commitments by country since 1974. The small decline from 1979 to 1980 was due primarily to a drop of over $100 million in commitments from the OPEC countries and their financial institutions. Development aid to the Sahel is around $40 per capita, which is three times the average of that to other developing countries (CILSS/Club du Sahel 1981). Given the existing commitments to developing the major river basins, the CILSS/Club du Sahel goals, and the recurring shortages of food, it is unlikely that aid to the Sahel will decline much in absolute terms. On the other hand, it would be unrealistic to expect real growth in aid similar to that experienced in 1973-1979.

As pointed out earlier, the Sahelian countries are dependent on outside funds for almost all their development efforts. Moreover, 90 per cent of the foreign funds invested in the Sahel are classified as official development assistance. Of the remaining 10 per cent, over half are export credits. Thus, outside private investment in the Sahel is very small indeed (CILSS/Club du Sahel 1981), and a totally inadequate basis for development.

Of the $1,500 million in assistance to the Sahel in 1980, approximately two-thirds was in the form of grants. The proportion, however, varies significantly among the different donors, presumably reflecting their respective philosophies regarding foreign aid. The traditional donors — the OECD countries — provided 86 per cent of their aid to the Sahel in the form of grants. In contrast, only one-third of the aid from the OPEC countries has been in the form of grants. OPEC aid, however, is largely untied — i.e. the recipient is not bound to obtain products and expertise solely from the donor country. This is in marked contrast to the policies of the OECD countries (Sardar 1981). Many of the OPEC countries also devote a much higher proportion of their GNP to development assistance. In 1980, for example, Saudi Arabia, Kuwait, and the United Arab Emirates each devoted 2-4 per cent of their GNP to development assistance, as compared to 0.27 per cent for the United States, 0.62 per cent for France, and 0.43 per cent for West Germany. These latter figures are significantly below the World Bank's recommendation that the industrialized countries should provide 0.7 per cent of their GNP as development assistance.

Another means of indicating the political nature of aid is to examine the debt of the Sahelian countries. In particular, there is a sharp contrast between the pattern of aid just described and the pattern of indebtedness. For example, Mauritania alone accounts for three-quarters of the debt of all Sahelian countries to the OPEC countries but only one-fifth of the total indebtedness. This is presumably due to the fact that Mauritania is largely Moslem, and OPEC aid — particularly in the beginning — was directed towards other Islamic countries. Similarly, Mali accounts for nearly all the Sahel-wide debt to the centrally planned economies, and this dates primarily from its close ties to the USSR shortly after independence (CILSS/Club de Sahel 1981). Senegal had the highest debt in 1981, $944 million — followed by Mauritania ($827 million), Mali ($738 million), Niger ($605 million), Upper Volta ($296 million), Chad ($201 million), and the Gambia ($71 million) (OECD 1981; World Bank 1983). Expressed as percentage of GNP, Mauritania's debt was the highest at 122 per cent, followed by that of Mali at 65 per cent. Senegal had to reschedule its debt in 1981 and 1982, while Chad, the Gambia, and Mali were all behind in their payments during the same period.

The pattern of debt for the other countries generally reflects the pattern of aid, with the industrialized countries carrying nearly half and multilateral institutions responsible for another quarter. In many cases the industrialized countries are simply converting past loans to grants, thereby avoiding having to provide new loans to make payments on past loans. Even though none of the Sahelian countries has been in serious danger of defaulting, this practice of cancelling past loans in lieu of repayment is likely to increase. For many of the older loans, interest rates are so low that repayment is primarily a political and symbolic act and of little economic significance to the lender.

In view of the variation in the amount and type of development assistance, it should not be surprising that development priorities also vary widely among donors. To a large extent this can be traced to the respective areas of competence of the donors, their perception of development priorities, and their future economic needs. Japan, for example, tends to concentrate on fisheries, mining, and transport, which are all areas in which Japan has considerable expertise. The first two can also be considered relevant to Japan's perceived long-term needs for food and raw materials. On the other hand, Canada is a relatively resource-rich country, so its emphasis on infrastructure, forestry, and agriculture can be ascribed to its expertise and perception of priorities.

This variation in donor assistance must somehow be reconciled with the designation by the Club du Sahel of self-sufficiency in food as the first priority of development. Although annual fluctuations in project financing make it difficult to identify trends, the fastest-growing aid sectors have, in fact, been forestry, mining, and basic budget/balance-of-payments support. The rapid relative increase in the first two of these — forestry and mining — is due partly to the very low level of support they received in the mid-1970s. Thus, by 1980 they still accounted for only 7.0 and 2.4 per cent of all development assistance respectively. The rapid increase in budget support is a much more ominous sign; in 1980 over 20 per cent of all development assistance was used for this purpose.

Another sign that only limited progress has been made towards development in general and food self-sufficiency in particular is the fact that food aid has increased at the same rate as general development assistance. For the period 1975-1980 food aid accounted for approximately 10 per cent of all foreign assistance. Overall, the proportion of assistance devoted to irrigated and rain-fed agriculture has increased, while livestock projects are receiving proportionately less funding than before.

Commitments for education have increased slightly faster than the overall increase in development aid. Increasing amounts of aid have also been directed towards infrastructure, which is one of the largest sectors for development assistance. Transport is viewed as a key element in facilitating future development, and there has been a large co-operative effort to improve the basic road system.

In summary, CILSS and the Club du Sahel are trying to establish priorities for the various donor agencies to follow, but these are non-binding. The donor agency must still respond to its own internal policies, the directives of the government, and the expertise and orientation of the country as a whole. Inevitably these local considerations have the highest priority.

In addition to these large-scale programmes that operate through governments and multilateral bodies, there are a number of governmental, quasi-governmental, and private groups whose collective contributions considerably increase the total amount of aid indicated in table 24. Data on these is very sketchy, but it is possible to give an indication of the type and magnitude of assistance being provided.

Nearly every industrialized country, for example, has some kind of official volunteer programme and an assortment of private volunteer organizations. In general, financial and material support for these volunteers is relatively small, but the value of the donated and often skilled labour can be quite significant. Since outside experts are typically the largest single cost of development assistance projects, a substitution of volunteers can effectively double the size of a given project. In practice, however, volunteers are often placed as teachers in local schools or other situations where the opportunities for positive change are limited. The number of volunteers is difficult to determine, but the Peace Corps figure of 500 volunteers in 1979 (GAO 1979) would suggest that there might be as many as 5,000 volunteers in the Sahel.

Probably exceeding the impact of the volunteers are the activities of the various private relief and development organizations. Data on these are even harder to come by, but total voluntary contributions have been estimated to equal about 10 per cent of offical development assistance, or 0.03 per cent of GNP (ODM 1978). Project listings imply that most are church-based, although not necessarily denominational. Ranging from Catholic Relief Services to the World Council of Churches and Oxfam, these organizations usually operate on a semi-volunteer basis and are involved in a wide variety of projects, including afforestation, education, health care, and the development of cottage industries. It should be noted

that these types of programmes usually originate in and are funded by those countries which contribute the most to development on a governmental level — i.e. the Western industrialized countries. Voluntary grants are estimated to equal 20 per cent of official development assistance in the United States and the Federal Republic of Germany and 29 per cent in Switzerland. In some countries these private organizations receive significant government support, and this again makes it difficult to obtain reliable statistics.

A more significant way to present figures on voluntary assistance is to express them in terms of GNP, and a list of donor countries ranked on this basis has a somewhat different order from one based on official development assistance. Norway (0.07 per cent), Sweden (0.06 per cent), and the United States and Canada (each 0.05 per cent) are among the most generous, while the voluntary contributions of France and Italy are estimated at less than 0.01 per cent of GNP. Altogether roughly $2,000 million dollars a year is transferred on a voluntary basis (ODM 1978), and, although this may be fairly limited in absolute terms, it is again the real value of the labour and expertise which must be considered. Furthermore, such assistance is untied and generally carried out on a grass-roots basis, so the impact is by no means a simple function of expenditure. In a recent review of anti-desertification efforts, for example, the executive director of UNEP indicated that small-scale projects run by non-governmental organizations were far more effective than large downward-directed projects (Tolba 1984). This tacit admission of failure, combined with the explicit recognition that the problem of desertification in the Sahel is becoming worse (Berry 1984), suggests that there is a need to look in greater detail at both current and past development efforts. Project evaluation is the general topic of the next chapter.

5. PROJECT EVALUATION

Project Management

The high level of aid flowing into the Sahel — $1,500 million in a non-drought year, or $40 per capita — suggests that one should be able to begin to see some impact. Effects might be measured in terms of the overall goal of improving the standard of living, the three goals of CILSS, or the design goals of particular projects.

One can also look at the effectiveness of the aid activities, including the selection and implementation of projects as well as the amounts and distribution of benefits. The questions of project formulation and delivery are important because they directly and indirectly affect the type of project selected and hence its impact on the rural resource base. These interactions, together with the different levels of analysis, mean that there can be nearly as many sets of criteria to evaluate aid programmes as there are types of development projects.

Finally, although this report concentrates on the UN system as a source of aid, and natural resources as a focus of development efforts, there is a great deal of similarity among donors and among sectors. Virtually all major donors must make a series of decisions regarding the location and objectives of projects and develop mechanisms to allow smooth implementation. Projects in the natural resources sector are usually treated in the same way as those in any other sector. While this may not necessarily be an optimal approach, it does mean that a somewhat more general discussion can have wide applicability.

Perhaps the first prerequisite of a meaningful evaluation is a clear definition of objectives and goals. For example, the World Bank must limit itself to projects that will offer a satisfactory rate of return and thus be able to meet the required repayment schedule; on a macro-scale finances are directed towards the neediest countries, but there is little evidence that on a micro-scale — within a country — they are consistently directed towards the neediest recipients. On the other hand, USAID projects are not necessarily concerned with the rate of return but rather with implementing activities that will become self-sustaining and thereby have a long-term effect; in 1973 USAID was specifically directed by Congress to give more consideration to the rural poor and less attention to capital-intensive or technologically oriented projects (USAID 1979a). Bilateral aid also tends to reflect the ideology of the donor country. Countries must decide, for example, whether to support local entrepreneurs and encourage a market economy or to support state farming enterprises at the expense of individual farmers. Furthermore, bilateral aid usually is an integral part of foreign policy, with the amount and type of aid related to the donor's perception of the receiving country's importance and "friendliness" (see chap. 4).

UNDP's funds, like those of the World Bank, are allocated among countries on the basis of a complex formula of population and poverty. Adherence to this allocation is stricter, but there is not the need to demonstrate a favourable cost-benefit ratio for each project. In fact, the recipient government tends to play the dominant role in determining the use of UNDP funds, as proposals for UNDP funding can only come from the concerned government. Of course, UNDP could refuse a project, at the risk of damaging relations with the host government; alternatively UNDP can urge the government to propose a certain project. In practice UNDP and the various project-identification missions work closely with the recipient government so as to suggest only projects that will ultimately be acceptable to the recipient government. Usually there is then an internal selection process during which the government, in consultation with UNDP, determines which of the suggested projects will actually be formally proposed. Since UNDP's expenditures are now limited to 55 per cent of the 1982–1986 IPF, this final selection has become more important to agencies competing to have their proposals selected and implemented.

In summary, there is a wide variety in goals and objectives and in the precision to which these are defined. In the Sahel the emergence of bodies such as CILSS and the Club du Sahel has led to unprecedented co-operation among donors and a universal endorsement of certain objectives, but each donor still maintains its own overriding values.

Despite these differences, it should be clear that all major aid organizations do follow the same basic steps in the provision of aid: (1) deciding on the allocation of funds on the macro-scale, either by country or economic sector, (2) staging preliminary talks and visits to identify potential projects that are mutually acceptable, (3) formulating and approving detailed project documents, (4) executing projects, and (5) evaluating completed projects. It may help, therefore, to go through these steps of allocation, project identification, formulation, execution, and evaluation to determine the relative strengths and failings of the varying approaches used by different organizations.

Allocation

Here the term "allocation" means the critical process of deciding who gets what on a global or regional scale. In the case of large international institutions, such as the World Bank and UNDP, complex formulas are used, while political considerations tend to dominate in the case of bilateral agencies. In the smaller UN agencies funds tend to be allocated on an ad hoc basis. As noted earlier, UNDP also operated on an ad hoc basis until it was realized that countries which didn't have the capability to formulate and initiate projects (i.e. the poorest and least-developed) were at a disadvantage compared to countries that had a more developed infrastructure, such as South Korea or Egypt. Thus the Sahelian countries, with the possible exception of Senegal, fared poorly in the aid race of the 1960s. The project-by-project approach also led to an excess of "salesmanship" by personnel from the various executing agencies as they tried to persuade UNDP and governments of the value of their particular projects (Jackson 1969). Another disadvantage of this approach is the potential for abuse, as powerful people tend to direct projects towards regions or countries where they have close ideological, political, or personal ties.

While the formula approach ensures a fairer distribution of funds on a regional basis, its disadvantage is that governments come to regard their allocation as free funds for use or abuse as they see fit; the money is to be spent in the country in a given period of time no matter whether that is the "best" possible use. UNDP and certain other agencies allocate funds for regional and global projects, but UNDP's Governing Council has put a strict ceiling on the proportion of funds that can be used in this way. Thus UNDP is increasingly seen as a source of resources which governments can then use as a basis for tapping the technical expertise of the UN agencies (ECOSOC 1978) or as a source of counterpart contributions for other (e.g. World Bank) projects.

Project Identification

Once the allocation of resources has been done on either a country-wide or a regional basis, the next step is to identify specific projects. Within UNDP efforts are being made to tie UNDP's programming cycles closely to the respective planning cycles of the host country, and this again helps the recipient country to better guide the project-identification

process. CILSS is attempting to do much of the project identification in the Sahel, in general accordance with the guidelines laid down by the Club du Sahel. Of course, many of the sectoral missions sponsored by CILSS include personnel from the major donors (UNDP, World Bank, USAID, etc.), so that the identification of potential projects may be a co-operative venture from the beginning. Nevertheless, it is those countries or organizations that do not have an institutional presence in the Sahel that are most likely to support CILSS-generated projects. Thus France and UNDP, while actively participating in CILSS, tend to be more independent in identifying projects.

The United Nations Sudano-Sahelian Office is also intimately involved in project identification by working closely with CILSS and by sponsoring missions to the Sahel — often on a multi-donor basis — in order to identify projects for funding. Other agencies, such as the World Bank, sponsor their own missions to a series of countries within a given region, and these typically concentrate on a specific sector of the economy (forestry, industry, agriculture, energy, etc.).

Project Planning

In practical terms, the planning of aid projects is simply a continuation of project identification but on a more formal basis. At least within the UN system this phase is generally initiated by a formal request from a government. The concerned agency then puts together a design team, composed mostly of outside experts and people from the agency's headquarters rather than local people. According to Mason and Asher (1973), FAO, Unesco, and WHO each have units whose primary purpose is to assist governments in project identification, with most of the units' costs being defrayed by the World Bank. UNDP works in much the same way, relying on experts from the different specialized agencies to assist in the formulation of large projects, and then reviewing the proposals at headquarters in New York.

In contrast USAID tends to rely more heavily on consultants, and there has been some criticism of the consultants for setting specifications for their own equipment, recommending that a given project be implemented, and then becoming the project contractor. In other words, their own interests become more important in defining a project than the needs of the local people. Hoben (1979), in his review of livestock projects in Africa, notes that planners are prone to be biased towards the public sector and the formal part of the private sector because these areas are more visible, there are more readily available data on them, and they can be tapped later as sources of government revenue. Similarly, there is often a bias towards certain commodities, such as meat rather than dairy products, hides, and skins, which don't play such a large role in the formal economy. These same factors can largely explain the usual emphasis on cash crops instead of subsistence crops. Hoben and other writers (e.g. Lele 1975) have noted that a variety of political considerations can influence where a project is sited, what its target audience is, and whether funding is available. Because of the limited time available in the field and the usual background of the design teams, physical aspects, such as land-use management and agricultural production, and technological fixes are usually the focus of concern rather than individual subsistence farmers or pastoralists.

If one is concerned with the long-term sustainability of production and minimizing the disruption of ecological systems, the extent to which environmental considerations are taken into account during the planning process is of central importance. A study by the International Institute for Environment and Development pointed out that procedures vary widely (IIED 1978). Of the agencies examined (UNDP, World Bank, regional development banks, European Development Fund), only the World Bank claimed to have a formal procedure for taking into consideration environmental impacts. Specifically it has set up an Office for Environmental and Health Affairs, and the task of a small group within this office is to review projects and, in principle, to force a restructuring where necessary to meet minimal environmental standards. The group is also responsible for preparing materials for use by project officers to help ensure that proper account is taken of environmental considerations. In reality, the small staff and heavy workload mean that only the more glaring environmental problems are noted in the review process and that project officers have little time to refer to the general guidelines regarding the environmental integrity of the projects they are concerned with (IIED 1978). The most effective way to incorporate environmental considerations is to ensure that the consultants and project staff involved with project planning and execution have the required awareness. This point becomes all the more critical in the case of the African Development Bank, the Arab Bank for Economic Development of Africa, and the European Development Fund, as they do not have any formal structure to review projects for their environmental impact (IIED 1978).

UNDP also lacks a formal structure for environmental review, but since it works through a variety of other agencies, institutionalizing any consideration of environmental impact — other than at the final review stage — will prove difficult. It should be noted that there is considerable variation in project procedures depending on the nature of the specific UNDP-sponsored activity. In UNDP's pre-investment and feasibility studies, environmental considerations are usually an explicit issue, whereas environmental issues may not be a concern in some of the technical co-operation projects, depending on the type of project and the executing agency. UNEP technically has the right to review UNDP projects with regard to environmental concerns, but this is not exercised in practice. UNDP does have basic administrative and referral machinery that could be used to ensure a proper environmental review, but — as in the case of the regional banks — this needs to be institutionalized and made a required step (IIED 1978). At least a formal commitment to these and related goals has been made by UNDP, UNEP, the World Bank, the European Development Fund, and the major regional banks (*New Scientist* 1980).

Among the bilaterial agencies, USAID has a formal procedure whereby every project must be examined early on and a decision made as to whether it will have a significant environmental impact. If there will be a significant impact, a full assessment must be prepared and approved at the same time as the project review paper is considered (USAID 1976b). In general these environmental assessments (or environmental impact statements) are prepared by outside consulting firms. Given the often limited experience of these firms in developing countries, especially in tropical areas, and the fact that there is no real constituency that reviews the reports critically, they tend to be superficial and based on extremely limited data. Extrapolation from temperate to tropical areas and from the United States to developing countries is often done without any real indication that conditions may be so different as to nullify the results. Furthermore, the preparation of an environmental-impact report in the project-planning stage does not necessarily mean that those concerns will be incorporated in the execution and evaluation stages.

Of course, concern for environmental impact is not limited to donors but can also be expressed by the recipient countries. Ideally it would be the recipient countries who would press upon the donors the need to take these factors into account, as they can draw on past experience and are familiar with the local situation. However, the great lack of trained manpower means that most developing countries, particularly in the Sahel, have much more basic and immediate concerns. It is also true that developing countries tend to be less concerned with environmental matters than the industrialized countries, as the former feel that other needs are much more pressing. Thus the World Bank has met resistance when occasional projects required additional expenditures for environmental safeguards such as pollution-control devices. On the other hand, the IIED report noted that the World Bank has refused to fund environmental safeguards that it deemed "unnecessary or overly sophisticated" (IIED 1978).

The planning of projects that will be supported by loans rather than grants is further complicated by the need to meet certain financial criteria. For natural-resource development projects, any thorough economic analysis is severely hampered by the expression of physical and biological resources in financial terms. These problems then tend to limit the extent to which environmental considerations are taken into account. In the 1978 review of the World Bank's forestry sector, the problem of adequately quantifying the direct and indirect benefits of forestry projects was "the main problem area common to forestry projects in all regions of the Bank" (World Bank 1978a).

A final criticism that has been made by virtually every author who has written about UN development efforts, either with regard to a specific project or on a more general basis, is the extensive delays involved in planning. Jackson (1969) provides the most extensive statistics, noting that the average time between receipt of the official request by UNDP and signature of the plan of operations was 26 months; for certain agencies the average was three years. To improve this rather dismal record, UNDP has raised the ceiling for projects requiring headquarters approval to $400,000. Similarly, the World Food Programme has instituted a "quick-action procedure" to simplify approval at headquarters and thus save time. A review of WFP's experience is instructive, as it shows that 90 per cent of the projects planned under this procedure were approved within 15 weeks (WFP 1978b); in contrast, only 6 per cent of projects following the normal procedures were approved within 15 weeks, while 43 per cent took more than one year. Disadvantages or problems were also noted in nearly half the quick-action projects, which provide an interesting commentary on the difficulties of project execution. Table 27 shows the results of an analysis of difficulties in the implementation of projects approved under WFP's quick-action procedure that might be attributable to the procedure.

The table speaks for itself, but it should be noted that all projects, especially emergency aid activities, are subject to similar failings. In the project reports comments are noted such as "However, the Government distributed the entire 3,000 tons of food to 410,000 beneficiaries instead of 75,000 [beneficiaries] over a period of 30 days instead of 100 days as originally approved," and "It has been reported by the WFP field officer that a very small quantity of food has been distributed in kind, while sales of WFP commodities continued without prior approval of WFP and without notification of the utilization of sales proceeds" (WFP 1977, 1978a).

Of course, other development agencies have similar problems, and it could be argued that delays are inevitable given the complex design procedures. A 1979 report on USAID's Sahel Development Programme noted that 15 to 40 months are required to design each project. Moreover, different phases of the design process are often handled by different teams, and the design may be based on one or more studies done by other consultants on specific issues. Major undertakings, such as dam or airport construction,

TABLE 27. Problems encountered in implementing WFP 'quick-action' projects

Analysis of projects and types of difficulties	% of projects with diffi- culties	% of all projects
Projects which encountered difficulties		48
Inadequate and/or hasty planning of project operations	27	
Inadequate arrangements for logistics	18	
Failures in general administration and supervision	18	
Food not acceptable (unfamiliar or poor quality)	14	
Reasons for project no longer valid	14	
Government budgetary allocations insufficient or not in time	14	
Other difficulties	6	
Total	111[a]	
Quick-action projects that encountered none of the above difficulties		48
Not applicable (project not started)		4
Total		100

Source: WFP 1978b
[a] More than one difficulty was identified for some projects.

usually have an initial project for the feasibility phase, another project for the planning phase, and a third project (or series of projects) for the actual construction. Since preliminary studies are usually a separate project, the long lead time can rarely be ascribed to precautionary studies.

Project Execution

Once a project document has been signed by the respective government(s) and donor(s), the next step is to orchestrate the input of funds, equipment, and personnel as quickly as possible and in the proper sequence. Since in all projects there is some kind of counterpart contribution, these local inputs must be co-ordinated with those from outside. This is an extremely difficult task, and it is a rare project which does not suffer from delays or undergo substantial revision in its execution. Through experience UNDP learned that, if it is to operate in the least-developed countries, it must adjust its requirements for counterpart contributions and provide inputs that in some of the wealthier developing countries would normally be provided by the countries themselves. These liberalization policies began to be implemented in the late 1960s, together with the adoption of country programmes (Inter-agency Consultative Board 1967). The distribution of responsibilities between donors and recipients will remain a matter for ongoing debate, with considerable variation among donors and projects.

With regard to the implementation of development projects, virtually every review in the literature identifies the same basic problems. These might be grouped into categories of (1) delays in obtaining outside experts and equipment, (2) failure of the concerned government to supply a proper counterpart contribution, (3) poor participation by the target population, and (4) lack of infrastructure.

The most comprehensive review of UN development efforts was made by Jackson in 1969. He analysed approximately 250 UNDP projects then under way and found that 50 per cent were behind schedule. Of these, 46 per cent were delayed because of problems with the counterpart contribution (usually personnel), 29 per cent because of delays in the recruitment of qualified outside experts or, less often, equipment delays, 6 per cent because of delays in fellowships, and 25 per cent because of other problems (some projects were delayed for more than one reason) (Jackson 1969). Another UNDP study in 1974 noted that 113 projects had been postponed by at least three months from their intended implementation date. A failure to recruit experts in good time accounted for 60 per cent of these delays, and the responsibility for this usually rested with UNDP. Shortage of fellowship candidates, general administrative delays, and project postponements or cancellations each accounted for approximately 5 per cent of the problems. Unspecified problems with the recipient government were cited in about 40 per cent of the 113 cases (UNDP 1975b). Problems with ongoing projects were also reviewed, and it was found that 35 per cent of the difficulties were due to problems with the UN inputs, 53 per cent to problems with government inputs, and 12 per cent to other problems (poor project agreements, war, drought, etc.).

Given these delays, the problems of matching expenditures to the budget for any given year become even more difficult. For example, at the end of 1968 the total difference between planned and actual expenditure for UNDP was $117 million, which exceeded the $112 million actually spent. In 1975–1976 the opposite problem occurred, with UNDP committing more funds than it had available. The resulting deficit of $36 million forced UNDP to cut back severely on its proposed projects. Then, when its financial situation improved in 1977, programme planning and implementation could not respond quickly enough, causing an excess of income over expenditures of $163 million, or 36 per cent (UNDP 1978c). A sophisticated programme-monitoring system has now been set up to help avoid similar oscillations in the future. Although this can do little to prevent any dislocation caused by unanticipated changes in the level of contributions to UNDP, there is usually some advance warning that contributions will not match expectations. The five-year planning cycle (IPF) also provides a longer period during which UNDP can match expenditures with income. For example, over the last three years it has simply progressively lowered the ceiling on IPF expenditures, with the current target being just 55 per cent of the original (and admittedly optimistic) IPF.

Again, the UN is not unique in these problems of implementation. The World Bank forestry sector review, for example, notes that the rate of tree planting consistently falls short of expectations, but does not detail why. In a review of the US Sahel Development Programme several examples of extensive delays in project implementation are given, with the implication that the recruitment and placement of properly qualified experts is a major problem (GAO 1979).

In the early 1970s Lele (1975) reviewed 17 rural development projects in Africa sponsored by the World Bank. Two of these were in Mali, and many of the constraints she identified were similar to those already discussed. In particular she emphasized the need to involve local officials, and that the lack of administrative and service personnel often posed a more severe limitation on the expansion of projects than the availability of funds. She also emphasized the need for projects to be consistent with national policies and the existing administrative structure. More planning was suggested in order to better anticipate the effects of a proposed project, but there is a minor contradiction in that greater flexibility is needed during implementation — at least in the case of pilot projects. However, these pilot projects are generally too resource-intensive to be repeated on a wider scale. Lele concludes that the first step should often be to improve the regional administrative capacity for effective planning and implementation of programmes directed towards only a few productive activities; if efforts are to be oriented towards individual farmers, the local people must be responsible. Either approach implies the presence of an effective infrastructure in communications and transport facilities, administrative centres, etc. Corroboration of Lele's analysis is found in the World Bank's forestry sector review, in which it is noted that "virtually all rural forestry programmes presented to the Bank in FY 78 . . . underestimated the institutional and sociological problems of how to obtain the support of village people for forestry, to secure the land for planting, and to protect young plantations from grazing and fire" (World Bank 1978a).

In addition to the problems discussed above, project implementation in the Sahel must take into account the uncertainties of politics and climate. Civil unrest in Chad has periodically made a shambles of the various aid programmes. For the most part, however, political uncertainties must lie beyond the scope of contingency planning. In contrast, one can at least estimate the chances for a given degree of climatic perturbation. Nevertheless, agricultural development projects seem almost always to assume average or better conditions. Many projects also set specific annual targets with regard to the number of acres to be treated or the number of farmers to be included. Adverse climatic conditions not only disrupt the projected activities but also may make the basis of the project unrealistic or irrelevant. The 1968–1973 drought had this effect, and the World Food Programme reports again provide some interesting case studies.

In the Gambia, for example, one WFP project was to provide food in small quantities in exchange for work on various development projects (road-building, etc.). However, drought in the preceding year had so reduced the harvest that the WFP food was used to feed farmers during the planting season. The shortage of food also resulted in the programme being expanded to include twice the number of beneficiaries but for only half of the planned period. Finally, makeshift means were used for the distribution of food, as the project truck arrived only after the project had finished. In other remarkably candid assessments, WFP noted that in a school feeding programme the poorest children couldn't pay even the minimal amount charged and were thus excluded. In a programme of aid to mothers and pre-school children, regular transport was available to only 6 of the planned 33 centres, unprepared food was distributed instead of fully cooked meals, and because the government could not properly implement the project it was terminated early, having distributed less than 5 per cent of the amount approved to its intended beneficiaries and having suffered 20 per cent losses due to pilferage. In another project the family size turned out to be five rather than the government estimate of eight, so that 50 per cent more man-days of work were available than originally foreseen. In general, WFP has had to demonstrate tremendous flexibility to cope with factors such as the staggered arrival of foodstuffs that were supposed to have been distributed together, the changing needs of the target population (or even a change in the target population), problems of distribution, pilferage, spoilage, and delays in the provision of equipment and funding. (It should be emphasized that these examples are being drawn from WFP not because its projects are less successful but simply because WFP has been more open about its shortcomings than most other multilateral and bilateral agencies.)

Evaluation

Critically important for improving the design and operation of future development projects is the step of evaluation. Most of the larger aid agencies have an evaluation section, but the reports emanating from the UN agencies are generally restricted. On the basis of interviews, experience, and the limited literature available, the problems with evaluation appear to be threefold.

First, an adequate data base is needed. This means that the initial objectives need to have been clearly defined, there should be quantitative data available on the participation in and effects of the project, and the respective reports should have been submitted by the project staff concerned. This last point — the timely submission of final reports — is again a common problem, and a waiting time of two years is not unknown (Jackson 1969; UNDP 1978c; Inter-agency Consultative Board 1967; GAO 1979).

The second requirement is for experienced, qualified evaluators who are familiar with the socio-economic context in which the project took place and are not biased towards the viewpoint of either the donors or the recipients.

The third point is that, once the evaluation is completed, the information needs to be condensed and put into a form useful for project officers, planners, government officials, etc. This last task is made difficult by the need to achieve a balance between generalizing too much, in which case the resulting guidelines are pious and vague, and being too specific, in which case the evaluation will be of limited applicability. Hence it may be best for evaluation offices to organize training sessions on specific topics for project planners and administrators. Some initial efforts in this direction are being made by UNDP's new Central Evaluation Office (UNDP 1984g).

Perhaps the biggest problems in carrying out an evaluation result from the various political forces involved in any development project. No agency, whether local, national, or multilateral, is fond of criticism, particularly when it could have adverse effects on future funding and the careers of the personnel involved. Similarly, those conducting the evaluation are often hesitant to offend the host government or the sponsoring agency, for they may be risking their own future involvement. Some agencies, such as the World Bank, have allowed the publication of articles by staff members on a wide variety of potentially sensitive topics, even though many of their in-house reports are restricted. While failing to complete evaluation reports or limiting access to them may be politically desirable in the short term, this means that the same mistakes may well be repeated, thereby making poor use of the available aid funds.

In summary, aid projects — whether multilateral or bilateral — tend to follow the same basic procedures and suffer from the same limitations. Delays in project formulation, project approval, and identification of project staff are nearly unavoidable, particularly in the more complex projects. Problems with co-ordination are inherent in almost any project anywhere in the world. These characteristics, coupled with the climatic and political uncertainty in the Sahel and the severe restrictions in infrastructure and locally available, trained personnel, mean that all aid projects in the Sahel are exercises fraught with uncertainty and frustration. It is, therefore, little wonder that these basic problems tend to overwhelm environmental considerations, especially when the latter are vague, unquantified threats to the long-term sustainability of production. For most aid agencies, day-to-day and year-to-year operations are the only ones that are relevant. Environmental considerations are given lip service, but they rarely stand in the way of a planned development project. It is likely, however, that these environmental factors will determine much of the development work that is to be done one or two decades hence.

Type and Impact of Projects

As has been noted in the first part of this chapter, different aid organizations have a variety of objectives or goals. Even if there is a consistency of objectives, there can be very different criteria for measuring success. Within the UN system there is a series of themes or catch-phrases that help to guide development efforts, if not actually serve as objectives. Typical examples are "integrated rural development", "self-reliant development", "assistance to the rural poor", and "technical co-operation among developing countries". The crux of the problem is how to measure progress towards these relatively vague and general goals, to say nothing of the more specific goals of each individual UN agency.

One of the proclaimed goals of UNDP is to act as a pre-investment agency, with UNDP-sponsored studies, surveys, or projects being taken up and implemented by other funding agencies such as the World Bank, regional banks, or even private capital. This definition of UNDP's role allows a more quantitative assessment of "success", and Jackson (1969) noted that of 114 survey projects, 42 had generated $1,800 million in investments, 27 had developed a second phase, 31 were still in the follow-up process, and 14 had not resulted in any further action.

UNDP estimates that from 1972 to 1981 its activities have led to over $33,000 million of additional investment. Just over half of this has come from public funds in the recipient country, and this would presumably include all the various counterpart contributions for UNDP projects. Another 28 per cent is derived from multilateral sources (primarily the World Bank) and 12 per cent from govern-

ments on a multilateral basis. Only $2,750 million of private investment has been generated as a result of UNDP's activities. UNDP has also provided some technical assistance support to $9,000 million of outside investments (UNDP 1982q).

Recent attempts to help the poorest countries in the first phase of searching for oil is another indication that UNDP still considers pre-investment activities one of its primary functions (DWB 1980). Most of the major dam-building projects on the large rivers in the Sahel also have been facilitated by pre-feasibility and evaluation studies organized through, if not sponsored by, UNDP. Hence, from a purely economic point of view, UNDP's activities in the pre-investment field have been relatively successful. Certain administrative innovations, such as the participation of World Bank and other personnel in UNDP's project-identification and evaluation missions, have significantly contributed to UNDP's success rate. This type of collaboration at the project-identification stage has also been adopted by other UN agencies.

On the other hand, the criterion of "outside funds invested per unit of UNDP activity" is not applicable to most UNDP projects. Many of UNDP's activities are directed at facilitating rural development in one or more sectors or at building up a country's infrastructure.

Economic success in rural development projects is very difficult to assess because of the different ways in which and sectors to which public and private capital can flow. Other factors, such as crop yields and rural health, can be evaluated on a quantitative basis, but it may be difficult to separate the effect of a particular project from other causal factors (Hopkins 1974) or to set benchmarks for "success". Clearly the final determination of success is the extent to which positive change is continued or expanded after the external support is withdrawn. However, in many ways it is easier for the sponsoring agency to continue projects than to initiate new ones. This, plus the never-ending nature of rural development, helps explain why some projects have been extended repeatedly beyond the original planning period, yet show few signs of long-term viability.

The criterion of the extent to which activities are taken over and run locally is even more important for projects designed to strengthen the local infrastructure. For example, it seems that the time required for the establishment of agricultural research and training centres has been consistently underestimated, to judge by the number of phase-two, phase-three, and even phase-four projects. One such centre in Mauritania was begun in 1964 and entered phase three 14 years later, with the hope that two more years of working with expatriates would finally qualify the national staff to take over. A similar project in Upper Volta encountered the usual difficulties in that the contribution of local staff at the working level was only half of what was expected, and at the technical level only one-third of the planned 636 counterpart man-months were realized. This, combined with periodic lapses in the provision of experts, made it extremely difficult to train counterpart staff to take over (UNDP/FAO 1969). Another factor is the problem of retaining trained personnel in a given project; in Upper Volta in 1978, 17 of the 18 trained veterinarians were working in administrative positions (GAO 1978). In their review of World Bank activities, Mason and Asher (1973) note that the World Bank has also been less than successful in training counterpart staff on the spot. Jackson (1969) provided the interesting statistic that 33 per cent of the projects initiated were expected to develop a phase two; this proportion is probably still accurate 16 years later.

In general, the lack of infrastructure and trained personnel in the Sahel make large-scale, capital-intensive projects such as roads and dams much easier to execute than people-oriented projects. The demands of capital-intensive projects in terms of counterpart contributions, complementary personnel, and local involvement are far less than most other types of rural development projects. Thus, these large infrastructure projects provide a convenient means of disbursing large sums of money, and bilateral agencies find that a large proportion of these funds can be recycled to their own country through the hiring of sub-contractors and the purchase of machinery and materials. Assuming that these capital-intensive projects are successfully completed, there still remain the questions of how the benefits are measured and distributed among the different segments of the affected population and how the capital improvements will be maintained.

Despite such considerations, the World Bank has been shifting its priorities away from classic, capital-intensive projects in transportation and electric power to agriculture. Priorities are also shifting within the agricultural sector. In the past, 50 per cent of agricultural loans were for irrigation, drainage, and flood control, but the Bank (and many other agencies) have become proponents of integrated rural development. This change has been caused by a number of factors, including the realization that many of the big dams have not achieved their goals and that the provision of credit in terms of either cash or materials has often helped only the medium- and high-income farmers, thus exacerbating the gap between rich and poor. Lele (1975) notes that the twin problems of providing credit — namely the lack of administrative manpower and the uncertain profitability of innovation through credit (i.e. uncertainty in ability to repay) — mean that alternative approaches, such as the creation of co-ops, need to be formulated. In her view co-ops would spread the risk and lessen the administrative work by providing credit on a group basis. Dupricz (1979), in reviewing integrated rural development projects in Niger, found that co-operatives were never fully adopted because they were imposed rather than developed in response to an actual need.

A critical conflict that has to be resolved when planning and evaluating rural development projects is the conflict between cash and subsistence crops. Many believe (e.g. Raynaut 1977; Dupricz 1979) that financial and technical assistance is always oriented towards export rather than subsistence crops. Any such bias presumably results from a combination of local and donor priorities and values. Donors presumably find it easier to work with commercial crops, for production is concentrated on fewer farmers, and the farmers are likely to be better off and better educated than their subsistence-cropping colleagues. By definition, their crops become part of the market system, so that their cultivation and management can be influenced by market forces. Local governments may emphasize cash crops for this latter reason, as well as a general desire to increase exports. It is also easier to tax and control those farmers who are active in the marketplace. Noting that Mali's cotton-seed production reached a record high in 1971-1972, Lofchie (1975) questions to what extent the 1968-1973 famine was due to drought and to what extent it was an indirect result of the emphasis on cash crops. In general an emphasis on the commercial sector has been criticized for having little effect on the standard of living of the subsistence population and for leading to food shortages in areas where marketing systems are inadequate (Lele 1975). Low food prices, while beneficial to the politically powerful urban population, can discourage food-crop production and thereby lead to a greater dependence on imported food. Similar arguments have been made against food aid, as this may also serve to lower incentives and thereby lead to lower agricultural production (Lappé et al. 1981). As might be expected, studies commissioned by the World Food Programme indicate that food aid does not articially depress food production provided the projects are well formulated (WFP 1978).

From an ecological point of view, projects that encourage a shift from subsistence cropping to cash-cropping have a much greater potential impact than projects that seek to improve subsistence farming. An increase in cash crop production usually depends on bringing new land into production and implies a degree of capital and credit availability that in turn facilitates mechanization, inputs of fertilizers, pesticides, and herbicides, the use of improved seeds, etc. Short-term economic considerations encourage further expansion onto even more marginal land and a reduction in the usual fallow period. In developing subsistence farming, change tends to be much more incremental, and there is typically much less expansion of the area under cultivation. Thus the potential impact on the environment is much less. Furthermore, it is typically the wealthier farmers who can afford to invest in cash-cropping, and an emphasis on cash-cropping will tend to push the subsistence farmer onto poorer quality land. In situations where a fallow period is normally used to restore soil fertility, a vicious circle can rapidly develop in which poor yields lead to shortened fallows and greater desiccation as a result of the reduced plant cover, which in turn causes a deterioration in soil quality through increased wind and water erosion, resulting in yet poorer crops and a further extension onto yet poorer lands (Wade 1974).

Another factor which is rarely attacked head on in rural development projects is the question of land tenure. Lele (1975) notes that for tenant farmers a large increase in yield is necessary before any technological innovations are adopted, while for land-owners any increase in yield will improve their economic condition, so innovations tend to spread more rapidly among the latter. Clearly this can lead to an increasing gap in incomes; yet most development projects do not come to grips with questions of land tenure because of the threat this would pose to the existing social, political, and economic order. As a result, Lappé and Collins (1977) question many current development policies and make a number of recommendations on public participation, self-reliance, criteria of success, etc.

Mixed farming projects, which combine animals (usually used also for traction) and crops, have also met with very limited success in the Sahel. While these can increase the cropped area, the labour required to care for the animals, the high initial and maintenance costs, and the shortage of fodder in the dry season, together with a variety of sociological factors, make this approach another theoretically logical concept that is exceedingly difficult to realize (Delgado 1978). Ferguson (1977) notes that animal-crop combinations are most feasible in areas that (1) have friable soils and a minimum of trees, (2) grow cash crops (usually groundnuts or cotton) to provide the necessary economic return, (3) have local herds from which the oxen can be drawn, and (4) have appropriate training, credit, and equipment. From an ecological viewpoint the keeping of more animals in the village would only exacerbate the pressure on the immediately surrounding vegetation and the circles of desertification often present. Long-term erosion must also be taken into account. Lewis (1979) noted that every farmer interviewed in Dukolomba in Mali offered or admitted that the plough wears out the soil more quickly than the hoe. Thus, animal traction may well require a host of other inputs — fodder crops, equipment, fertilizers — that the average farmer cannot justify unless land is abundant and the farmer concentrates on cash crops.

On the basis of past experience, Mason and Asher (1973) suggested that there are two main strategies appropriate for agricultural development: it is possible either to focus on a cash crop over a wide area or to work comprehensively in one area with high agricultural potential (i.e. with good soil, high availability of water, access to markets, etc.). However, the long-term sustainability of both strategies is still open to question (NAS 1983).

Selected Sectoral Reviews

To further illustrate these resource-development problems, it is useful to look at several sectors in greater depth. The forestry sector is of particular interest because the shortage of fuelwood has been a major development issue only in the last 10 to 15 years. A tremendous amount of aid funds and effort have been directed to this area with generally unsatisfactory results. In contrast, livestock development has been a major concern for a much longer period of time, although the results again can be considered mixed at best.

Forestry Projects

In the forestry sector, the availability of wood was the subject of one of the first reports from the Special Sahelian Office after the 1968-1973 drought (Raeder-Roitzsch 1974). This painted a rather dire picture of demand outstripping supply, and this type of logic, combined with rapid increases in the price of fossil fuels, triggered a rapid increase in aid for forestry-related activities. From 1975 to 1982 an estimated $160 million was spent in the Sahel, with most of these funds being devoted to the establishment of new plantings. The average cost of these afforestation efforts has been approximately $800 per hectare.

In reviewing forestry activities in the Sahel since 1972, Weber (1982) concluded that only 25,000 ha of new plantations have been successfully established. Of these 25,000 ha, perhaps one-third produce little or no wood because of fires, grazing, or their protected status (e.g., green belts around urban areas). Overall, Weber estimates the survival rate of the newly planted trees at only 10 to 20 per cent. Efforts in the area of training, infrastructure, and inventory have been more successful, but the basic problem of an assured fuel supply is far from being solved.

In general the technical obstacles are few, as one can draw on the experience of both English and French foresters in West Africa and the Sudan, as well as related work in countries such as India and Australia. The primary problem is one of local participation. As Weber (1982) states, "The common denominator of success is the way projects have been administered in the field, how the local population was approached and how project activities are being carried out so that local interests are stimulated and respected.'' Without active involvement by the local people, fires, grazing, and trampling take a heavy toll. Active opposition in the form of uprooting is not unknown, for the farmers and pastoralists often view state-sponsored forestry as a competing land use (Howe and Gulick 1980).

Staff, transport, and tools are also limiting. As an example, Howe and Gulick cite one office in Upper Volta that was responsible for 10,920 km^2 but had only one mobylette (motor-scooter) and 30 litres of fuel per month. The sheer impossibility of effectively policing large, diffuse areas of wood production only emphasizes the absolute necessity of working within the context of the needs of the local people.

A shift from expropriating land for government-owed plantations to more social forestry will require significant change in the attitudes and policies of the Sahelian countries (Weber 1982). For people to invest labour and possibly capital in protecting the natural vegetation and planting trees, they must receive benefits greater than their investments; this usually requires a stable land-tenure system that recognizes the rights of the rural inhabitants. In view of the increasing pressure on the land, there must be a shift in attitudes and government regulation from designating and protecting government forests to working with local inhabitants to establish wind-breaks, village wood-lots, and agro-forestry systems (World Bank 1978b). As noted by Le Houerou (1978), a continuing decline in woody vegetation in the Sahel will cause massive disruption to the life-styles of both the nomadic and the sedentary inhabitants of the rural areas.

Livestock Development Projects

The production of livestock is the most common use of land in the Sahel, and its high visibility has made it an important focus of development for a relatively long time. On the other hand, there has been relatively little in the way of long-term studies. To understand the controversy surrounding the effectiveness of livestock projects, it is necessary to understand the historical background. In this respect the Niger case study presented at the 1977 UN Conference on Desertification (UNCOD 1977a) provides an outstanding example of the problems of pastoralists in a world in which they have decreasing control. From a position of dominanace over (or at least co-existence with) sedentary farmers, the pastoralists have seen a consistent bolstering of sedentary farmers and cash-cropping at their expense, first by the colonial power and then more strongly as the post-independence governments have taken hold and established more effective communication and transportation networks.

The initial desire of the government bodies was primarily to control and pacify the nomads. To reduce farmer-

pastoralist conflict and to protect the traditional pastures from erosion, a variety of regulations were promulgated. For example, in 1962 Niger prohibited the growing of crops north of the 400-mm isohyet (Ferguson 1977), and in Tunisia and Syria crops were prohibited on slopes greater than 15 per cent. None of these regulations have been effectively enforced (FAO 1975), and the Niger government has gone so far as to protect farmers who migrated north of the designated boundary (UNCOD 1977a). Thus, the declining power of the pastoralists has resulted in the encroachment of sedentary farmers onto traditional grazing lands, a breakdown of traditional boundaries between the various pastoral groups, and an increase in large stock compared to small stock because of the shortage of shepherds (caused in part by the end of slavery) (UNCOD 1977a).

Over the past few decades efforts have been made to improve the lot of the pastoralist, with the initial emphasis being on the provision of veterinary services and animal-disease control. Rinderpest and pleuropneumonia were wiped out in many areas, although it first had to be learned that veterinary services are under-utilized when the tax collector accompanies the vaccinator (Horowitz 1979). In order to make more areas available for dry-season grazing and thus increase total production, various well-drilling programmes were undertaken. It was thought that these wells would also help to stabilize the pastoralists — a goal that was deemed desirable (FAO 1962) for social, medical, and educational reasons and was accepted by governments for political and economic, if not humanitarian, reasons. At least in the area of the Niger case study, the initial management scheme for the wells was based on controlling access and having the user pay, but because the government did not want to appear to be favouring any single group and feared difficulties in collecting the fees, these management policies were not implemented. As a result, areas that previously had water only in seasonal pools or shallow, hand-drawn wells now had deep boreholes, diesel pumps, and abundant water. The proper spacing of these high-volume bore-holes with low-volume shallow wells was supposed to result in an even distribution of pasture use between wet and dry seasons. If certain areas allocated for dry-season use did show signs of degradation, the pumps could be shut off to prevent over-use. However, this was rarely done, and it is widely agreed (UNCOD 1977a; Horowitz 1979; Hoben 1979) that the construction of boreholes has led to an over-concentration of animals around the few watering points, with circles of degradation of up to eight kilometres in radius around each borehole and the destruction of most trees within several kilometres. These circles of over-grazing were exacerbated by the 1968–1973 drought, for the seasonal watering points dried up earlier than usual, leading to an even greater concentration of animals at the wells and a disappearance of the surrounding vegetation. Most animals then died of hunger rather than thirst. Percentage losses varied among species, as cattle need water every day and thus could not graze far from the wells, while sheep and goats need water only once every two days and camels every five to ten days. This allowed camels to forage further afield, where the concentration of animals was much less, resulting in a proportionately lower death rate during the drought.

While a clean water supply is essential for the health and development of rural populations, these documented circles of desertification would suggest that there is little justification for providing water beyond immediate human needs unless there is an accompanying management strategy (Horowitz 1979). The provision of water for livestock must include a means to limit pasture use. Restrictions can be either technological (e.g. shallow wells where water must be drawn by hand and which may dry up, or means to limit the operation of the pumps to a short time) or sociological (e.g. granting control over a water source or area to a specific group of pastoralists). Since technological solutions are more amenable to planning, most livestock projects have been conceived in this vein, but none can be considered an unqualified success. This results in a continuing controversy over the best approach. For example, ranching schemes allow complete control over access, number of cattle, and intensity of use, and therefore can prevent degradation of pastures, but they have not demonstrated economic viability or social acceptability to the nomads in the Sahel (Wade 1974). Horowitz (1979) and Bernus (1971) note that some pastoral groups oppose the construction of any public wells, preferring instead to pay for shallow wells where they will have control of access.

Although past well-drilling programmes have tended to result in desertification in the immediate vicinity of the wells, it is not clear whether there has been a widespread decline in the quality and productivity of Sahelian rangelands. Often a long-term decline in pasture production has been assumed in order to help to justify a particular action, but World Bank reports, for example, have come down on both sides of the degradation/no-degradation issue. Hoben (1979) notes that the data can often be contradictory, depending on the location, time of observance, and observer bias.

The problem of assessing vegetation change in the Sahel is vastly complicated by the irregularity in rainfall. Horowitz (1979, citing Bille 1974 and Swift 1977) notes that above-ground plant production varied on a single site from 1,300 kg per hectare in a "good" year to 590 kg per hectare in a "bad" year and virtually nothing in 1972. This decline in production is typically accompanied by a reduction in the numbers of some of the higher-quality forage species (Bernus undated; Bremen and Cissé 1977). Some authors

(e.g. Stebbing 1937) have claimed a general shift southward in the desert margin, while others note that as the rains return the vegetation exhibits a remarkable resilience (Le Houerou 1978; Warren and Maizels 1977). In general there is agreement that intensive grazing does cause an overall shift towards weedy species with a shorter life-cycle. There is also little doubt that grazing pressures have intensified. In 1970, at the end of a period of relatively wet years, the animal population was estimated to be twice the 1930 figure and one-third higher than the 1960 estimate (Wade 1974). A recent NAS study (1983) suggests that there has been both a decline in actual productivity and a decline in the desirable species, and that the increased dominance and numbers of cattle are the main cause.

Since heavy grazing can have certain effects similar to those of low rainfall, it is difficult to separate animal-induced changes from climate-induced changes. Fortuitous timing and management allowed the separation of these factors on a ranch in Mali which receives an annual average precipitation of 590 mm. In those areas which had little or no grazing pressure the 1970–1973 drought caused a significant decline in woody and herbaceous species that

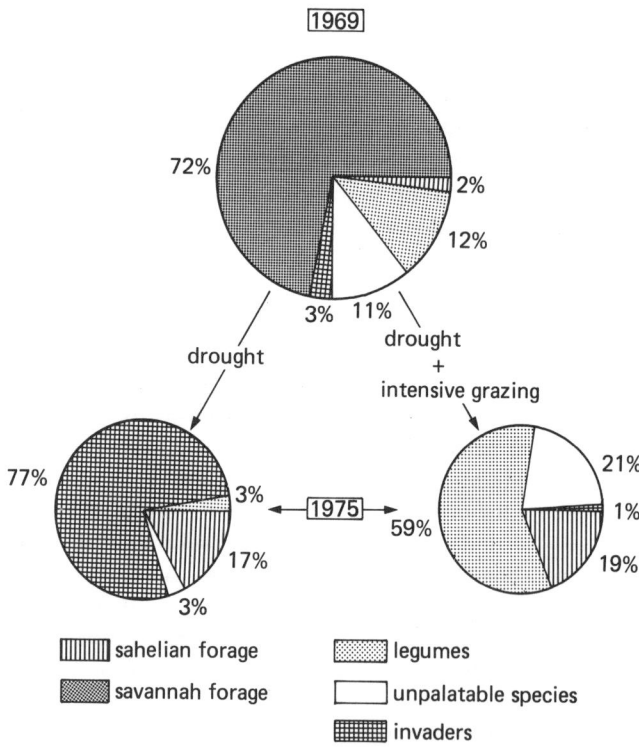

FIG. 6   Changes in the species composition of a pasture in the Sahelo-Sudanian zone due to drought versus changes due to a combination of drought and heavy grazing. "Savannah forage" here refers to the generally preferred fodder species found in the moister region just to the south of the Sahel. (From Bremen and Cissé 1977)

were near the northern limits of their distribution, and these tended to be replaced by invader (weedy) species rather than more northern (xerophytic) species (fig. 6). The changes in the herb layer were more pronounced, with mean coverage in lightly grazed areas dropping from 40 per cent to 25 per cent and standing crop reduced by nearly half. In areas that were also heavily grazed there was a clear substitution of ephemeral legumes and poor quality grasses for some of the preferred fodder species. Woody plants exhibited similar trends, with an increase in coverage due to protection from grazing, a shift in species composition due to drought, and a loss of the palatable species in the heavily grazed area (Bremen and Cissé 1977).

Degraded areas that are completely protected from grazing show complete recovery (Le Houerou 1978), but the rate should be measured in terms of years rather than of months. Herbaceous species that disappear during drought quickly reappear when precipitation levels return to normal values, but recovery in the shrub and tree layer is, of course, much slower. Even with abundant rainfall primary productivity does not return immediately to pre-drought levels (UNCOD 1977a), and Bremen and Cissé (1977) postulate that nitrogen may be more limiting than water in the initial stages of recovery.

Fire is another controversial topic, some seeing it as destroying the limited forage available, while others see it as releasing nutrients and stimulating growth. A number of efforts have been made to control burning, but these have been generally unsuccessful. Both Kucera (1978) and Warren and Maizels (1977) state that burning during the dry season consumes low-quality fodder and stimulates growth by releasing nutrients and reducing competition. By discouraging shrubs, fire can help lessen the incidence of tsetse and trypanosomiasis, but the decline of woody species correspondingly reduces the availability of dry-season fodder and fuelwood. Hence, fire-breaks are not necessarily beneficial in the Sahel or Sudanian zones and are not socially or economically viable.

The training of personnel has been very inadequate, as Mauritania, for example, had only nine veterinarians in 1978 (USAID 1979b).

The improvement of transportation and communication links has not drastically altered the traditional marketing pattern but has helped to encourage the expansion of sedentary farmers and a system of exports that has shifted beef consumption to urban consumers in Lagos, Abidjan, and Dakar rather than the local farmers (Abercrombie 1975). The development of ranch projects has been beset by serious administrative and financial difficulties, has disrupted the traditional land-use system, and does not

facilitate adjustments in grazing intensity in accordance with annual variations in productivity.

In summary, the results of past attempts to improve livestock productivity have been mixed at best. Wells have increased dry-season utilization but disrupted traditional rights and led to severe localized degradation. The simplistic appeal of an easily implemented technological fix has continued to attract donors to well-drilling, and local governments have taken the political credit without the attendant responsibility. The provision of veterinary services "has tended to be counterproductive except where accompanied by marketing or stock production control programmes that have been adequate to control the growth of animal units" (Ferguson 1977). More generally, an FAO sociologist has said, "One of the basic factors in the situation is overpopulation, both human and bovine, brought about by the application of modern science."

A wide variety of projects are now being designed that build to varying degrees on traditional social groups and their respective lands. Practical assessment is impossible at this early stage, but success or failure will still provide a better idea of how the various traditional socio-economic systems operate, and thus will provide a better basis for future project design. To a certain extent the concept of local management is inconsistent with large-scale projects, such as the recurring theme of stratified livestock production. In such a plan, animals are supposed to be progressively shifted south for final weight gain and slaughter close to the urban markets. In a broad functional sense this is close to the traditional practice of taking the animals far to the south in times of drought. While stratified livestock production was the basic idea behind SOLAR (one of the six transnational projects proposed during the UN Conference on Desertification), implementation on an international basis in the Sahel is now recognized as impossible. Even in one country, the economic and social barriers to establishing such a system are severe. Proposals to establish industrial-style feedlots near the major markets and abbatoirs (slaughterhouses) are equally impractical, primarily for economic reasons (Horowitz 1979; Ferguson 1977).

The integration of animals with sedentary farming is another logical approach that has serious social and economic flaws (Delgado 1978). Others advocate game ranching or the use of drought-adapted species such as camels, but these also will pose a variety of social and economic difficulties. Clearly a technological fix is not possible, nor will there be a painless solution. Some shift in the pattern of settlement and/or the means of livelihood is necessary if widespread, irreversible degradation of pasture lands is to be avoided.

6. CONCLUSIONS

Having reviewed the historical, political, and environmental aspects of aid to the Sahel and attempted to analyse the impact of development projects, a few general conclusions emerge together with some specific recommendations. First, it is remarkable how dominant a role political considerations play in the entire process of providing development assistance. At each stage in the process (defined here as allocation, identification, planning, execution, and evaluation) some combination of micro- and macro-scale political forces are influencing the use of public funds. This is not to say that development assistance is not well-intentioned or that the motives in providing aid are anything but the most humane. Rather, the term "political considerations" must be taken in the broadest possible sense, in that every decision involves certain values and beliefs and no decision is based solely on objective considerations. On the macro-scale, for example, decisions must be made on the level of aid to different countries, on whether it will be provided on a bilateral or a multilateral basis, and on the sectoral allocation (e.g. for family planning, infrastructure, or agricultural development). On the micro-scale, one must identify the intended beneficiaries and select a specific geographical area. In an agricultural development project, a decision must be made whether assistance is to be provided to all farmers, landless farmers, or co-operatives. Aid projects inevitably reflect a particular interpretation of a problem, and the more people-oriented projects inevitably have a greater subjective component.

Why has Senegal historically had a much higher level of development aid? The obvious answer is that it has a stronger infrastructure and therefore a higher absorptive capacity, but is that not a result of an earlier emphasis on Senegal, which itself is partially due to the more pleasant climate of Dakar as compared to Nouakchott or Niamey? To what extent are projects concentrated in those areas where the ruling party or dominant ethnic group have their roots? Why are donor countries often willing to co-ordinate their activities but reluctant to pool their resources, preferring instead to work on a bilateral basis? Why do certain countries give more support to certain UN agencies and not others? Why has there consistently been a policy to sedentarize nomads and to support farmers in their historical conflict with the nomads? Simple answers are difficult to come by, but each of these questions points

out that motivations are complex and depend on much more than a purely objective analysis of needs and priorities. It is probable that our failure to develop a comprehensive theory and understanding of development processes has resulted in tremendous variability in development policies and approaches. While this often can be considered beneficial, it also facilitates a greater intrusion of political and ideological considerations into aid policies than might otherwise be the case.

It is primarily in the political sphere that the drought can be considered to have brought some benefit to the Sahel. Because it focused attention on the sub-Saharan region of West Africa, aid programmes have increased considerably over what they otherwise would have been. Certainly the United States would not have been likely to contribute hundreds of millions of dollars to a region with relatively little strategic value, nor would there have been a UN Sudano-Sahelian Office to further stimulate project formulation and funding. In turn CILSS and the Club du Sahel, unique among developing countries, probably would not have been formed, and they certainly would not have played such a prominent role in determining the priorities and conditions for development aid. Even though donors still fund CILSS-recommended projects as they see fit, CILSS and the Club have led to regional and donor-recipient dialogues that are unique and undoubtedly beneficial.

"Better co-ordination" is the single inevitable recommendation that comes out of virtually any aid-review panel or study, but as a concrete goal it is something of a mirage. Without a complete restructuring of the bilateral and multilateral aid system, one can talk only of sharing experience and knowledge and of preventing two agencies from doing the same work in the same geographic area. Effective co-ordination implies both a willingness to surrender some control to a central authority and an agreement on basic issues; both of these present very serious barriers. It should perhaps be emphasized that co-ordination in the Sahel is not a single process but must be done on three levels: (1) internationally, among both donors and the CILSS countries; (2) at the national level, among both donors and the respective government departments in the recipient country; and (3) in the field, directly exchanging knowledge and experience. On the international level co-operation is taking place at the regular meetings of CILSS, the Club du Sahel, and their respective technical and working group meetings. CILSS is also establishing national committees, but it remains to be seen how effective these will be in enhancing co-operation at either the national or international levels. Perhaps most important is co-ordination at the working or field level, but this is largely dependent on the individuals concerned (GAO 1978; Inter-agency Consultative Board 1967) and thus not easily mandated.

Within the UN system an inordinate amount of time and funds are spent on "co-ordination", when the problem actually stems from the fractured nature of the system. In theory each agency has its own niche, but in practice almost any given activity could be carried out by any one of several agencies. Each agency uses its own broad mandate to jealously protect its historical niche while trying also to expand the scope and volume of its activities. Hence, co-ordination efforts are unable to achieve much other than the appeasement of the governing bodies, each of which requires assurance that its efforts are essential and unique.

From a managerial and operational point of view the UN system is inefficient, if not on the verge of being ludicrous, and many of Jackson's (1969) criticisms are equally applicable today. The United Nations has an Advisory Committee on Co-ordination, which consists of the head of each agency, but this is relatively ineffective. Concrete results seem to be limited to a standardization of project categories and terminology. Agreements between agencies are generally only on paper and are usually ineffective in determining jurisdiction. Each agency sets its own independent course according to the broad outline determined by its governing council, and the director typically has considerable latitude in determining priorities and the means of execution. With the exception of UNDP and its associated agencies, projects are established on an ad hoc basis as funds and political (in the broad sense) preferences dictate. Each agency also has its own administrative procedures, local personnel, and regional offices, and the confusing network of these is documented by Renninger (1979). He argues that the complete inconsistency in terms of regional offices and responsibilities not only makes it difficult for governments to work with UN agencies but also prevents an effective complementarity of programmes between agencies. In contrast, I posit that the clustering and standardization of regional offices which Renninger recommends would just be a superficial solution for a much deeper problem.

In some countries the UNDP Resident Representative has been renamed the Resident Co-ordinator and is the acknowledged leader among equals for all UN activities in a given country. While this is a major step forward, the Resident Co-ordinators still do not have control over the location or content of non-UNDP projects. This means that their effectiveness in avoiding duplication is primarily at the early stages of project selection and formulation.

A clear example of the difficulties of co-ordination at the international level is the fate of the transnational projects to combat desertification. Formulated as part of the Action Plan to Combat Desertification and presented to the UN Conference on Desertification in 1977, these seven projects were to establish green belts north and south of the Sahara, stratify livestock production in the Sahel, and survey and manage several regional aquifers, all on an international basis. Each of these has now been abandoned, although parts of a few have been taken up as national programmes. At the March 1980 meeting of the Consultative Group for Desertification Control (DESCON) only one regional project was submitted to donors — a meteorological centre for the Sahelian countries — and the director of DESCON noted, "In future they [transnational projects] will have to be designed to cater for the needs of individual countries included in the project. Individual governments would also be involved in the execution of these projects" (*Uniterra* 1980).

At present there are enough co-ordination and joint programming meetings in the UN system to keep at least one professional officer in each agency doing nothing but attending these. Requests for information from the agencies on their activities in a specific field are constantly received, with the replies to such requests being dutifully compiled, distributed, and ignored. Internecine warfare is a constant preoccupation with some, and can take the place of concrete action (witness the battle between Unesco and UNEP over environmental education, which nearly destroyed the Tbilisi conference in 1978). In short, the present proliferation of agencies is not only inefficient but also counter-productive. Furthermore, the agencies were not created to conduct technical assistance programmes, yet this often constitutes half of their disbursements (Jackson 1969).

The alternative would be to restructure the UN system, creating five to ten super-agencies under one central authority with centralized budgets, and with special sections or agencies responsible for technical assistance. Since most agency heads or governing boards would be unwilling to surrender some of their influence, the likelihood of change is very small. On its own the United Nations is taking agonizingly slow and painful steps towards at least ensuring proper consultation — e.g., the creation of the World Food Council to work with FAO, the World Food Programme, and the International Fund for Agricultural Development.

In the meantime there is constant pressure to create

new bodies to look after specific problems or topics. The mythology is that such bodies will attract new funding that would not otherwise be available, and that creating a new agency with a specific mandate will help resolve the problem. However, the major donors have been increasingly reluctant to add to the cacophony; so new bodies have been created within existing agencies. Among the most recent are the Desertification Control Unit (1977) in UNEP and the Science and Technology Interim Fund (1979) under UNDP. Neither of these is receiving anywhere near the support they were originally designed to attract. Nevertheless, vicious squabbles take place over who is to control these new funds, and since the major donor countries tend to indicate their displeasure by making no or token contributions, the question of control becomes moot. At least part of the reason for the attempted proliferation of new agencies is that developing countries view certain agencies, particularly UNDP and the World Bank, as Western-dominated and therefore not very responsive to their needs and views. Another factor is the need for the United Nations to demonstrate some concrete action with regard to a given set of problems.

One can theorize that as the world economy continues to exhibit relatively little growth, contributions to many of the smaller agencies will drop off. There already seems to be a tendency for the smaller agencies to utilize an increasing percentage of their funds for keeping the door open and thus to have almost no project capability. This in turn further inhibits their fund-raising capability. A class distinction may be developing in the UN agencies — on one hand the large, well-established agencies such as WHO and FAO, whose funding will allow them to keep more or less abreast of inflation, and on the other the smaller agencies who will fall into a vicious circle of less funding and fewer activities. This "marginalization" of some agencies may eventually force a certain amount of restructuring, but in the meantime these marginal agencies continue in their inefficient ways.

A more recent phenomenon with uncertain implications is the tendency for countries to withdraw from those UN agencies whose behaviour is inconsistent with their national goals and values. The United States pioneered this approach with its withdrawal from the International Labor Organisation in 1978. Presumably this forced the ILO to tilt more towards the viewpoint of the United States, which rejoined the organization two years later. It is too early to predict if the withdrawal of the United States and Great Britain from Unesco is again a short-term lever to produce desired change or a semi-permanent withdrawal that could seriously damage the United Nations' efforts to serve as a universal forum. Certainly the withdrawals have set a dangerous precedent which may already have weakened the commitment of individual countries to the United Nations. The

threat of withdrawal may also result in a certain conservatism in the specialized agencies, as they can't afford to offend their major donors. Of course, this conservatism may also lead to a reduction in the level of political rhetoric.

Operationally there seem to be a number of possibilities for agencies to carry out their work more effectively. The first of these is to provide the field offices with as much control as possible, thereby obviating the need for protracted discussions with headquarters and automatically reducing much of the paper work. The ability of the UNDP Resident Co-ordinators to implement projects of up to $450,000 is a very positive step in this direction. The World Food Programme has its quick-action procedure which gives it the possibility of responding quickly to a country's needs for food aid or food-for-work programmes. These efforts must be contrasted with the fact that development projects that proceed through normal channels take an average of two years before they are ready to be implemented.

A major problem for the United Nations is the uncertain level of medium-term and long-term contributions. While UNDP's 1976 fiscal crisis was brought on more by mismanagement than by declines in contributions, it still took three years before it could re-establish an equilibrium between project formulation, project implementation, and the availability of resources. In the past the UN agencies have been accustomed to growth in real terms, but it appears that at least in the near term there will be no real growth for most, and a decline in real terms for others. UNDP's indicative planning figures for 1982–1986 are now simply ideals rather than realistic targets. Although this has been recognized for some time, the severity of the decline was not, and UNDP is being forced to slow down the rates of project formulation and approval as well as lay off staff. It may be that UNDP's five-year planning cycle will create its own cycle of expenditures; when times are good, the last year will be a frenetic scene of activity; if contributions are down, the last couple of years will be devoted to keeping the remaining projects on track. In this context the oft-extended, long-term projects may actually help to ease the fluctuations in expenditures. As noted earlier, changes in UNDP's funding then have major repercussions throughout the entire UN system.

For a number of reasons, uncertainties in funding plague those UN agencies that are supported by assessed contributions as well as those that rely on voluntary contributions. First, although support by assessed contributions suggests some long-term stability, the precise level of support changes with each biennial budget. Second, most agencies depend on outside funds for most of their technical assistance activities, and generally these are subject to the same fluctuations as any other voluntary contributions. Third, countries have the right to withdraw from an organization, although advance notice is required. Finally, and perhaps most importantly, currency fluctuations can have a tremendous effect on expenditures and income. An increase in the value of the US dollar can be very beneficial when assessments are in dollars and expenditures are in other currencies, but the effect can be disastrous when voluntary contributions are made in local currencies and many expenditures are in dollars (e.g. when an organization is based in New York and must pay salaries in dollars). Particularly in the past few years, the dollar has shifted by 10 or 20 per cent in relation to other major currencies within a few months, and this makes forward planning and budgeting a very risky business.

While bilateral agencies are not nearly so subject to currency fluctuations, they must be prepared for major shifts in funding as the political winds shift in both the originating and the recipient countries. Given the problems of formulating, signing, and implementing large develop-ment projects, continuity in funding must be assured in order to prevent a rush of poorly planned projects when shifts in priorities occur or additional funding materializes.

In the case of most natural resource projects in the Sahel, long-term commitments and flexibility in planning are absolutely essential because of the severe climatic fluctua-tions. If one is trying to introduce animal traction in a dryland farming scheme, for example, what happens if an unusually dry year comes, or a swarm of locusts destroys many of the crops and thus the poor farmer's credit? Rondinelli (1977) describes the different theories that govern development project planning, with one extreme being that detailed planning and preparation is impossible since implementation is uncertain, and the other — the management science approach — being that projects must be planned in their entirety. Such arguments become meaningless out of context, however, for the desired degree of planning depends on the capability of the project officials to anticipate and respond to problems, and also on the degree of certainty that one can attach to items such as the timely arrival of equipment and ex-perts. Since all projects involve government counterpart contributions as well as outside funds, the uncertainty is usually high and the value of detailed planning doubtful. A detailed planning phase is essential only to develop a consensus on what needs to be done and how, and the phasing of the various inputs, including the delineation of respective contributions and responsibilities.

Hence the first step in project planning must be to specify the goals of the project clearly. Who is the target audience? And is improved production, equity, or the meeting of basic needs of primary importance? Then the approximate

means can be suggested and the basic feasibility (e.g., economic, ecological, social) evaluated, with the results of the basic feasibility assessment feeding back into the identification of means to achieve the set goals. Detailed planning is only needed in order to provide a starting point for the feasibility analysis and assignment of the respective costs and responsibilities. Only when there will not be a competent designated project manager on the spot should it be necessary to spell out every step to be taken. The one aspect that is typically neglected in the planning process is a discussion of alternative scenarios — what to do in case of drought; what might be some unexpected side effects. While these need not be explored in great detail, an initial discussion will ensure a broader sense of agreement on the goals of the project and provide a base for future actions.

With the advantage of hindsight, criticism is too easily given, but the continuing lack of emphasis on education and training, despite the acknowledged need, is difficult to understand. Time and time again projects are frustrated, delayed, or ineffective because of a lack of counterpart technical and administrative staff. It has been estimated that 7,000 agricultural, stock farming, and rural develop-ment experts and technicians are needed in the Sahelian countries to carry out present development plans (OECD 1976). Most projects do provide for the training of coun-terpart staff, but they often are pushed upstairs into administrative positions where their technical training is of little use. UNDP estimated in 1976 that two-thirds of total field expenditures — on the order of $350 million — was spent on outside experts. Yet less than 10 per cent of its expenditures were for training in 1978 and 1979 (UNDP 1980).

Similar problems are encountered with regard to the provision of counterpart funding. Most development agencies require some contribution of funds and man-power to be provided by the recipient country as a gesture of commitment and good will. Increasingly it has been realized that the cumulative requirements of the various aid projects pose a tremendous burden to these countries, and also that the required provision of counter-part funds is one mechanism to force a country to accept the priorities of the donor. Hence there has been a tendency within the UN system to adopt a more liberal attitude towards counterpart contributions, particularly in the Sahel. In some cases UNSO or UNDP may provide the counterpart contribution, which then allows the country to obtain much larger funds from outside. Traditionally the division between outside assistance and the counter-part contribution was made on the basis of foreign exchange costs versus local costs, especially in capital-intensive telecommunications or transportation projects and in the middle or upper tier of developing countries. For agricultural and rural development projects, however, many of the costs are local, and in such projects in the poorer countries the donors must provide the bulk of the local costs as well.

A more difficult problem is that of recurring costs, especially in view of the fact that most aid agencies are reluctant to commit funds or to support projects for more than a few years. Assuming a ten-year development programme in the Sahel at a rate of $1,000 million per year, Beazer and Pulley (1978) calculate that, under normal procedures, this would involve $6,800 million of aid, $3,200 million of counterpart investment by the recipient countries, and $3,600 million of recurring costs, all over the ten-year period. Since the counterpart investment alone would amount to 40 per cent of projected annual government revenues, donors working in the Sahel must be prepared to provide virtually all the investment funds. Similar problems arise with the foreign exchange component of the recurring costs, especially since the bulk of this would occur after the initial investment is completed. In short, aid should not be regarded as a "free lunch", either economically or in terms of political priorities.

There are also a variety of environmental trade-offs associated with rural development and the acceptance of aid funds in general. Obviously the most significant of these are associated with the expansion of both irrigated and dryland farming, water resources development, and shifts in farming practices.

Perhaps the most significant projects now under way are the construction of dams on the Senegal River. On the positive side, these should open up vast new areas for irrigation, generate electricity, prevent salt-water intrusion, and facilitate inland navigation. On the other hand, 10,000 people will need to be resettled; the seasonally flooded pastures and farmlands will largely be lost; there could be negative effects on the important inland fisheries; and the incidence of water-borne diseases such as schistosomiasis and onchocerciasis could increase (Hunter 1981). Experience elsewhere indicates that salinization and a variety of crop pests have been serious problems (NAS 1983), and the development of new areas has barely exceeded the rate at which old areas have been abandoned (Club du Sahel/CILSS 1980). Since irrigated agriculture requires such high capital and recurring costs, as well as a relatively sophisticated management structure, it is usually these non-environmental factors that are instrumental in deciding whether a given project is to be implemented. Once a project is under way, however, inadequate management can easily result in environmental problems (such as disease, pests, and salinization) becoming the dominant concerns.

The development of the livestock industry, through the provision of veterinary services and watering points, has also resulted in a variety of environmental problems. In some areas localized over-grazing and the resulting desertification is so severe that the overall balance of the development effort must be considered negative. Once a few deep wells are provided, local deterioration of soils and pastures will occur rapidly unless grazing pressure is controlled. In the past it was thought that an entire network of watering points would relieve the pressure on a few spots, but it now appears that this only serves to expand the scope of the problem. Access must be limited in time, or by ethnic group, or in the quantity of water made available, but this is politically sensitive and difficult to enforce. Some may advocate the fencing of land for large commercial ranches, but group management is difficult and individual management may violate the general development goals of equity and assistance to the poor.

Mechanization of dryland farming and a switch to cash-cropping are two other, interrelated rural development activities designed to increase income and productivity, but they may have a number of negative side-effects. Among these are a decline in soil fertility and a breakdown of soil structure, an increasing need for imported fertilizers, and an increase in erosion. Similarly, the provision of credit can lead to a disparity in incomes and an intensification of farming without the necessary soil conservation measures. Experiences in the Sahel and elsewhere indicate that unless mechanization and other innovations are introduced on a collective or co-operative basis, the rich farmers are likely to get richer and the poorer farmers are likely to become tenant farmers or to be pushed onto even more marginal land, further accelerating the process of desertification.

Few of these environmental problems can be considered particularly new. Over-grazing, reduction in the forest cover, and expansion of dryland farming have all been known to occur as a result of climatic change, population shifts, or economic considerations. One key difference seems to be that many of the means to adjust to changed conditions have been lost. Today's pastoralists and dryland farmers are hemmed in by a much larger rural population, stable political boundaries, and fixed land boundaries. There are fewer opportunities for either short-term or long-term migration in response to normal climatic variation. Social structures which served to spread risk and share resources are being weakened or lost.

The rapid increase in population is also forcing a much more intense use of resources and a much faster rate of development than in the past. An annual population growth rate of 2.5 per cent means that all production, services and infrastructure must double every 28 years just to maintain present inadequate standards; very few countries in the industrialized world would be able to cope with such demands. Put these needs in a highly variable climate, and the reason for periodic inputs of food aid is clear. Under these conditions, it is almost inevitable that some environmental degradation will occur.

These and other questions arise with almost any natural resource development project, yet there are few indications that the lessons of the past will not be repeated. For example, obvious questions in an afforestation scheme are who will prevent the animals from eating or trampling the seedings, and who is to provide the required watering and weeding during the first couple of years? The attempt to answer such simple questions leads to the more fundamental problem of how costs and benefits will be distributed. Obviously the local people must perceive a project to be in their own interests or else its chances for success are negligible. This in turn implies that donors must listen to the local people rather than imposing their own value-laden ideas. Unfortunately most donors are not willing to undertake such time-consuming or humbling tasks; their constraint is usually to disburse funds as quickly and efficiently as possible.

There is a very real problem resulting from the fact that some 80 per cent of all development assistance flows through bilateral or multilateral channels on an official basis. As public institutions, both UN and bilateral development agencies are dependent on annual contributions and are required to be efficient. Since efficiency is defined in terms of funds disbursed, there is real pressure for development to be conceived in units of short-term capital-intensive projects, despite general recognition that small-scale people-to-people projects are the most effective. More than once a successful small-scale project has been adopted as the blueprint for a large-scale activity, only to result in failure because there was not the same basis of trust, understanding, and responsiveness (including local controls). In many cases it might be better to provide small supporting grants for the multitude of on-going private and volunteer efforts.

To be effective, aid must be offered in a genuine spirit of co-operation and without preconceived ideas. As indicated above, the very nature of development assistance — despite the dedication of the individuals involved — makes this extremely difficult for both practical and philosophical reasons. The alternative, however, is that poorly conceived development assistance will foster both social unrest and a deterioration of the natural resource base, forcing ever more people onto marginal land and into a marginal existence. Then, when the next, inevitable set of dry years occur, this dispossessed segment of the population will bear the growing burden of suffering.

LIST OF ACRONYMS

ADB	African Development Bank	ODM	Ministry of Overseas Development (United Kingdom)
ADF	African Development Fund		
AFESD	Arab Fund for Economic and Social Development	OECD	Organisation for Economic Co-operation and Development
CDF	Capital Development Fund (United Nations)	OMVS	Organisation pour la Mise en Valeur du Fleuve Sénégal (Organization for the Development of the Senegal River)
CFA	Committee on Food Aid Policies and Programmes		
CILSS	Comité Permanent Inter-états de Lutte contre la Sécheresse dans le Sahel (Permanent Interstate Committee for Drought Control in the Sahel)	OPE	Office for Projects Execution (UNDP)
		OPEC	Organization of Petroleum Exporting Countries
		OPI	Office of Public Information (United Nations)
DESCON	Consultative Group for Desertification Control	OSRO	Office of Sahelian Relief Operations (FAO)
DTCD	Department of Technical Co-operation for Development (United Nations)	SSO	Special Sahelian Office (United Nations)
		UNCHS	United Nations Centre for Human Settlements (also known as Habitat)
ECA	Economic Commission for Africa (United Nations)	UNCOD	United Nations Conference on Desertification
ECB	Environment Co-ordination Board (United Nations)	UNCTAD	United Nations Conference on Trade and Development
ECOSOC	Economic and Social Council (United Nations)	UNDP	United Nations Development Programme
EDF	European Development Fund	UNDRO	Office of the United Nations Disaster Relief Co-ordinator
EEC	European Economic Community		
FAC	Food Aid Convention	UNEP	United Nations Environment Programme
FAO	Food and Agriculture Organization of the United Nations	Unesco	United Nations Educational, Scientific and Cultural Organization
FRG	Federal Republic of Germany	UNFPA	United Nations Fund for Population Activities
FY	fiscal year		
GAO	Government Accounting Office (United States)	UNFSSTD	United Nations Financing System for Science and Technology for Development
GATT	General Agreement on Tariffs and Trade	UNGA	United Nations General Assembly
IAEA	International Atomic Energy Agency	UNHCR	Office of the United Nations High Commissioner for Refugees
IBRD	International Bank for Reconstruction and Development (also known as the World Bank)		
		UNICEF	United Nations Children's Fund
		UNIDO	United Nations Industrial Development Organization
IDA	International Development Association (part of the World Bank group)	UNITAR	United Nations Institute for Training and Research
IFAD	International Fund for Agricultural Development (United Nations)		
		UNSO	United Nations Sudano-Sahelian Office
IEFR	International Emergency Food Reserve	UNU	United Nations University
IFC	International Finance Corporation (part of the World Bank group)	UNV	United Nations Volunteers
		UPU	Universal Postal Union
ILO	International Labour Organisation	USAID	United States Agency for International Development
IPF	indicative planning figure		
ITC	International Trade Centre (UNCTAD/GATT)	WFC	World Food Council (United Nations)
		WFP	World Food Programme (United Nations/FAO)
ITU	International Telecommunication Union		
LDC	least-developed country	WHO	World Health Organization
NGO	non-governmental organization	WMO	World Meteorological Organization
NIEO	New International Economic Order		

REFERENCES

AAAS. 1977. "Nairobi Seminar on Desertification: Statement." American Association for the Advancement of Science (and five other co-sponsoring organizations), Washington, D.C.

Abercrombie, F.D. 1975. "A sectoral approach to the cattle industry in West Africa." *Development Digest*, vol. 13, no. 2 (Apr.).

ADB/ADF. 1984. African Development Bank/African Development Fund: Annual report, 1983. African Development Bank, Abidjan, Ivory Coast. (ADB-ADF/BG/AR/83)

Adefolalu, D.O. 1983. "Desertification in the Sahel." Mimeo.

Allen, S. 1974. "The Sahel starts to bloom again." *African Development*, vol. 8, no. 12.

Beazer, W.F., and L.B. Pulley. 1978. "Foreign aid and the domestic costs of Sahel development projects." US Agency for International Development, Washington, D.C.

Bernus, E. 1971. "Possibilities and limits of pastoral watering plans in the Nigerian Sahel." ORSTOM, Paris. Mimeo.

——. Undated. "The impact of human activity upon the Sahelian ecosystems." Mimeo.

Berry, L. 1975. "The Sahel: Climate and soils." In *The Sahel: Ecological approaches to land use*. MAB Technical Notes. Unesco Press, Paris.

——. 1984. "Desertification in the Sudano-sahelian region, 1977–84." *Desertification Control* (UNEP, Nairobi), 10: 23–28.

Bille, J.C. 1974. "Recherches écologiques sur une savane Sahélienne du Ferlo septentrional, Sénégal: 1972, année sèche au Sahel." *La Terre et la Vie*, 28: 5–20.

Boeckm, E., et al. 1974. *Study of the actual situation of livestock breeding in the countries of the Sahel and preventive measures to be considered*. Commission of the European Community.

Bon, D., and K. Mingst. 1980. "French intervention in Africa: Dependency or decolonization." *Africa Today*, 27 (2): 5–20.

Boudet, G. 1975a. "Improvement of pasture and livestock exploitation in the Sahel: Proposals for management and land use." In *The Sahel: Ecological approaches to land use*. MAB Technical Notes. Unesco Press, Paris.

——. 1975b. "Pastures and livestock in the Sahel." Ibid.

Bradley, P.N. 1977. "Vegetation and environmental change in the West African Sahel." In P. O'Keefe and B. Wisner, *Land use and development*. International African Institute, London.

Bremen, H., and A.M. Cissé. 1977. "Dynamics of Sahelian pastures in relation to drought and grazing." *Oecologia*, 28: 301–315.

Brown, B.J. 1977. "The United Nations and disaster relief in the Sahel." Ph.D. thesis, University of Denver, Denver, Colo., USA.

Caldwell, J.C. 1975. *The Sahelian drought and its demographic implications*, Overseas Liaison Committee Paper No. 8. American Council on Education.

CILSS. 1978. Energy in the development strategy of the Sahel. CILSS/Club du Sahel.

CILSS/Club du Sahel. 1981. Official development assistance to CILSS member countries, 1975–1980. (Sahel D (81) 163)

Club du Sahel. 1980. The development of irrigated agriculture in the Sahel: Review and perspectives. Club du Sahel/CILSS. Mimeo.

——. 1982. Food self-sufficiency and ecological balance in the Sahel countries. Note by the Club du Sahel Secretariat, Paris.

Club du Sahel/CILSS. 1980. The Sahel drought control and development programme, 1975–1979: A review and analysis. (SAHEL D (80) 101)

Clyburn, L. 1974. *Grazing patterns in the Sahel-Sudan region*. Technical Staff Paper. US Agency for International Development, Washington, D.C.

Cockrum, E.L. 1976. "An ecological view of the Sahel-Sudan region of sub-Saharan West Africa." In P. Paylore and R.A. Haney, eds., *Proceedings of the West Africa Conference*. University of Arizona, Tucson, Ariz., USA.

Davidson, B. 1974. *Africa in history*. Paladin Books, Frogmore, St. Albans, UK.

Delgado, C.L. 1978. "Livestock versus food-grain production in southeastern Upper Volta: A resource allocation analysis." Ph.D. thesis, Cornell University, Ithaca, N.Y., USA.

Dupricz, H. 1979. "Integrated rural development projects carried out in Black Africa with EDF aid: Evaluation and outlook for the future." Paper for the Commission of the European Communities, Luxembourg.

DWB. 1980. *Diplomatic World Bulletin* (New York), vol. 10, no. 12.

ECOSOC. 1978. Governing Council of the United Nations Development Programme, Report on the Twenty-fifth Session. Official Records, 1978, supplement 13. UN Economic and Social Council, New York.

——. 1981a. General progress report of the Executive Director. (E/ICEF/681)

——. 1981b. Aperçu des programmes par pays: Tchad. (E/ICEF/P/L.2063(REC))

——. 1981c. Country programme profile: Mali. (E/ICEF/P/L.2069 (REC))

——. 1981d. Country programme profile: Mauritania. (E/ICEF/P/L.2070(REC))

——. 1981e. Country programme profile: Senegal. (E/ICEF/P/L.2072(REC))

——. 1981f. Country programme profile: Upper Volta, (E/ICEF/P/L.2076(REC))

——. 1982. Report of the United Nations High Commissioner for Refugees. (E/1982/29)

El-Khawas, M. 1976. "A reassessment of international relief programmes." In M.H. Glantz, ed., *The politics of natural disaster*. Praeger, New York.

FAO. 1965. *Conservation in arid and semi-arid zones*. Food and Agriculture Organization, Rome.

——. 1973. *Ten years of World Food Programme development aid: 1963-1972*. Rome.

——. 1975. Drought in the Sahel: International relief operations, 1973-1975. Rome.

——. 1977. *Annual Fertilizer Review*. Rome.

——. 1979. Programme and budget for 1980–1981. Rome.

——. 1981a. Programme of work and budget for 1982–1983. Rome.

——. 1981b. Report of the Conference of FAO. Rome. (C81/REP)

Faulkingham, R.H. 1977. "Ecologic constraints and subsistence strategies: The impact of the drought in a Hausa village, A case study from Niger." In D. Dalby et al., eds., *Drought in Africa*. International African Institute, London.

Faure, H., and J.-Y. Gac. 1981. "Will the Sahelian drought end in 1985?" Nature, 291: 475–478.

Ferguson, D.J. 1977. *A conceptual framework for the evaluation of livestock production development projects and programs in sub-Saharan West Africa*. US Agency for International Development, Washington, D.C.

Franke, R.W., and B.H. Chasin. 1980. *Seeds of famine: Ecological destruction and the development dilemma in the West African Sahel*. Allanheld, Osman and Co., Totowa, N.J., USA.

GAO. 1978. The Sahel development program: Progress and constraints. Comptroller General's report to Congress. Government Accounting Office, Washington, D.C.

——. 1979. US development assistance to the Sahel — Progress and problems. Government Accounting Office, Washington, D.C.

Gillet, H, 1975. "Plant cover and pastures of the Sahel." In *The Sahel: Ecological approaches to land use*. MAB Technical Notes. Unesco Press, Paris.

Greene, M.H. 1975. "Impact of the Sahelian drought in Mauritania." *African Environment*, 1 (2): 22–21.

Grove, A.T. 1978. "Geographical introduction to the Sahel." *Geographical Journal*, 144 (3): 407–415.

Guest, I. 1980. "UN disaster relief is called incompetent." *International Herald Tribune* (Paris), 12 Nov.

Hanson, A.H. 1960. "Nile and Niger: Two agricultural projects." *Public Administration*, 38: 339–352.

Hoben, A. 1979. "Lessons from a critical examination of livestock projects in Africa." AID Program Evaluation, Working Paper No. 25. Office of Evaluation, US Agency for International Development, Washington, D.C.

Horowitz, M.H. 1979. "The sociology of pastoralism and African livestock projects." Workshop on Livestock in Africa. US Agency for International Development, Washington, D.C. Mimeo.

Howe, J.W., and F.A. Gulick. 1980. "Fuelwood and other renewable energies in Africa: A progress report on the problem and the response." Overseas Development Council, Washington, D.C.

Hunter, J.M. 1981. "Past explosion and future threat: Exacerbation of red water disease (Schistosomiasis haematobium) in the upper region of Ghana." *Geojournal*, 5 (4): 305–313.

IAEA. 1977. *20 years: International Atomic Energy Agency*. Vienna.

——. 1982. Annual report for 1981. Vienna.

IFAD. 1978. "IFAD: The International Fund for Agricultural Development." Rome.

——. 1979. "IFAD: What it is and how it works." Rome.

——. 1982. Annual report, 1981. Rome.

IIED, 1978. *Banking on the biosphere?* International Institute for Environment and Development.

ILO, 1980. Programme and budget proposals for 1982–1983. International Labour Organisation, Geneva.

——. 1982. Programme and budget, 1984–1985. Geneva.

——. 1984. Programme and budget, 1986–1987. Geneva.

Inter-agency Consultative Board. 1967. Annual report for 1967. United Nations, New York.

Jackson, R.G.A. 1969. *A study of the capacity of the UN Development System*. United Nations, Geneva.

Kucera, C.L. 1978. "Grasslands and fire." Paper presented at Fire Ecology Conference, East-West Center, Honolulu, Hawaii, USA.

Lamb, R. 1979. "Can chemicals alone control river blindness?" *Earthscan Bulletin* (London), vol. 2, no. 8 (Nov.).

Lappé, F.M., and J. Collins. 1977. *Food first*. Houghton Mifflin Co., Boston, Mass., USA.

Lappé, F.M., J. Collins, and D. Kinley. 1981. *Aid as obstacle*.

Institute for Food and Development Policy, San Francisco, Calif., USA.

Lateef, N.V. 1980. *Crisis in the Sahel: A case study in development cooperation*. Westview Press, Boulder, Colo., USA.

Laya, D. 1975. "Interviews with farmers and livestock owners in the Sahel." *African Development*, vol. 1, no. 2 (Apr.).

Le Houerou, H.M. 1978. "Recovery from desertization." *Development Digest*, vol. 16, no. 1.

Lele, U. 1975. *The design of rural development: Lessons from Africa*. Johns Hopkins University Press, Baltimore, Md., USA.

Lewis, J. "The status of the ox-drawn plow in Dukolomba, 1975." In M.H. Horowitz, *The sociology of pastoralism and African livestock projects*. US Agency for International Development, Washington, D.C.

Lofchie, M.F. 1975. "Political and economic origins of African hunger." *Journal of Modern African Studies*, Dec., pp. 551–567.

Lopez, S.P., et. al. 1980. "Aspects of international intellectual co-operation." United Nations University, Tokyo, Mimeo.

Mabbutt, J.A. 1979. *Proceedings of the Khartoum Workshop on Arid Lands Management*. United Nations University, Tokyo.

Manshard. W. 1979. *Some geographical aspects of resource use and management in the arid and semi-arid zones*. II: *The case of the Sahel*. Tübingen Geographische Studien, no. 80.

Marnham, P. Undated. *Nomads of the Sahel*. Report no. 33, Minority Rights Group, London, England.

Mason, E.S., and R.E. Asher, 1973. "The World Bank since Bretton Woods." *Development Digest*, vol. 11, no. 3 (July).

Matlock, W.G., and E.L. Cockrum. 1976. "Agricultural production systems in the Sahel." In M.H. Glantz, ed., *The Politics of Natural Disaster*. Praeger, New York.

Monod, T. 1975. "La zone sahélienne nord-équatoriale." Manuscript.

NAS, 1983. *Environmental change in the West African Sahel*. National Academy Press, Washington, D.C.

Nature, 1982. "Where now for UNEP?" 297: 349–350.

New African, 1977. "Upper Volta in desperate straits." Vol. 2, no. 6.

New Scientist, 1980. "Banking on the environment." 7 Feb.

Nicholson, S. 1982. *The Sahel: A climatic perspective*. Club du Sahel, Paris.

——. 1983. "The climatology of sub-saharan Africa." In *Environmental change in the West African Sahel*. National Academy Press, Washington, D.C.

ODM. 1978. British aid statistics, 1973-1977. Ministry of Overseas Development, London.

OECD, 1976. "Development strategies for the Sahel: The Club des Amis du Sahel." In *Review of Development Co-operation*. Organization for Economic Co-operation and Development, Paris.

——. 1981. *External debt of developing countries*. Paris.

Office of International Studies, 1978. *Science and technology for managing fragile environments in developing nations*. School of Natural Resources, University of Michigan, Ann Arbor, Mich., USA.

Overseas Development. 1981. "UK joins challenge to big FAO budget rise." No. 84.

Raeder-Roitzsch, J.E. 1974. *Institutional forestry problems in the Sahelian region*. Special Sahelian Office, United Nations, New York. (ST/SSO/32)

Rasool, S.I. 1982. "Are Sahelian droughts predictable?" *Nature*, 297: 19–20.

Raynaut, C. 1977. "Lessons of a crisis." In D. Dalby et al., eds., *Drought in Africa*. International African Institute, London.

Renninger, J.P. 1979. *Multination co-operation for development in West Africa*. Pergamon Press, New York.

Robarts, R.C. 1974. *French development assistance: A study in policy and administration*. Sage Publications, Beverly Hills, Calif., USA.

Rondinelli, D.A., ed. 1977. *Planning development projects.* Dowden, Hutchinson and Ross, Inc., Stroudsberg, Penn., USA.

Ruthenberg, H. 1974. "Artificial pastures and their utilization in the southern Guinea savannah and the derived savannah of West Africa." Stuttgart-Hohenheim. Unpublished.

Salifour, A. 1975. "When history repeats itself: The famine of 1931 in Niger." *African Environment*, 1 (2): 22-48.

Sardar, Z. 1981. "How good is Arab aid for the Third World?" *New Scientist,* 22 Oct., pp. 233-235.

Schove, D.J. 1977. "African droughts and the spectrum of time." In D. Dalby et. al., eds., *Drought in Africa*. International African Institute, London.

Seifert, W.W., and N.M. Kamrany, 1974. *A framework for evaluating long-term strategies for the development of the Sahel-Sudan region*, vol. 2. Center for Policy Alternatives, MIT, Cambridge, Mass., USA.

Sheets, H., and R. Morris. 1974. *Disaster in the desert*. Humanitarian Policy Studies. Carnegie Endowment for International Peace, Washington, D.C.

Sikes, S.K. 1972. *Lake Chad*. Methuen, London.

Singh, M. 1973. "Why regional development banks?" *Development Digest, vol. 11, no. 3.*

SSO. 1973. *Livestock: Survey of the range recovery and animal production sector in the Sudano-Sahelian zone*. Special Sahelian Office, United Nations, New York. (ST/SSO/10)

Stebbing. E.P. 1937. *The forests of West Africa and the Sahel.* W.R. Chambers Ltd., London.

Stoop, W.A. 1981. "Cereal-based intercropping systems for the West African semi-arid tropics, particularly Upper Volta." In *International Workshop on Intercropping*. ICRISAT, Pantancheru, Andhra Pradesh, India.

Swift, J. 1976. "Desertification and man in the Sahel." CILSS/UNSO/FAO Consultation. (FO:RAF/305/4)

———. 1977. "Sahelian pastoralists: Underdevelopment, desertification and famine." *Annual Review of Anthropology* 6: 475-478.

Thimm, H.-U. 1979. *Development projects in the Sudan*. United Nations University, Tokyo.

Tolba, M.K. 1984. "Harvest of dust." *Desertification Control* (UNEP, Nairobi), 10: 2-4.

UN. 1968. *Everyman's United Nations.* Office of Public Information, United Nations, New York.

———. 1978. United Nations Conference on Desertification. New York.

———. 1980. *Basic facts about the United Nations*. Dept. of Public Information. UN, New York.

UN Chronicle. 1983. "UNEP: Assistance to developing countries stressed." 20 (7): 113.

———. 1984. "Shortfall in pledge payments forces IFAD programme cuts." 21 (2): 97-98.

UNCHS. 1982. Activities of the UN Commission on Human Settlements (Habitat). (HS/C/5/2)

UNCOD, 1977a. Case study on desertification: The Eghazer and Azawak region, Niger. UN Conference on Desertification, Nairobi. (A/CONF. 74/14)

———. 1977b. Draft plan of action. Nairobi. (A/CONF.74/3)

———. 1977c. Desertification: An overview. Nairobi. (A/CONF.74/1)

UNDP. 1971. Country and inter-country programming: Chad. UNDP Governing Council, 13th session, New York. (DP/GC/CHD/R.1)

———. 1973a. Country and inter-country programming: Gambia. UNDP Governing Council, 17th session, New York. (DP/GC/GAM/R.1)

———. 1973b. Country and inter-country programming: Mali. UNDP Governing Council, 17th session, New York. (DP/GC/MLI/R.2)

UNDP. 1973c. Country and inter-country programming: Niger. UNDP Governing Council, 17th session, New York. (DP/GC/NER/R.1)

———. 1973d. Country and inter-country programming: Senegal. UNDP Governing Council, 17th session, New York. (DP/GC/SEN/R.1)

———. 1973e. Country and inter-country programming: Senegal. Recommendations. UNDP Governing Council, 17th session, New York. (DP/GC/SEN/R.1)

———. 1973f. Country and inter-country programming: Upper Volta. Note by the Administrator. UNDP Governing Council, 16th session, New York. (DP/GC/UPV/R.1)

———. 1973g. Country and inter-country programming: Upper Volta. UNDP Governing Council, 16th session, New York. (DP/GC/UPV/R.1)

———. 1975a. UN Revolving Fund for Natural Resources Exploration. UNDP Governing Council, New York.

———. 1975b. Report of the Administrator for 1974. New York. (DP/111)

———. 1977a. Country programme for Chad. UNDP Governing Council, New York. (DP/GC/CHD/R.1)

———. 1977b. Country programme for Gambia. UNDP Governing Council, New York. (DP/GC/GAM/R.2)

———. 1977c. Country programme for Mali. UNDP Governing Council, New York. (DP/GC/MLI/R.2)

———. 1977d. Country programme for Mauritania. UNDP Governing Council, New York. (DP/GC/MAU/R.1)

———. 1977e. Country Programme for Niger. UNDP Governing Council, New York (DP/GC/NER/R.2)

———. 1977f. Country programme for Senegal. UNDP Governing Council, 1977. (DP/GC/SEN/R.2)

———. 1977g. Country programme for Upper Volta. UNDP Governing Council, New York. (DP/GC/UPV/R.2)

———. 1978a. UN Capital Development Fund: Annual report of the Administrator for 1977. UNDP Governing Council, 26th session. (DP/305/Annex II)

———. 1978b. United Nations Sahelian Office. UNDP Governing Council, 25th session, New York. (DP/326)

———. 1978c. Budgetary, administrative and financial matters. UNDP Governing Council, 25th session, New York. (DP/336)

———. 1979a. Assistance to drought-stricken areas of Africa and adjacent areas. UNDP Governing Council, 26th session, New York. (DP/400)

———. 1979b. Action taken in 1978 by organs of the United Nations and related agencies. UNDP Governing Council, 26th session.

———. 1979c. Information on the regular and extra-budgetary programmes of technical co-operation in 1978. UNDP Governing Council, 26th session. (DP/381)

———.1979d. The UN Revolving Fund for Natural Resources Exploration: Report of the Administrator. Governing Council, 26th session, New York. (DP/368)

———. 1979e. United Nations Capital Development Fund. UNDP Governing Council, 26th session.

———. 1980. Annual report of the Administrator for 1979. UNDP Governing Council, 27th session. (DP/460)

———. 1981. Programme planning: Preparations for the third programming cycle, 1982-1986. UNDP Governing Council, 28th session. (DP/519)

———. 1982a. The 10-year record: The record in 1981. UNDP Governing Council, 29th session. (DP/1982/G/Add. 1)

———. 1982b. Annual review of the financial situation, 1981. UNDP Governing Council, 29th session. (DP/1982/49)

———. 1982c. Third country programme for the Gambia. UNDP Governing Council, special session. (DP/CP/GAM/3)

———. 1982d. Third country programme for Mali. UNDP Governing Council, New York. (DP/CP/MLI/3)

UNDP. 1982e. Second country programme for Mauritania. UNDP Governing Council, special meeting. (DP/CP/MAU/2)

———. 1982f. Third country programme for the Niger. UNDP Governing Countil, special meeting. (DP/CP/NER/3)

———. 1982g. Third country programme for Senegal. UNDP Governing Council, special meeting. (UNDP/CP/SEN/3)

———. 1983. Third country programme for Chad. UNDP Governing Council, 30th session. (UNDP/CP/CHD/3)

———. 1982h. Third country programme for the Upper Volta. UNDP Governing Council, special meeting. (DP/CP/UPV/3)

———. 1982i. Annual report of the Administrator for 1981: Basic programme data. UNDP Governing Council, 29th session. (DP/1982/G/Add. 2)

———. 1982j. UN Capital Development Fund: Annual report of the Administrator for 1981. UNDP Governing Council, 29th session. (DP/1982/38)

———. 1982k. Annual report of the Administrator for 1981: Special funds and activities. UNDP Governing Council, 29th session. (UNDP/1982/G/Add. 1/Annex)

———. 1982l. United Nations Volunteers: Annual report of the Administrator for 1981. UNDP Governing Council, 29th session. (DP/1982/37)

———. 1982m. Report of the Executive Director on the UNFPA experience with the system of priority countries. UNDP Governing Council, 29th session. (UNDP/1982/30/Add. 1)

———. 1982n. UN Fund for Population Activities: Report of the Executive Director on allocations to projects in 1981. UNDP Governing Council, 29th session. (DP/1982/23/Add. 2)

———. 1982o. Evaluation of UNFPA projects. UNDP Governing Council, 29th session. (DP/1982/32)

———. 1982p. Compendium of approved projects. New York. (UNDP/MIS/Series A/No. 13.)

———. 1982q. Annual report of the Administrator for 1981: Supplementary programme data. UNDP Governing Council, 29th session. (DP/1982/6/Add. 2 and 3)

———. 1982r. Second regional programme for Africa. UNDP Governing Council, special meeting. (DP/RAF/2)

———. 1983. Third country programme for Chad. UNDP Governing Council, 30th session. (UNDP/CP/CHD/3)

———. 1984a. United Nations Financing System for Science and Technology for Development. UNDP Governing Council, Geneva. (DP/1984/49)

———. 1984b. Programmes in energy development. UNDP Governing Council, Geneva. (DP/1984/37)

———. 1984c. United Nations Volunteers. UNDP Governing Council, Geneva. (DP/1984/43)

———. 1984d. UNSO-UNDP/UNEP joint venture. UNDP Governing Council, Geneva. (DP/1984/51)

———. 1984e. United Nations technical co-operation activities. UNDP Governing Council, Geneva. (DP/1984/42)

———. 1984f. Agency support costs. UNDP Governing Council, Geneva. (DP/1984/62)

———. 1984g. Information on UN system regular and extra-budgetary technical co-operation expenditures in 1983 financed from sources other than UNDP. UNDP Governing Council, Geneva. (DP/1984/66 Annex)

———. 1984h. Ex post facto report on agency support costs. UNDP Governing Council, Geneva. (DP/1984/62)

———. 1985. United Nations Special Fund for Landlocked Developing Countries. UNDP Governing Council, Geneva. (DP-1984/53)

UNDP/FAO. 1969. Final Report, Agricultural Training and Demonstration Centre, Matourkou, Upper Volta. (FAO/SF:63/UPV-1)

UNDRO. 1979. "Emergency relief assistance in the Sahelian region, 1977–78." UNDRO Newsletter, no. 8. Geneva

UNEP. 1975. UNEP: 1975 annual review. Centre for Economic and Social Information/OPI, United Nations, New York.

UNEP. 1978a. Report of focal points. UN Environment Programme, Nairobi. (UNEP/FP/R.1)

———. 1978b. Report on implementation of the fund programme in 1977. Nairobi. (UNEP/GC.6/13)

———. 1980. Co-ordination questions. UNEP Governing Council, Nairobi. (UNEP/GC.8/4)

———. 1982a. The implementation of the Environment Fund programme in 1981: Report of the Executive Director. UNEP Governing Council, tenth session. (UNEP/GC.10/10)

———. 1982b. The management of the Environment Fund. UNEP Governing Council, tenth session. (UNEP/GC.10/11, Add. 1, Add. 2)

———. 1982c. Implementation of the Plan of Action to Combat Desertification. UNEP Governing Council, tenth session. (UNEP/GC.10/9)

———. 1984. Annual report of the Executive Director, 1983. Nairobi.

———. 1985a. Annual report of the Executive Director, 1984. Nairobi.

———. 1985b. Implementation of the Plan of Action to Combat Desertification: Report of the Executive Director. Nairobi. (UNEP/GC.13/7)

Unesco. 1979. Approved programme and budget for 1979–80. Paris.

———. 1981. Approved programme and budget for 1981–83. Paris. (21 C/5)

———. 1984. Approved programme and budget for 1984–85. Paris. (22C/5)

UNFPA. 1982. UN Fund for Population Activities: 1980 report. New York.

———. 1983. 1982 report. New York.

UNGA. 1978. Office of the United Nations Disaster Relief Co-ordinator: Report of the Secretary-General. UN General Assembly, New York. (A/33/82)

———. 1979a. Development and international co-operation: Multilateral development assistance for the exploration of natural resources. New York (A/34/532)

———. 1981a. Proposed programme budget for the biennium 1982–83. UN General Assembly Supplement No. 6. New York. (A/36/6)

———. 1981b. Evaluation of the Office of the United Nations Disaster Relief Co-ordinator. Joint Inspection Unit Report No. 11, 1980. (A/36/73)

———. 1981c. Office of the UN Disaster Relief Co-ordinator: Report of the Secretary-General. (A/36/259)

———. 1981d. Report of the Executive Director of the UN Institute for Training and Research. (A/36/14)

UNHCR. 1984. Report on UNHCR assistance activities in 1983–84 and proposed voluntary funds programmes and budget for 1985. UN General Assembly, New York. (A/AC.96/639)

———. 1985. Report on UNHCR assistance activities in 1984–85 and proposed voluntary funds programmes and budget for 1986. UN General Assembly, New York. (A/AC.96/657)

UNICEF. 1982. Annual report. United Nations Children's Fund, New York.

UNIDO 1978. Country sheets. Industrial Development Board, 13th session, Vienna.

———. 1982. Annual report of the Executive Director, 1981. Industrial Development Board, 16th session. (ID/B/280/Corr. 1)

———. 1985. Annual report of the Executive Director, 1984. Industrial Development Board, Vienna.

Uniterra. 1980. "Positive support for desertification control." Vol. 5, no. 4 (Apr.).

UNSO. 1979. An analytical review of the priority desertification control projects submitted to the UNSO desertification control planning and programming missions to the Sudano-Sahelian countries. United Nations Sudano-Sahelian Office, New York.

UNSO. 1982. United Nations Sudano-Sahelian Office: Information note. New York.

UNU. 1983. *The United Nations University today.* United Nations University, Tokyo.

USAID. 1976a. Proposal for a long-term comprehensive development programme for the Sahel. Report to the US Congress. US Agency for International Development, Washington, D.C.

———. 1976b. Guideline for preparation of initial environmental examination. Washington, D.C. Mimeo.

———. 1979a. Congressional presentation, FY 1979. Washington, D.C.

———. 1979b. Assessment of the environmental effects of the proposed developments in the Senegal River basin: Partial report for livestock. Washington, D.C. Draft.

———. 1980a. Sahel livestock industry status and development strategy. Washington, D.C.

———. 1980b. Sahel regional country development strategy statement, FY 82. Washington, D.C.

———. 1982. Sahel development programme: Annual report to Congress. Washington, D.C.

Wade, N. 1974. "Sahelian drought: No victory for Western aid." *Science*, 185 (4147): 234-237.

Warren, A., and J.K. Maizels, 1977. "Ecological change and desertification." UN Conference on Desertification, Nairobi. (A/Conf. 74/7)

Weber, F. 1982. "Review of CILSS forestry sector: Program analysis papers." Forestry Support Programme, USAID/US Department of Agriculture, Washington, D.C.

Westebbe, R.M. 1968. "Mauritania: Guidelines for a four-year development programme." IBRD, Washington, D.C.

WFP. 1975. "Sahel stop press." *World Food Programme News*, Oct.-Dec.

———. 1977. Emergency operations: Report by the Executive Director. World Food Programme, Committee on Food Aid, third session, Rome. (WFP/CFA/: 3/6)

———. 1978a. Emergency operations: Report by the Executive Director. World Food Programme, Committee on Food Aid, fifth session, Rome.

———. 1978b. Assessment of the quick-action procedure. World Food Programme, Committee on Food Aid, fifth session, Rome.

WFP. 1978c. A survey of studies of food aid. World Food Programme, Committee on Food Aid, fifth session, Rome (WFP/CFA:5/5-6)

———. 1978d. "Programme will serve as focal point for Sahel relief supplies." *WFP News.*

———. 1981a. Annual report of the Executive Director on the development of the programme: 1980. Rome. (WFP/CFA: 11/4)

———. 1981b. Audited accounts for 1980. Rome. (WFP/CFA: 12/17)

———. 1981c. Report of the twelfth session of the Committee on Food Aid and Programmes. Rome. (WFP/CFA: 12/22)

———. 1981d. Emergency operations. Rome. (WFP/CFA: 12/5-A)

White, J. 1973. "The African Development Bank." *Development Digest*, vol. 11, no. 3.

WHO, 1978. Proposed programme and budget, 1980-81. World Health Organization, Geneva.

———. 1980a. Proposed programme budget for the financial period 1982-83. Geneva. (WHO PB/82-83)

———. 1980b. Proposed programme budget, 1982-83. World Health Organization, Regional Office for Africa, Brazzaville. (WHO AFR/RC30/2)

———. 1984. *The work of WHO, 1982-83.* Geneva.

Williams, R. 1977. "Club du Sahel: A new approach to problems of least developed countries." United Nations Conference on Trade and Development. (TD/B/AC.21/G)

Winstanley, D. 1976. "Climatic changes and the future of the Sahel." In M.H. Glantz, *The Politics of natural disaster.* Praeger, New York.

WMO. 1975. Drought. Special Environment Report No. 5. World Meteorological Organization, Geneva.

———. 1982. Annual report of the World Meteorological Organization. Geneva.

———. 1985. Annual report of the World Meteorological Organization. Geneva.

World Bank. 1978a. Review of Bank forestry sector activity, FY 78. Washington, D.C. Mimeo.

———. 1978b. Forestry. Sector policy paper. Washington, D.C.

———. 1981. *World Development Report, 1981*. Washington, D.C.

———. 1983a. *World Development Report, 1983*. Washington, D.C.

———. 1983b. The World Bank: Annual Report, 1983. Washington, D.C.

Compte rendu du Séminaire sur la gestion des terres arides en Afrique de l'Ouest

Edited by Jean Gallais

Bringing together reports (in French) presented at a symposium held in Ouagadougou in 1981, this book reviews ongoing and planned arid land management programmes in the Sahel region. Also covered are strategies for the application of present knowledge, the exchange of traditional methodologies, and problems encountered. Important issues for research are identified, including social, demographic, and environmental changes, and courses of action are recommended.

NRTS-19F/UNUP-421   ISBN 92-808-0421-9
80 pages, 21.4 x 28 cm, paper-bound, US$9

Agro-forestry in the African Humid Tropics

Edited by L.H. MacDonald

A comprehensive view of agro-forestry possibilities and practices in the African humid tropics. The report brings together information from fourteen countries in Africa, both French- and English-speaking. While it concentrates on the African humid tropics, many of the themes are also relevant to tropical Asia and Latin America.

NRTS-17/UNUP-364   ISBN 92-808-0364-6
163 pages, 21.4 x 28 cm, paper-bound, US$12

Agroforesterie en Afrique tropicale humide

French edition of the above.

NRTS-17F/UNUP-467   ISBN 92-808-0467-7
179 pages, 21.4 x 28 cm, paper-bound, US$15

Transforming Natural Resources for Human Development: A Resource Systems Framework for Development Policy

by Kenneth Ruddle and Dennis A. Rondinelli

This introductory volume to the Resource Systems Theory and Methodology Series presents an original and in-depth study of the relationship between natural resources and human development, summarizing the experiences of the past two decades and offering realistic guidelines for future action. It is concerned with methods of transforming natural resources for human development — an approach that can both generate greater economic growth with social equity and protect and enhance the natural resource base on which social and economic progress depend.

NRTS-22/UNUP-469   ISBN 92-808-0469-3
87 pages, 21.4 x 28 cm, paper-bound, US$15

Obstacles to Tree Planting in Arid and Semi-arid Lands: Comparative Case Studies from India and Kenya

by Jeffery Burley

A concise overview of the problems of meeting the growing need for timber, fodder, and fuel in arid and semi-arid lands. The contrast between India and Kenya is quite striking. This publication will serve as a valuable guide not only to technical specialists but to a much broader range of people who are concerned with self-sustaining development, particularly in arid and semi-arid lands.

NRTS-18/UNUP-391   ISBN 92-808-0391-3
52 pages, 21.4 x 28 cm, paper-bound, US$7

The Impacts of Opencast Mining on the Rivers and Coasts of New Caledonia

by E. Bird, J.-P. Dubois, and J.A. Iltis

Mineral exploitation has been the basis of economic development in New Caledonia during the past century. This study examines the general landforms of the country and the economic factors that have influenced the development and fluctuations in intensity of mining. It then documents the extent of landscape modification caused by mining and its impact on river and coastal resources.

NRTS-25/UNUP-505   ISBN 92-808-0505-3
53 pages, 21.4 x 28 cm, paper-bound, US$9

Social, Economic, and Institutional Aspects of Agro-forestry

Edited by J.K. Jackson

The transfer of agro-forestry techniques to areas that appear biologically suitable may still be hindered by social, economic, or institutional problems. These collected papers examine issues relating to the adoption of agro-forestry systems: cost/benefit analysis, the role of community and governmental organizations, land tenure and land-use planning, legal aspects, and educational requirements. Case studies from several tropical countries are included.

NRTS-23/UNUP-502   ISBN 92-808-0502-9
97 pages, 21.4 x 28 cm, paper-bound, US$9

Arid Zone Settlement in Australia: A Focus on Alice Springs

by D.N. Parks, I.H. Burnley, and S.R. Walker

Human settlement in remote arid regions is the focus of this work. Based on studies in central Australia, it discusses ecological characteristics of urban zones in relation to urbanization; migration, attitudes, and lifestyles of settlers; and provision of community services.

NRTS-26/UNUP-506   ISBN 92-808-0506-1
129 pages, 21.4 x 28 cm, paper-bound, US$10

Ecology in Development: A Rationale for Three-Dimensional Policy

by Brian Spooner

This monograph urges the integration of social and natural science approaches to ecological problems in development planning. It discusses the current state of ecological knowledge and theory in relation to development, changing perceptions of human beings' relation to nature, and the underlying moral problems of management and welfare.

NRTS-21/UNUP-458   ISBN 92-808-0458-8
58 pages, 21.4 x 28 cm, paper-bound, US$9

Natural Resources and Rural Development in Arid Lands: Case Studies from the Sudan

Edited by H.R.J. Davies

Case studies of four pressing problems of dryland resource management: dura (*Sorghum vulgare*) production and its parasite buda (*Striga hermonthica*), the impact of improved rural water supplies on the environment, the use of wood resources in the Nuba Mountains, and planners' and participants' differing perceptions of development.

NRTS-24/UNUP-504   ISBN 92-808-0504-5
84 pages, 21.4 x 28 cm, paper-bound, US$15

HOW TO ORDER

UNU publications may be ordered from the distributors listed below. In countries not covered by any distributor, orders, accompanied by a cheque or money order in either dollars or yen payable to the United Nations University, specifying the UNUP number and the full title, should be sent to Distribution and Sales, Academic Publication Services, The United Nations University, Toho Seimei Building, 2-15-1 Shibuya, Tokyo 150, Japan.

The Middle East

United Schools International, Arab Regional Office, PO Box 726, Bahrain

Asia and the Pacific

Hunter Publications, 58A Gipps Street, Collingwood, Victoria 3066, Australia
Kinokuniya Bookstore Co. Ltd., Journal Dept., PO Box 55, Chitose, Tokyo 156, Japan
Maruzen Company Ltd., Import and Export Dept., Dai-3 Maruzen Bldg., 2-16-1 Nihonbashi, Chuo-ku, Tokyo 103, Japan (for orders from outside Japan)
National Book Store, Inc., PO Box 1934, Manila, Philippines
P.T. Bhratara Niaga Media, Jl. Oto Iskandardinata III/29, Jakarta 13340, Indonesia
Segment Book Distributors, D-17/B Kailash Colony, New Delhi — 110048, India
Tayyab M.S. Commercial Services, PO Box 16006, A-2/3 Usman Ghani Road, Manzoor Colony, Karachi — 44, Pakistan
Toppan Company (S) Pte. Ltd., 38 Liu Fang Road, Box 22, Jurong Town Post Office, Jurong, Singapore 22

North America

Sales Section, United Nations, New York, NY 10017, USA
Unifo Publishers Ltd., PO Box 37, Pleasantville, NY 10570, USA
Unipub, 10033-F King Highway, Lanham, Maryland 20706, USA

Europe

Sales Section, United Nations Office at Geneva, Palais des Nations, CH-1211 Geneva 10, Switzerland
Fritzes Kungl. Hovbokhandel, Regeringsgaten 12, Box 16356, 10327 Stockholm, Sweden
Her Majesty's Stationery Office, Publications Centre, 51 Nine Elms Lane, London SW8 5DR, UK
Keesing b.v., P.B. 1118, 1000 BC Amsterdam, Netherlands
Licosa, Via Lamarmora, 45, PO Box 552, 50121 Firenze, Italy
Mundi-Prensa Libros, S.A., Castelló 37, Madrid 1, Spain
Trismégiste, 4, rue Frédéric-Sauton, 75005 Paris, France
UNO-Verlag, Simrockstrasse 23, D-5300 Bonn 1, FRG

NRTS-20/UNUP-422

United Nations Sales No. E.86.III.A.3
01000